- Why the rise of the "knowledge worker" leads to new principles of managing people—so that companies can really mean it when they say employees are their most important asset
- How to collaborate with customers to build wealth together
- How the knowledge economy affects you personally and in your career; and how to capitalize on the opportunities it presents

Read *Intellectual Capital* as if the future of your company and your career depend on it. They do.

JOHN ABBOTT

THOMAS A. STEWART is an award-winning member of the board of editors of *Fortune* magazine. He pioneered the field of intellectual capital in a series of landmark articles that earned him an international reputation as the chief expert on the subject. The Planning Forum called him "the leading proponent of knowledge management in the business press," and Business Intelligence, a British research group, gave him a special award for his outstanding contributions to the field. He lives in Manhattan.

Intellectual CAPITAL

Intellectual
CAPITAL

THE NEW WEALTH OF ORGANIZATIONS

THOMAS A. STEWART

DOUBLEDAY / CURRENCY

NEW YORK LONDON TORONTO SYDNEY AUCKLAND

FOR MORE ON CURRENCY AND ITS RESOURCES,

SEE INFORMATION AT THE BACK OF THIS BOOK

A CURRENCY BOOK
PUBLISHED BY DOUBLEDAY
a division of Bantam Doubleday Dell Publishing Group, Inc.
1540 Broadway, New York, New York 10036

CURRENCY and DOUBLEDAY are trademarks of Doubleday, a division of
Bantam Doubleday Dell Publishing Group, Inc.

Library of Congress Cataloging-in-Publication Data
Stewart, Thomas A., 1948–
Intellectual capital: the new wealth of organizations / Thomas A. Stewart.
p.   cm.
Includes index.
1. Creative ability in business.   2. Success in business.
3. Human capital.   I. Title.
HD53.S74   1997
658.4′06—dc21   96-47491
CIP

ISBN 0-385-48228-0
Copyright © 1997 by Thomas A. Stewart
All Rights Reserved
Printed in the United States of America
March 1997
First Edition
1   3   5   7   9   10   8   6   4   2

To Amanda, Pamela, and Patrick
My only wealth

Contents

Foreword

Information and knowledge are the thermonuclear competitive weapons of our time. Knowledge is more valuable and more powerful than natural resources, big factories, or fat bankrolls. In industry after industry, success comes to the companies that have the best information or wield it most effectively—not necessarily the companies with the most muscle. Wal-Mart, Microsoft, and Toyota didn't become great companies because they were richer than Sears, IBM, and General Motors—on the contrary. But they had something far more valuable than physical or financial assets. They had intellectual capital.

By "intellectual capital" I don't mean a clutch of Ph.D.s locked up in a lab somewhere. Nor do I mean intellectual property (such as patents and copyrights), though that is one part of intellectual capital. Intellectual capital is the sum of everything everybody in a company knows that gives it a competitive edge. Unlike the assets with which business people and accountants are familiar—land, factories, equipment, cash—intellectual capital is intangible. It is the knowledge of a workforce: the training and intuition of a team of chemists who discover a billion-dollar new drug or the know-how of workmen who come up with a thousand different ways to improve the efficiency of a factory. It is the electronic network that transports information at light speed through a company, so that it can react to the market faster than its rivals. It is the collaboration—the shared learning— between a company and its customers, which forges a bond between them that brings the customer back again and again.

In a sentence: *Intellectual capital is intellectual material—knowledge, information, intellectual property, experience—that can be put to use to create wealth.* It is collective brainpower. It's hard to identify and harder still to deploy effectively. But once you find it and exploit it, you win.

You win because today's economy is fundamentally different from yesterday's. We grew up in the Industrial Age. It is gone, supplanted by the Information Age. The economic world we are leaving was one whose main sources of wealth were physical. The things we bought and sold were, well, *things;* you could touch them, smell them, kick their tires, slam their doors and hear a satisfying thud. Land, natural resources such as oil and ores and energy, and human and machine labor were the ingredients from which wealth was created. The business organizations of that era were designed to attract capital—financial capital—to develop and manage those sources of wealth, and they did it pretty well.

In this new era, wealth is the product of knowledge. Knowledge and information—not just scientific knowledge, but news, advice, entertainment, communication, service—have become the economy's primary raw materials and its most important products. Knowledge is what we buy and sell. You can't smell it or touch it; even that satisfying *thud* from a slammed car door is probably the result of clever acoustical engineering. The capital assets that are needed to create wealth today are not land, not physical labor, not machine tools and factories: They are, instead, knowledge assets.

Pundits and consultants speak of a new economy and call the change a "paradigm shift"—a term I have just used for the first and last time in this book. The P-word allows us to agree on something, to nod sagely—"Yup, that's what it is all right, a P-shift if ever I saw one"—without bothering to figure out what we're actually agreeing upon. Hip companies call themselves "learning organizations," a vague vogue term for a corporate culture that cherishes continuous improvement—but in 1996, six years after Peter Senge's excellent book *The Fifth Discipline* popularized the learning-organization concept, participants in a busy Internet forum devoted to the subject engaged in a lively discussion about the need to figure out what "learning organization" means. That's typical. For years, I heard people talk about "the information economy," or "the Knowledge Era," but did not know what they meant.

I suspected that no one else knew, either, including many of the people doing the talking. What is this great transformation? How does it change the nature of commerce and the task of management? How is it that companies and other organizations manage knowledge? How do they find it, store it, sell it, move it around, keep it refreshed, relevant, and up-to-date? How does the Information Age affect me, personally, in my work and career?

Although the answers to those questions have not been clear, it's obvious that we live in a time of dramatic, fundamental economic change. The signs are as inescapable as neon in Times Square. The comfort of a long career at a big company—gone. The every-other-year promotion from assistant-this to associate-that—gone. The giant corporation, which came into being at the beginning of the twentieth century and has dominated its economic life ever since, while not gone, has lost its hold. Two thirds of the companies listed on the inaugural *Fortune* 500 list in 1954 had either vanished or were no longer big enough to make the list on its fortieth anniversary. Between 1979 and 1994, the number of people employed by America's biggest industrial corporations fell by nearly a third, from 16.2 million to 11.6 million. In place of these faltering behemoths are companies like the U.S. subsidiary of Nokia, a Finnish electronics company, which has annual sales of approximately $160 million—and just five employees. Or Nike, a shoemaker that makes no shoes—its work is research and development, design, marketing, and distribution, all knowledge-intensive services—which has $334 thousand in sales for each employee, versus $248 thousand in sales per employee for the median *Fortune* 500 company. Or companies like Netscape Communications, whose chairman, Jim Clark, owns stock worth about three quarters of a billion dollars, in a company that didn't exist three years ago.

In a confusing business landscape, it's no wonder management trends and fads come and go as quickly as good witches and bad witches in the Land of Oz. There's reengineering, then there's "beyond reengineering." There's the Third Wave and there's the Second Curve. There's twenty-first-century manufacturing and there's post-industrial society. There's the power of leadership and there's the power of followership. There's the virtual corporation and the agile corporation; the web, cluster, and shamrock organizations; the intelligent enterprise and the learning organization. There's even a fad denouncing management fads.

In place of fads, this book offers understanding: a look at what's causing change and what you can do—for yourself, for the company where you work—to prosper in the Information Age.

The idea that a new, knowledge-based economy is emerging has been like a new tennis ball—fuzzy, but with a lot of bounce. As we will see, it's becoming less fuzzy every day, and more tangible. This book will show how, in fact, seemingly vague ideas of "managing knowledge" and "leveraging intellectual capital" can yield results and agenda items that employees, managers, and leaders can do something about—real work, not fancy talk. We'll take intellectual capital and look under the hood, so to speak, to show how the stuff works and how to make it work better. Old-style business organizations don't manage knowledge well—they weren't designed to. Now business must learn to manage knowledge. Someone who knows how to walk and run on land has to learn new skills to swim and dive and get around in water; in a similar way, the skills individuals and companies need to succeed in their new environment, the knowledge economy are, in many cases, different from the ones they are used to.

▼ We'll learn why most companies don't manage their corporate brainpower—the most important asset they have—and see how untold billions of dollars of revenues and profit await those who learn how to do it;

▼ We'll see how intellectual capital can free up other capital, such as equipment, cash, and inventory, liberating financial resources, increasing corporate agility, and dramatically increasing profitability;

▼ We'll learn important new principles of managing people in an information economy—so that companies can really mean it when they say "people are our most important asset";

▼ We'll see why, when knowledge is power, power flows downstream toward customers, giving them vastly more influence on the companies that sell to them, and we'll see how a company—any company—can reposition itself to share in that new wealth;

▼ We'll discover some surprising counterintuitive truths about managing in the Knowledge Era; for example, we'll learn how planned ignorance can sometimes be more valuable than knowledge, and why business leaders, who spend much of their time trying to construct management systems, would do better figuring out ways to make those systems disappear;

▼ We'll see why and how new models of organizational design will forever supplant familiar bureaucratic and hierarchical schemes;

▼ We'll see how the emergence of a new economy affects careers—for everyone—and what new strategies will help you succeed.

Intellectual assets have always mattered, but not at all as much. The medieval guild, one of the first forms of incorporation, represents one way of managing knowledge assets—when knowledge is scarce, you hoard it, give it an aura of magic and mystery, and bar the inner sanctum to all but a few initiates. It's a form of knowledge management that survives today in contemporary guilds and priesthoods like medicine and the law, the College of Cardinals, and, of course, the corporate computer services department. In 1768, a Swede named J. Westerman wondered why his country's shipyards and ceramics factories were only half as productive as their British and Dutch counterparts. The report of his investigation—called *Om de svenske närigarnes undervigt genetmot de utländske dymedelst en trögare arbetsdrift*, meaning, of course, "On the Inferiority of Swedish Compared to Foreign Manufacturers Because of a Slower Work Organization"—showed that the Swedes and their competitors used essentially similar machinery. It wasn't fixed assets that gave the Brits and Dutch an advantage, Westerman found, but the intelligence with which the machines were employed. In this century, the pyramidal corporation and later the invention of the business unit came about to manage knowledge—to collect and interpret financial data and to fund new technologies.

What's new? Simply this: Because knowledge has become the single most important factor of production, managing intellectual assets has become the single most important task of business. It wasn't always so. In 1940, Buckminster Fuller wrote a long article in the tenth anniversary issue of *Fortune* magazine. It was full of the quirky, marvelous stuff that makes Buckminster Fuller such fun to read: He juxtaposed the production of silk stockings with the number of radios in use with the number of tons of coal shipped with the number of industrial machines on factory floors. . . . When he'd added it all up, Fuller had demonstrated a fundamental change in what moved the economy. In the late nineteenth century, Fuller showed, the best way to measure economic activity was to look at the use of raw materials—how much coal was mined, how much steel was made. By 1940, that had changed. The measurements that really showed how vigorously the economy was working involved the use of energy: kilowatt hours of electricity produced, gasoline consumed, kilometers traveled by rail or air. Thinking of that time, retired Citicorp chairman Walter Wriston recollected: "When I was a kid in the bank, the key economic indicator we looked at was freight-car loadings." Then he went on: "Who the hell cares about them now? What we need is a way to measure the knowledge we bring to the work we do."

Muscle power, machine power, even electrical power are steadily being replaced by brainpower. Peter Drucker says that the amount of labor needed to produce an additional unit of manufacturing output has fallen 1 percent a year since 1900, as machines have taken over jobs that muscles once did. After World War II, the amount of raw material needed for each increase in manufacturing GDP began falling at about the same rate. A few years later—beginning about 1950—the amount of energy manufacturers needed began to fall, again at 1 percent a year for any given unit of additional output. What's taken the place of matter and energy is intelligence. Since the turn of the century, the number of educated workers on company payrolls has risen, according to Drucker, at that same 1 percent annual rate. We still speak of the United States, Japan, and Western Europe as "the industrialized world," but that is a misnomer. Agriculture, construction, manufacturing, and mining employ fewer than one in four Americans and, as we will see, even those people work principally with their heads rather than with their backs and hands. We are all knowledge workers now, working for knowledge companies.

I first heard the term "intellectual capital" from a sausage-maker. He is Ralph Stayer, the CEO of a Wisconsin company called Johnsonville

Foods. In the fall of 1990, he and I got into a wide-ranging conversation about what wealth is. Time was, Stayer said, that natural resources—land, minerals, fisheries—were the most important source of national wealth and the most important asset of corporations. Then capital—money, capital goods like machines and factories—became paramount. Now that was giving way to brainpower, to "intellectual capital." Interesting, we agreed, that this paramount asset isn't tracked by accountants the way land and financial capital are.

I was intrigued; "hooked" is probably a better word. When I first came to *Fortune*, I knew next to nothing about how to read financial statements, though I had had business experience. People around the office quote *Fortune*'s founder Henry Luce as having said, "It's easier to teach a poet how to read a balance sheet than it is to teach an accountant how to write," and I was the most recent test case. Possibly my ignorance made it easier for me to believe that what is not on balance sheets is more important than what is.

My first exploration of intellectual capital became a brief article in a package of stories about new ideas in business, published in January 1991. Charlie Burck, who edited the piece, suggested I do a longer story, which became "Brainpower," published that spring. A few months later, a Swede who worked for an insurance company named Skandia phoned to say that he was coming to New York and to ask if he could visit me. In my office he handed me his business card. *Leif Edvinsson*, it read, *Director, Intellectual Capital*. I was floored. Leif explained that he had been interviewing for a job with Jan Carende, head of Skandia's Assurance and Financial Services division, and had shown "Brainpower" to him, saying, "This is what your company should do: Manage intellectual capital." Carende agreed, and said: "You do it."

There weren't many of us, then, interested in the subject; now it's become hot. My second cover story about knowledge assets ("Intellectual Capital," in October 1994) got tons of mail—more than any story I'd written before except one. Every day new letters, new phone calls, new questions come from CEOs, managers, consultants, and others: What do you know about knowledge management? How can I find out more? Who is doing interesting work on intellectual capital? Have you got any hard figures about return-on-investment in knowledge assets? If I needed proof that the age of intellectual capital has arrived, it came in the middle of the writing of this book, when I got a phone call from an executive recruiter, who told me that he had established what was proving to be a successful speciality as a headhunter for companies looking for chief knowledge officers and other leaders in knowledge management.

We've come a long way in half a decade, but a longer road lies ahead. This story is still unfolding. Nevertheless, it is possible—and it is time—to make sense of the information economy, to demonstrate how and why knowledge has become the most important asset of a company or of any organization, to show how knowledge can be measured and managed to improve performance, and to reveal how managers and workers—you and I—can thrive in the Knowledge Era. It's time to knock the fuzz off the tennis ball.

How to Read This Book

I've tried to do two things here. One is practical. It is, I hope, the principal contribution to this book that it shows how to find, manage, and grow intellectual capital—that it offers a framework upon which business people can build useful and valuable strategies for competing in the Information Age. It's not enough to prattle sagely and sublimely about the knowledge economy: Investors, managers, and individuals need to know what to do about it.

I've tried to help them in three ways. First, because you can't lift a bucket without a handle, this book provides a vocabulary and a structure for working with corporate knowledge and knowledge assets—language, rules, and principles of intellectual capitalism that allow managers to put it into practice. In particular, in Part Two we'll take our working definition of intellectual capital—intellectual material that can be used to create wealth—and open it up to craft an agenda that managers can apply to practical business problems. In addition, throughout the book you will find plenty of examples—stories, case histories—of companies that have successfully identified and exploited intellectual capital. They're the proof of the pudding; they will also, I hope, inspire readers to see how they can do the same. Third, I've suggested ways in which readers might come up with their own recipes—approaches and strategies where profit might be found.

I've resisted the temptation to offer simple formulas and checklists.

Too many business people—bad business people—want someone to give them plug-and-play answers. Too many business books—bad business books—indulge them. This isn't a cookbook. I'm not competent to write one, and neither is anyone else: The whole field of intellectual capital is too new; besides, as we will see, knowledge work and intellectual assets tend to be unique, customized things. I'll count this book a success if it inspires many chefs to come up with ideas far beyond any I could imagine. I recognize that some of you may be impatient types, reading this only because your laptops are out of power and the flight isn't over yet. If you are chiefly interested in the practical stuff of management and careers, you will find most of what you are looking for in Part Two, in the second and third chapters of Part Three, and in the Appendix.

But this book is also, I hope, more than a practical one: an attempt to make sense of the dramatically changing world in which we work. The emergence of the Information Age and the sudden ubiquity of information technology are among the biggest—no, they are the biggest—stories of our time. They are everywhere and affect everything. Jet engines changed transportation, nylon altered clothing, television shook up news and entertainment, and these technologies indirectly affect us all. But computers touch every industry, and change the work of everyone—steelworker, secretary, farmer, financial planner. Not since Edison domesticated electricity has a technology revolutionized life the way this one has. It can prepare an invoice, animate a velociraptor, and sew a seam. The technology of information, a revolution in itself, is only a fraction of the larger revolution, the Information Age.

Even for readers in a hurry there's much to be said in favor of looking at the whole picture. Revolutions—and this is a no-fooling revolution—have consequences that go far beyond anything anyone can predict. Surviving and thriving in such times require peripheral vision as well as focus, adaptability as well as power. The better you can understand the large forces—the tectonic plates—reshaping our world, the better you will be able to cope with the surprises they are certain to throw at us. These days, keeping your nose to the grindstone is a big, shortsighted mistake.

By the same token, I hope that those who come to this book motivated by a desire to learn about the larger forces will spend time with the seemingly practical chapters. Like a lot of people who grew up in the 1960s, I once thought business and management were pretty dreary. I had no idea, when I first came to *Fortune*, how wrong I had been.

Work is where change happens and where it hits. Too much of what passes for discussion of the Great Issues of the Day comes out of the Washington bureaus of newspapers and television networks. That's like trying to make sense of the tide by watching the froth on the wave. It's remarkable, and wrong, that so little of the workaday challenges of men and women finds its way into literature and art or into discussions of public affairs. Back in the 1930s, defending the decision to found a School of Business Administration, Harvard University president Abbott Lawrence Lowell wrote: "The vast bulk of the American people are engaged in business of some kind, and are not to be disparaged therefor . . . Anyone who sees in his own occupation merely a means of earning money degrades it; but he that sees in it a service to mankind ennobles both his labor and himself."

Acknowledgments

A writer is only as good as his sources, teachers, and muses. I have been lucky in all three. Hundreds of people contributed to this book by graciously spending the time to be interviewed, by sharing their ideas, or by pointing me to people to talk to. I cannot name them all here, but I would particularly like to thank Debra Amidon, Weston Anson, Brian Arthur, Warren Bennis, Larry Bossidy, Keith Bradley, Michael Brown, Bruce Bunch, Andrea Costa, Quinn Cummings, Donald Curtis, Tom Davenport, Stan Davis, Desi DeSimone, Leif Edvinsson, Gunnar Eliasson, Robert K. Elliott, Fran Engoran, Liam Fahey, Jac Fitz-Enz, Terry Curtis Fox, Estee Solomon Gray, Michael Hammer, Peter Henschel, Joyce Hergenhan, Glen Hiner, Bob Immerman, Bipin Junnarker, Julia Kirby, David Klein, Valdis Krebs, Judy Lewent, Jordan Lewis, Judith A. Lewis, Christopher Locke, Myron Magnet, Thomas Malone, Brook Manville, Barbara Martz, Ron Mitsch, Rich Moran, Brian Murray, David Nadler, David Norton, Paul O'Neill, Frank Ostroff, Gordon Petrash, Joseph Pine, George Pór, Al Posti, Larry Prusak, Bill Raduchel, Robert Reich, Leon Royer, Paul Saffo, Hubert Saint-Onge, Charles Savage, Patricia Seeman, Richard Shattun, Chuck Sieloff, Charles Silver, Doug Smith, Ralph Stayer, Charles L. Stewart, Patrick Sullivan, David Teece, Jill Tottenberg, Tom Waite, Robert Walker, Arian Ward, Jack Welch, Etienne Wenger, John Hazen White, Oliver Williamson, and Betty Zucker.

I owe an enormous debt of gratitude to past and present colleagues and editors at *Fortune*. Among a crowd of ministering angels, let me polish the halos of a few. Charlie Burck shepherded me through my first work on this subject; nobody plays with ideas better than Charlie, and his conversation was a great gift. Peter Petre has been an ardent advocate of this work since its inception. Geoffrey Colvin always helped, always contributed superb ideas; my prose has never been abused by a more elegant, unobtrusive, and effective editor; I'm especially thankful to him, *il miglior fabbro*, for allowing me to borrow a few sentences of his own prose. Brian Dumaine has been both generous in letting me write about this subject in my column, "The Leading Edge," and extremely good at helping me clarify my thinking.

I've had splendid luck in the three men who have been managing editor of *Fortune* during my time here. To Marshall Loeb I owe a huge debt for hiring me in the first place, and for his support and good editing over the first five years of my life at *Fortune*. To Walter Kiechel, thanks for his wit and intellectual companionship, and for carving out a capacious place for writing like this. To John Huey, *Fortune*'s managing editor today, my great gratitude for encouraging this project from the beginning, allowing me the time off I needed to complete it, and being a hell of a guy.

Current and former members of *Fortune*'s superb reporting staff—especially Joyce Davis, Patty de Llosa, Therese Eiben, Kristin Dunlap Godsey, Ani Hadjian, Christopher Harris, Cindy Kano, David C. Kaufman, Sandra L. Kirsch, Rebecca Lewin, Stephanie Losee, Sally Solo, Ricardo Sookdeo, Melanie Warner, and Wilton Woods—saved me from making many an error in articles in which I first explored this topic. Joe McGowan earns my special thanks, not only for checking some of my articles but also for his brilliant and remarkably efficient research help with the manuscript. Research doesn't come better than

Joe's, and writers don't come more grateful than I. What's right in this book is right in no small part to these people. What's wrong, *c'est à moi.*

I little imagined when I tried to encourage Harriet Rubin to work for me, in the days when I worked in book publishing, that I would one day be writing a book for her. Judging by what I've seen from the writer's side of the desk, I was right to have wanted her then. My agent, Kristine Dahl of International Creative Management, has been a superb advocate and friend. I've been lucky in both, and am grateful.

In a book about knowledge and the management of knowledge, it's appropriate—and inevitable—that I offer thanks to the staff of one of the world's miraculous repositories of the stuff, the New York Public Library, whose shelves yielded much that was indispensable to this book and where I mostly wrote it. To Barbara Tuchman, who gave the library the money that created the Wertheim Study where I worked, a stranger's (and fan's) special thanks. I am grateful, too, for another miracle, for which the phrase *sine qua non* ought to have been coined; this book could never have been written without Apple Computer's wonderful little machine, the Powerbook that accompanied me everywhere. Scarcely a day went by that it didn't make easier, more productive, or even possible. Anyone who thinks it silly to thank a computer has never owned a Mac.

My wife, Amanda Vaill, and my children, Pamela and Patrick, are owed more thanks than I can possibly give them. This book would not have begun without Amanda's urging; it would have been far less good without her reading and advice; and it would not have been written without her support, forbearance, cheer, and love. As for the children: Even someone inured to seeing his words in print feels special about their appearing in a form where they'll endure, perhaps, long enough for his children to read them when they have to wrestle with adult responsibilities. Anything I write here will, I hope, never matter to them as much as the fact that I love them—but I hope they'll one day think their father got some of this stuff right, too.

PART ONE

The Information Age

CONTEXT

THIS WAS THE TRIUMPH OF "ARTIFICIAL WEALTH,"
CLAIMED SOME PEOPLE. BUT WAS NOT ARTIFICIAL
WEALTH A MASTERPIECE OF HUMAN ACHIEVEMENT?
—FERNAND BRAUDEL

CHAPTER 1

The Knowledge Economy

NOTHING SOLID IS ITS SOLID SELF.
—WALLACE STEVENS

C onsider a beer can. Open it if you want, but consider the can. If it is symbolic of anything, it is an emblem of blue-collar industrial work, an everyday accessory for "Joe Six-Pack," union member, factory worker. But it is far more: It is an artifact of a new, knowledge-based economy, evidence of how knowledge has become the most important component of business activity. To see how this is so is to begin to understand an extraordinary transformation, the emergence of the Information Age.

Three decades ago, that can would probably have been steel. Aluminum companies have always wanted to replace steel wherever it is used; indeed, they have long been imbued with an almost missionary zeal to peddle the metal, which was considered a miraculous substance when it was introduced to the public at an international exposition in Paris in 1855. Although aluminum is the most common metallic element in the earth's crust, refining it was outrageously expensive, requiring costly chemicals or even more costly electric power from batteries. In the nineteenth century, aluminum cost so much that King Christian X of Denmark ordered up an aluminum crown and France's conspicuously consuming Emperor Napoleon III had a dinner service made of it, which he used for guests who deserved something fancier than mere gold. Not till electricity became plentiful and cheap did aluminum find much of a commercial market. (Electricity remains the single largest cost in making aluminum.) By the 1950s, steel's lucrative can-making business had become an obvious target, but not an easy one to hit. Even with cheap power, aluminum costs more than steel; breweries and soft-drink bottlers weren't about to switch to a pricier material for a mere container. But aluminum is also easier to work than steel, and in that fact the industry found its chance: Steel's price advantage could be overcome if the industry could exploit aluminum's malleability to manufacture a can that used less metal than steel cans required. In 1958, the Adolph Coors Company developed a seven-ounce aluminum can, first used by a small Hawaiian brewery, but the process did not lend itself to mass production. Five years later, Reynolds Metals invented a way to mass-produce a twelve-ounce can. The first customer: Hamms, a Midwestern brewery. Within four years, Coca-Cola and Pepsi-Cola began using aluminum cans; today, the steel beverage can is almost nonexistent in the United States—steel's market share is about 1 percent—and it is losing ground in international markets.

That first aluminum can represented a triumph of know-how over nature. Weighing just .66 of an ounce, about half what a steel can weighed, the aluminum container substituted knowledge—years of research—for raw material. Since then, improvements in manufacturing processes, subtle changes in the alloys used to make can sheet, and other brainpower investments have steadily reduced the amount of metal in a can. Today, empty, your beer can weighs just .48 of an ounce, about three fourths as much as Reynolds's first can. The can contains less material and more science. The beer may have a head, but the can is about 25 percent knowledge.

One of the world's largest factories making can sheet stands in Alcoa, Tennessee, a town built in the 1930s by the giant aluminum maker; Alcoa put it there to get an inexpensive hydroelectric power from the Tennessee River. The factory originally made dozens of products—even aluminum phonograph records; now it makes only ingot and, from the ingot, can sheet. In the factory, huge bars of gleaming metal—74 inches wide, 21 inches thick, 20 feet long, each weighing 35,000 pounds—pass through a series of rolling mills until they have been flattened to a thickness of about one one-hundredth of an inch, the same as a couple of sheets of paper. The 20-foot ingot becomes a sheet more than 3,000 feet long; and over all that length the metal varies in thickness by no more than one *ten-thousandth* of an inch.

Now, having squeezed and rolled raw material out of their product, aluminum makers are going after its other major physical ingredient, electricity: Can sheet made with melted, recycled metal uses only 5 percent of the electricity needed to make ingot from scratch, which explains why about two out of three aluminum cans are recycled. It still holds twelve ounces of beer, but the can itself contains dramatically less material and energy—and more brains.

Finish your beer. Pick up the can. You can crush it with one hand. Yet when it's full, that same can is strong enough to be stacked in towers six feet high on the floor of a supermarket, piled in the back of a delivery truck, jounced over potholed roads, slammed around and dropped by delivery crews, chilled in a 35-degree refrigerator, or baked in 95-degree sun. What holds it up? Not the metal—crushing it shows that. No, what keeps the can rigid, strong enough to withstand pressure of up to ninety pounds per square inch, is the gas inside: carbon dioxide bubbles in a Bud or a Coke, a shot of nitrogen in a can of tomato juice. Less metal—less energy—held up by something you can neither see nor feel: Joe Six-Pack's Industrial Age talisman has become an icon of the Knowledge Age, the economy of the intangible.

Knowledge has always been important—not for nothing are we *homo sapiens*, thinking man. Throughout history, victory has come to people on the cutting edge of knowledge: to the primitive warriors who learned how to make weapons of iron, who defeated foes armed with bronze; to American business, for a hundred years the beneficiaries of the world's most comprehensive system of public schools, which provided them with its best-educated workforce. But knowledge is more important than ever before. Our stock of intellectual capital matters because we are in the midst of an economic revolution that is creating the Information Age.

To understand what intellectual capital is, why it is so important, and how to grow and manage it, it's crucial to understand what "the Information Age" means. It isn't a slogan to sell home fax machines and extra phone lines. This and the next two chapters of this book will show you how knowledge has come to play the dominant role in our economy, our companies, and our jobs. Knowledge has become the preeminent economic resource—more important than raw material; more important, often, than money. Considered as an economic output, information and knowledge are more important than automobiles, oil, steel, or any of the products of the Industrial Age. We'll begin to see how knowledge and knowledge assets operate and manifest themselves, and we'll understand why managing intellectual capital should be business's first priority.

Welcome to the Revolution

Let us not use the word cheaply: *Revolution*, says Webster's, is "a sudden, radical, or complete change . . . a basic reorientation." To anyone in the world of business, that sounds about right. The changes surrounding us are not mere trends but the workings of large, unruly forces: globalization, which has opened enormous new markets and, a necessary corollary, enormous numbers of new competitors; the spread of information technology and the hell-for-leather growth of computer networks; the dismantling of the many-tiered corporate hierarchy—the characteristic architecture of industrial organization—and the politically charged downsizing and job disruption that attend it, an uninvited guest bearing an unwanted gift, like Carabosse at the christening of the girl who will be the Sleeping Beauty.

Growing up around these is a new Information Age economy, whose fundamental sources of wealth are knowledge and communication rather than natural resources and physical labor. Reigning over it, the late twentieth-century equivalent of the robber barons, is a new generation of tycoons, billionaires not by dint of the oil they pump or the steel they forge but by virtue of a product or a service that may have no physical reality—for example, the millionaires of Netscape, whose Navigator software gets into your computer via modem straight from Netscape's servers, almost never taking on a tangible form, or the billionaires of Microsoft, which owns no factories, whose executives have constructed Puget Sound mansions every bit as vulgarly luxurious as those built in Newport, Rhode Island, by the tycoons of the last century. These transformations—globalization, computerization, economic disintermediation, and intangibilization (an ugly word, but somebody has to use it)—are related. Like logs on a fire, each causes the others to burn more brightly. In the light they cast and in their flickering shadows we sense that business and society are in the midst of change comparable in scale and consequence to the one our great- and great-great grandparents endured.

It has become a cliché to compare this late twentieth-century event—the emergence of the Information Age—to the dislocations and transformation that marked the Industrial Revolution a century and a half ago. Trite but nonetheless true, and it's worth recalling a little of that history for two reasons: first, because it helps to sense the sheer magnitude of what's in store for us; second, because there are instructive parallels between some of the economic pain of our time and the struggles of the Industrial Revolution.

The Industrial Revolution began earlier in Great Britain and France than it did in the United States, where it picked up steam, as it were, after the Civil War, which industrialized the American North as it laid waste the agriculture of the South. The extent of the change can be seen in the astonishing growth of railroad freight service: In 1860, the year before war began, 55 million tons of goods traveled by rail; in 1870, five years after the war ended, 72.5 million tons; in 1885, 437 million tons.

Those first industrial workers—laborers, clerks, foremen, bosses—lived lives their forebears could not have imagined. The idea that people would show up in large numbers at factories and offices, to the same place at the same time, was new. Their fathers commuted to work by walking to the shed or the field after breakfast; this notion of a set time and place to work was weird, unnatural, ungodly. Before the Industrial Revolution, time itself, for most people, was measured by the sun, if it was measured at all; the clocks in one town might be set differently from the clocks in the next hamlet down the pike. In the United States, time wasn't standardized until the nineteenth century, at the insistence of the railroads, which needed to publish train schedules. The eight o'clock whistle, the boss, the manager, the nine-to-five job, the kids at school, the wife at home—these are inventions of the Industrial Age.

It was often violent and it wasn't pretty, as Dickens's brutal *Hard Times* (1854) and Karl Marx and Friedrich Engels's rousing *Communist Manifesto* (1848) show. The overstuffed mansions of the new industrialist class and the effulgent smokestacks of their factories shadowed and begrimed the alleys and hovels of industrialism's have-nots. The old rich, who had made their money from land or the fruits of land like farmstuffs, ores, furs, and timber, loathed the robber barons as much as their employees did. Ideas and knowledge mattered in all of this, of course; the schoolbook version of the Industrial Revolution is a narrative of inventors and inventions: James Watt, Eli Whitney, Thomas Edison. But the idea that mattered most was the accumulation of capital. Those first factories flourished not because they were superior to artisans' workshops in terms of what they made or how efficiently they made it—i.e., output per hour—but because hard-nosed factory owners paid less for labor than owner-artisans would have paid themselves and pocketed the difference. They thus built up capital to invest in expansion, at the same time that improvements in transportation—paved roads, railways, steamships—made it feasible to produce goods for consumption by far-away customers, not just neighbors. Eventually the Industrial Revolution enormously expanded the middle class and raised living standards for all; but at first it actually widened the already yawning gap between rich and poor, just as the Information Revolution is widening it today.

Wars of mass destruction—starting with the Civil War and moving on to the most violent of them all, World War II—coincided with the economy of mass production. One can make a persuasive case that these wars were won in factories rather than on battlefields, which simply ratified the results. It is more than a coincidence that the failure of American arms in Vietnam occurred about the same time as the competitiveness crisis of American industry. In 1971 the dollar was cut loose from gold; there followed the first Arab oil embargo in 1973, the Plaza Accord devaluing the greenback against the Japanese yen, and the rise of Japan's electronics and automobile industries—which was significantly aided by Japanese companies' adept scavenging of American research and technology. The Industrial Age was dying and, though few saw it, something new was struggling to be born.

But that came later. In the springtime of the Industrial Revolution, wealth was created in new ways. Shortly after the Civil War, in 1869, farm goods accounted for nearly 40 percent of U.S. gross domestic product; half a century later, after the end of the First World War, the farmers' share of national output had fallen to 14 percent. (Today it is 1.4 percent.) With the shift from agriculture to industry and from farm to city, whole new businesses appeared—for example, the meatpacking industry. Meat packers were a new middleman, something that wasn't needed when people grew their own and wasn't possible before railroads and refrigeration. Forty years ago, two of the ten biggest companies in America were meat packers.

Sometime between 1910 and 1920, it came to pass that the majority of Americans lived in towns rather than in rural areas. As World War I doughboys sailed home from fighting the Hun in France, a popular song writer wondered, "How you gonna keep 'em down on the farm after they've seen Paree?"

You couldn't: Today only 3.4 million Americans work in agriculture, 2.8 percent of the labor force, and even that tiny percentage continues to fall.

What Is the Information Economy?

Now we're at it again.

Asks George Bennett, founder of Symmetrix, a consulting firm in Lexington, Massachusetts: "If two percent of the population can grow all the food we eat, what if another two percent can manufacture all the refrigerators and other things we need?" Good question. The parking lot of General Electric's appliance factory in Louisville, Kentucky, was built in 1953 to hold 25,000 cars. Today's workforce is 10,000. In 1985, 406,000 people worked for IBM, which made profits of $6.6 billion. In 1987 *Fortune* hailed IBM's longtime leader Thomas J. Watson, Jr., who retired in 1971, as "the most successful capitalist in history." A third of the people, and all of the profits, were gone by 1993. Automaker Volkswagen has said it needs just two thirds of its present workforce. In 1996, AT&T announced it would eliminate 40,000 jobs, about three fifths of them in its newly spun-off manufacturing arm, Lucent Technologies. Manufacturing's share of U.S. employment has plunged, from 34 percent of the workforce in 1950 to 16 percent today, and about a third of those people are not production workers, being instead accountants, managers, designers, marketers, and other people who work primarily with information.

"The downsizing of America" (as the *New York Times* called it in a somewhat overwrought series of stories early in 1996) has become a major political issue, beneath which courses very real anxiety. But downsizing, though it is an element of the plot, is not the story. The story is the Information Revolution's reinvention of business, economic life, and society. Just as the Industrial Revolution wrought havoc in the countryside and in the swelling town, this new event will transfigure and disfigure all it touches—and it will touch everything.

It's difficult to track how knowledge changes the economy because it takes so many wildly different forms. Economists call it a "heterogeneous resource," and well they might; management reports, library books, bursts of electrons in cyberspace, and water-cooler gossip are all forms of information. How does one person's laboratory study of the biochemistry of the virus that causes AIDS compare to another's book about the paintings of Caravaggio or a third person's report about Toyota's sales in Thailand? As we'll see, people trying to manage corporate knowledge often get tangled up by the problems of deciding what's important knowledge and what's not.

Economists, bless 'em, can sidestep such nettle patches: If you can express it in dollars, that's good enough. A number of people have tried to measure the "information sector" of the economy in dollar terms. In 1994, *Business Week* proposed "a new statistical system designed for the Information Age," dividing the economy into three sectors: Goods (most manufacturing, along with mining and utilities); Services ("people-oriented" ones such as auto repair, banking, elementary and secondary education, health care, hotels, etc.); and Information (advertising, communications, computers and software, higher education, entertainment, publishing, the securities industry, etc.). By that reckoning, about 15.3 percent of the American labor force is in the information sector. *Business Week*'s rough cut wasn't bad, but it was arbitrary. For instance, why were high schools and banks stuck in the service sector while colleges and stock brokerages got into the glamorous information sector? It also missed taking a look at a question that's more interesting, and far more important to businesses and the people who work in them than the mere classification of industries into sectors: What role does knowledge play in the entire economy—and in my company, and in my job—not just in the "information sector"?

An answer to that fundamental question appeared long before most people ever imagined asking it. In 1962, Princeton University economist Fritz Machlup published *The Production and Distribution of Knowledge in the United States*, later expanded into an eight-volume work under the general title *Knowledge: Its Creation, Distribution, and Economic Significance*. Machlup attempted to measure the economic value of knowledge production, and concluded, using 1958 data, that 34.5 percent of the gross national product of the United States could be allocated to the information sector. In 1977, the U.S. Department of Commerce published a Ph.D. dissertation called *The Information Economy*, written by Marc Porat, later the CEO of General Magic, a communications software developer in Silicon Valley. Using 1967 data, the most recent available to him, Porat first defined a "primary information sector." Into it he put the entire contribution to GDP of such industries as communications, banking and finance, professional services, and education, plus an estimate of what portion of other industries' output was devoted to information; for example, he put about three fifths of value-added in the electrical machinery business into the information sector because it came from typewriters, computers, printing presses, telephones and their switches, copiers, and so on.* Added up, the numbers were stunning: The information sector was 25.1 percent of GDP (including government), and it generated 43 percent of all corporate profits.

More than that, actually: Porat next identified a "secondary information sector," which he said "includes all the information services produced for internal consumption by government and noninformation firms. . . . For example, a portion of an automobile's market price pays for the R&D, management, and advertising services necessary to bring the product to market." That, he figured, was worth an additional 21 percent of GDP, for a grand total of over 46 percent.

Porat probably put too much into his information sector, though he left out kitchen sinks. Nevertheless, those statistics, from just be-

---

* Value-added is statistician-speak for the difference between the cost of materials and supplies and the price received for finished goods: The difference between everything bought from outside and the money you get for everything people buy from you. Value-added, widely used as a basis for taxation in Europe, is used to calculate GDP to prevent double-counting, which would occur if one simply added up sales. For example, the steel in a car is sold several times—by the iron mine to the steel mill, by the steel mill to the carmaker, and by the carmaker to the consumer.

fore the decadence of the Industrial Revolution became apparent, show the dimensions of the revolution. Alas, no one has brought Machlup's and Porat's numbers past 1980, when Machlup's disciples estimated that the knowledge industry was 36.5 percent of GDP, but it is obvious that the "information economy" continues to expand: Just look at the growth of the computing, communications, and entertainment industries. Every country, company, and individual depends increasingly on knowledge—patents, processes, skills, technologies, information about customers and suppliers, and old-fashioned experience. Even Pope John Paul II recognized the growing importance of "know-how, technology, and skill" in his 1991 encyclical *Centesimus Annus*, writing: "Whereas at one time the decisive factor of production was the land, and later capital . . . today the decisive factor is increasingly man himself, that is, his knowledge."

Knowledge has become the primary ingredient of what we make, do, buy, and sell. As a result, managing it—finding and growing intellectual capital, storing it, selling it, sharing it—has become the most important economic task of individuals, businesses, and nations.

This has been hard-to-grasp stuff, but no longer is it *recherché*. The primacy of brainpower is everywhere evident, if you look.

The Knowledge Content of Practically Everything

Look at the "knowledge content" of everyday goods and services. The laptop computer on which I am composing these words—a Macintosh PowerBook 5300c purchased in 1995, and I love it and cannot understand why anyone has anything but a Mac—but I digress—weighs 6.2 pounds. It has 8 megabytes of RAM and a 500 megabyte hard drive, a color screen, and a processing speed of 100 megahertz, which was fast when I bought it. The original IBM personal computer, introduced in 1981, came in three pieces—keyboard, monochrome monitor, central processing unit—that tipped the scales at 44.3 pounds. The keyboard alone weighed 6.1 pounds, about what my laptop does. Instead of RAM and a hard drive, the first PC had something called "user memory," all of 16 kilobytes of it. Counting just RAM, not the hard drive, my Mac has a brainpan about 500 times bigger than the old PC's in a body about one-seventh the size. That's a 3,500-fold higher ratio of intelligence to silicon, metal, plastic, wire, and other physical attributes.

We see the same change in machine tools, the metal-cutting and metal-shaping lathes, drills, and dies used in factories. More than half the money spent on them is for computer numerically controlled tools. These CNC machines, each with a built-in microprocessor to guide its drill bits and other tools, are to the old mechanical machine tools what a personal computer is to a manual typewriter. Says Jodie Glore, vice president of the automation group at industrial-controls powerhouse Allen-Bradley: "The electro-mechanical boxes we used to sell had a macho feel. You could tell that they cost a lot. Now it's 'You see this disk . . . ?' "

The new Boeing 777 airliner, designed entirely on computers without paper drawings or mockups, has three on-board computers, and only two engines. The aircraft is powered by petroleum; more than half the cost of finding and extracting the petroleum is information.

A typical automobile, powered by information-rich gasoline, has more microchips than sparkplugs. A car's electronics cost more than the steel in it.

Steel, of course, was the quintessential manufactured product of the early twentieth century. Its value came from the physical effort of extracting the ore from the Mesabi Range in Minnesota, shipping millions of tons of it to Pittsburgh or Birmingham, then laboring in hellish conditions to transform it into steel in the mills. We still make a lot of steel, of course, but the physical part of steelmaking is far less important than it was. A big producer like Bethlehem used to need three or four man-hours of labor to make a ton of steel. Now Nucor Steel has revolutionized the business of sheet steel with a process that requires sophisticated computers—it can't work without them—and requires only forty-five man-minutes of labor per ton. The intellectual component has grown and the physical component shrunk.

Now consider the quintessential manufactured product of the late twentieth century: the microchip. The value of all the chips produced today exceeds the value of the steel produced. What makes them valuable? Certainly not their physical component. Chips are made mainly from silicon, that is, from sand, and not much of it. The value is mainly in the design of the chip, and in the design of the complex machines that make it. It is in the intellectual content, not the physical.

About four out of five of the dollars Levi Straus spends to made a pair of blue jeans go to information, not to make, dye, cut, and sew denim.

Overall, by the estimate of James Brian Quinn of the Tuck School of Business at Dartmouth College, information has become the source of about three fourths of value-added in manufacturing. In the heyday of old-fashioned manufacturing, it made sense for companies to gather under one roof as much as possible of what they needed for their work. Henry Ford's vertically integrated factory on the River Rouge in Detroit, where Ford made its own steel, its own parts, and, of course, cars, was one of the industrial wonders of its time. Today, Information Age advances in logistics, computer-aided design, and communication permit companies to outsource factory work—the very work that once defined them. Three out of ten large U.S. industrial companies outsource more than half their manufacturing. According to *Purchasing* magazine, in 1995 the average company spent nearly five times more on purchased parts, supplies, and services than it did just four years before. U.S. automakers today make none of their own steel and fewer than half the parts that go into their cars. Chrysler outsources 70 percent. It's an exaggeration, but not an outrageous one, to say that the Big Three are chiefly design studios and marketers, not manufacturers.

In a word, manufacturing is dematerializing. We are witnessing, say Lehigh University professors Steven Goldman, Roger Nagel, and Kenneth Preiss, "the convergence of goods and services . . . It is forcing a reconceptualization of what we mean by the terms 'production' and 'product.' "

And, of course, more and more we buy pure knowledge in the service sector. A partner in a New York law firm doesn't charge $400 an hour because his physical assets—his desk, his bust of Oliver Wendell Holmes—are so costly; you're paying for his brainpower. Industries that transport information are growing faster than those that transport goods: International voice telephone traffic has been increasing at about 16 percent a year; data traffic about 30 percent a year, Internet traffic faster still.

In air transportation, *all* the profits are in information: The *Official Airline Guide* is profitable, but the airlines collectively lost billions in the early 1990s—losses that would have been greater had they not been partly offset by profits from their reservation systems. Only 10 percent of the revenues of AMR, American Airlines' parent company, come from fees charged by its Sabre reservation system, but in 1995, after the airlines returned to profitability, Sabre produced 44 percent of the company's pretax profits. Indeed, one could say that air travel has become two different industries: the flying industry, which is marginally profitable at best, and the information-about-flying industry, which makes money hand over fist.

Even money has dematerialized. Time was, when nations traded currencies, officials of the Federal Reserve Bank of New York loaded gold bars onto trolleys and rolled them from one country's basement vault to another; today, some $1.3 *trillion* in currency is traded every day, and never takes tangible form:

> Money has been changing from a standard unit of value—a fixed and limited asset, a substantial and absolute "truth"—into something ethereal, volatile, and electronic. Over the last twenty-five years it has been moving from a government-mandated equivalency—$35 equals one ounce of gold, a concept first developed five thousand years ago—to a new electronic form. It has become nothing more than an assemblage of ones and zeros, the fundamental units of computing. It is these ones and zeros, representing money, that are piped through miles of wire, pumped over fiber-optic highways, bounced off satellites, and beamed from one microwave relay station to another. This new money is like a shadow. Its cool-gray shape can be seen but not touched. It has no tactile dimension, no heft or weight . . . Money is now an image.

Like the Industrial Revolution, the Information Revolution affects everything. Americans need so much less muscle power than we used to that the Department of Agriculture recommends we live on 2,000 calories a day—far less than the 3,700 calories we do consume, which is why stadium seats are too narrow, and less than the 3,752 calories that were the average daily diet of the slaves on George Washington's plantation in 1790, few of whom, one presumes, were pudgy. Thanks to research into high-yielding hybrid grains, farmers produce about five times more corn per acre than they could in the 1920s; put another way, today's ear of corn is 80 percent knowledge.

For military strategists, information is assuming the role that factories played for a century. Today's armed forces invest much more than yesterday's in training and education. During the Vietnam War, when educated people did their damnedest to avoid the military, 15 percent of U.S. military personnel had not graduated from high school; today 99.3 percent are high-school graduates; the percentage with postgraduate degrees has more than doubled. The Persian Gulf War displayed the devastating power of "smart bombs"—cruise missiles and the like—where a huge amount of information and intelligence deliver pinpoint and much more effective destruction with much less TNT than the strategic bombing of World War II or the carpet bombing of Vietnam. Now, Pentagon strategists are imagining wars that will not be fought on battlefields or in factories, but in the unseen realm of information. The primary targets in future wars are likely to be information systems, including financial services and telephone systems as well as military-command setups; studying how to launch or defend against "a Pearl Harbor attack on our information infrastructure" is keeping the lights burning late in the Pentagon. At Fort McNair in Washington, D.C., an Information Resources Management College has been added to Army, Naval, and Air War Colleges of the National Defense University. In war as in peace, the physical component has shrunk, the intellectual grown.

Brian Arthur, an economist who divides his time between Stanford University and the Santa Fe Institute, summarizes the shift this way: In the old economy, people bought and sold "congealed resources"— a lot of material held together by a little bit of knowledge. (Think of an ingot of aluminum, for example, made of bauxite and huge amounts of electricity according to a 100-year-old smelting process.) In the new economy, we buy and sell "congealed knowledge"—a lot of intellectual content in a physical slipcase. (Think of a piece of computer software, or a new aircraft, most of whose cost is R&D.)

The new economy will transform the old and reduce its relative importance, but will not kill it. Microsoft chairman Bill Gates, to date the preeminent capitalist of the Knowledge Age, spends his money on a big house and fancy cars, tangible stuff indeed. The Industrial Revolution did not end agriculture, because we still have to eat, and the Information Revolution will not end industry, because we still need those beer cans. No one can say for certain what new ways of working and prospering this revolution will create; in a revolution the only surety is surprise. But it's already obvious that success in a knowledge-based economy depends on new skills and new kinds of organizations and management.

The new era is already here, but its social and economic transformations have not even peaked. The transition may be difficult. As Neal Soss, chief economist for C.S. First Boston, puts it: "Adjustment is the dismal part of the dismal science." And, as Robespierre might have observed on his way to the guillotine, this time it's personal—for the inescapable tumult involves your company and your career.

CHAPTER 2

The Knowledge Company

STICK CLOSE TO YOUR DESKS AND *NEVER GO TO SEA*
AND YOU ALL MAY BE RULERS OF THE QUEEN'S NAVEE!
—W. S. GILBERT

Y ou would be hard-pressed to find a single industry, a single company, a single organization of any kind, that has not become more "information-intensive"—dependent on knowledge as a source of what attracts customers and clients and on information technology as a means of running the place. In this chapter, we'll look at the Information Revolution inside the walls of corporations to see what it means to be a "knowledge company." We'll look first at the enormous growth in the sheer *amount* of information companies handle. Second, we'll see what they *do* with it—how companies use information to replace inventories, warehouses, and other physical assets, saving both money and time. Finally, we'll look at how knowledge-intensive companies are organized differently from traditional outfits.

Take, for instance, a little company called InterDesign, located in Solon, Ohio, a few miles east of Cleveland. Like most businessmen who do not have to report to public shareholders, founder and chief executive Robert Immerman is reluctant to disclose financial details about his company, but he will say that InterDesign's annual sales are near $20 million, and that it's profitable. InterDesign began in 1974 importing and hawking wood products such as Scandinavian-designed boxes, lamps, and other items. Now its product line is almost entirely plastic—plastic clocks, refrigerator magnets, soap dishes, wastebaskets, and the like, designed by Immerman's people and manufactured to their specifications by factories that work under contract to the company. Wal-Mart, Kmart, and Target are customers, as are hundreds of housewares stores.

There's not a high-tech item in the InterDesign catalog, unless you count digital clocks, but computers have changed the business. In the past fourteen years, InterDesign's employment has tripled. The total space it occupies has quintupled. Sales have octupled. But the number of megabytes of computer memory the company uses has gone up thirtyfold. In 1985 Immerman dug deep and found $10,000 to buy a used disk drive that had 288 megabytes of storage—capacity that cost a couple of hundred dollars in 1996. Says Immerman: "In the seventies we went to the Post Office to pick up our orders. In the early eighties we put in an 800 number. Late eighties, we got a fax machine. In 1991, pressured first by Target Stores, we added electronic data interchange." Now more than half of InterDesign's orders arrive via modem straight into company computers. Errors in order entry and shipping have all but disappeared. Immerman says: "We had fifty weeks perfect with a big chain, then one week we missed part of the order for one item on a long list—and they're on the phone wondering what's wrong." Staffers who used to work the phones taking orders now bend over computer screens tracking sales by product, color, customer, region—valuable information that Immerman once couldn't afford to collect. Time and money that he once had to spend keeping track of today's business have been liberated and redirected toward research and innovation—new designs, new products—that are the basis of tomorrow's business.

InterDesign's story is typical. Practically every package deliverer, bank teller, retail clerk, telephone operator, and bill collector in America works with a computer. Like sand in a beach house, information gets in everywhere. Managing this flood of knowledge—not just invoices and messages and figures, but also patents, processes, employees' skills, technologies, knowledge of customers and suppliers, and old-fashioned experience—is more than ever what determines whether a company succeeds or fails.

How Companies Are Becoming More Knowledge-Intensive

If you want to figure out what a business is doing, follow the money. The trail leads straight to information. Companies make two basic kinds of expenditure. One is capital spending—money invested in property, equipment, and other assets that are expected to last for a while and whose ultimate benefit—the return on the investment—will be spread out over time. In addition to capital equipment, organizations also make long-term investments in, for example, research and development and training; these are also a form of capital spending, although accounting rules insist that they usually be treated like the other kind of corporate spending, expenses. Expenses, the second reason companies cut checks, are day-to-day costs: payroll, raw material, supplies, advertising, shipping, rent, etc. The distinction between capital spending and expenses is not always clear-cut, which is one reason accountants earn big bucks, but it is very clear that the Information Age has drastically changed both kinds of expenditures.

Take capital spending, which is tracked by the U.S. Department of Commerce's Bureau of Economic Analysis. Detailed BEA figures show private-sector spending on traditional, Industrial Age capital goods—engines and turbines, electrical distribution and control apparatus, metal-working machinery, materials handling and general industrial equipment, machinery for services, equipment for mining and oil fields, agriculture, and construction—has held more or less steady, at about $110 billion a year, since 1982. It has sagged in time of recession, bulged in boom times, but always around that $110 billion-a-year figure.

Capital spending for information machines has ballooned, however. In 1982, American companies spent $49 billion on computers and telecommunications gear. By 1987, that sum had grown to $86.2 billion, and it kept going. Plotted on a graph, the two lines—Industrial Age and Information Age capital spending—cross in 1991. That year, spending for production technology was $107 billion and information technology spending was $112 billion. Call that Year One of the Information Age. Ever since, companies have spent more money on equipment that gathers, processes, analyzes, and distributes information than on machines that stamp, cut, assemble, lift, and otherwise manipulate the physical world.

Those figures are impressive, but they understate investment in information-moving equipment. They do not factor in the newfound intelligence of some "old economy" equipment such as computer-controlled machine tools; nor do they fully account for the fact that a dollar spent on computers today buys much more processing power than ever: In the first half of the 1990s, while corporate spending for computer hardware almost doubled, the amount of processing power that money bought rose nearly threefold. Nor do they include expensed investments in knowledge, such as research and development. Some companies, including many in Japan, spend more on R&D than they do on all forms of capital equipment. Says Fumio Kodama, a professor of innovation policy at Saitama University near Tokyo: "If R&D investment begins to surpass capital investment the corporation could be said to be shifting from being a place for *production* to being a place for *thinking.*"

What has that money bought? Consequences are difficult to predict, even in the short run. For businesses, the first effect of change is usually to improve what already exists—to do something faster, better, cheaper, or more. These effects, note sociologists Lee Sproull and Sara Kiesler in *Connections,* a book about the effects of electronic networks on organizations, are "the anticipated technical ones—the planned efficiency gains or productivity gains that justify an investment in new technology," and estimating them is hard enough. But change creates second-order effects as well, unanticipated, impossible-to-predict consequences and opportunities. Gottlieb Daimler, Ransom Olds, and their friends and rivals thought they had improved the horse. They had no way of knowing that the automobile would fill the countryside with suburbs—which, in turn, created thousands of jobs building roads and houses, making lawn mowers, selling tulip bulbs, and delivering pizza.

We can barely begin—but we can begin—to see how the Information Revolution alters organizations. Partly the difficulty arises from the peculiar nature of its core technology, information-processing machines. Writes Harvard Business School professor Shoshana Zuboff:

> Information technology is characterized by a fundamental duality . . . On the one hand, the technology can be applied to automating operations according to a logic that hardly differs from that of the nineteenth-century machine system—replace the human body with a technology that enables the same processes to be performed with more continuity and control. On the other, the same technology simultaneously generates information about the underlying productive and administrative processes through which an organization accomplishes its work. It provides a deeper level of transparency to activities that had been either partially or completely opaque. In this way information technology supersedes the traditional logic of automation.

Information technology speeds up activities like adding a series of rows and columns of figures, but a corporation becomes a true knowledge company when it becomes aware of and involved in the "deeper level," where information is pursued for its own intrinsic value and not simply to automate or report on other activities. It will find itself involved in new realms of activity, such as:

Mining valuable detail: Some hotel chains, for example, keep track of their customers' favorite morning newspaper or preferences for smoking or nonsmoking rooms. MCI made its "Friends and Family" program a huge success that rival AT&T couldn't copy because the latter wasn't able to keep equally detailed records.

Running simulations: Simulation is now the main way in which geologists look for oil: Data gathered from aerial photography, seismographs, and subterranean probes are combined into a virtual image of what's underground, then analyzed by computer. All kinds of other new business activities can be performed in the intangible realm of what-if: What if we raised the price? added more thrust to the engines? acquired Universal Widget? It's through simulations that Boeing designed its 777 jetliner, and it was through simulation that Merck made its decision to acquire Medco Containment services (see Chapter 9).

Making a business out of knowledge itself: Information-intensive companies often become information vendors. IBM, for example, gets more revenue from selling computer services than from selling computers; Ryder doesn't just rent trucks but also sells logistics management.

The all-pervading, unconfined nature of knowledge—the sand in the beach house, invisible even when you feel it underfoot—confounds anyone trying to sort out how knowledge-intensive organizations work. It is in this context—automation and efficiency racing hip-to-hip with fumbling, perhaps foolish, not-yet efficient new ventures and new work—that one can begin to understand why there has been enormous controversy about what organizations have to show for all the money they poured into computers. Managers have intuited all along that information technology boosts productivity. For years, however, economists failed to find any gains, and puzzled over the "productivity paradox": If the stuff didn't do any good, why did companies keep buying it?

Many of those studies turn out to be gravely flawed. Some, for example, looked at industry-level data, and found that each dollar spent on high-tech capital earned back only eighty cents—that is, it was a waste of money. That result is not surprising when you think about it. Wal-Mart has spent more than a billion dollars on information technology, and done it so cleverly that it cut costs, improved service, wooed customers from competitors like Kmart, and sold more stuff out of each store. But very little of the productivity gain showed up in industry-level statistics. Some of it left the industry altogether, ending up in consumers' pockets as they benefited from lower prices. Some simply moved from one company's coffers to another's—a dollar gained for Wal-Mart, a dollar lost by Kmart—so that Wal-Mart's productivity gain would be canceled out by Kmart's loss. And since Kmart and every other discount retailer invested heavily in information technology, too, the industry-wide total would of course show a net loss in productivity. But did Wal-Mart waste its money? Of course not.

Data at the company level is what is relevant, and it is extremely hard to get; some economists have been forced to rely on 1978–82 figures—ancient history for computers. Recent company-level figures tell a more accurate story. In 1993, two economists at MIT, Erik Brynjolfsson and Lorin Hitt, with current data from annual surveys of companies' spending on computers gathered by International Data Corporation (IDC), reinvestigated. They found an astonishing eight-to-one difference between the return on investment in "computer capital" and the return from investments in other capital equipment. A year later, the ratio had climbed to ten to one. Those numbers are undoubtedly high: The "computer capital" numbers included computers alone—PCs, terminals, minicomputers, mainframes, and supercomputers—but not essential but ancillary gear such as network wiring, routers, and telecommunications equipment. In addition, because of the rapid improvement in information technology, computers are replaced more often than, say, machines for extruding plastics, so the investment depreciates faster.

It is nevertheless clear that spending for equipment that creates, codifies, manipulates, and distributes information has become more productive than investment in equipment that makes and moves material goods.* It is worth noting that the reward for investing in intellectual capital goods is similar to the return on investment in another form of knowledge capital, research and development: Columbia University professor Frank Lichtenberg measured the return on investment for spending on new plant and equipment—that is, physical capital—versus the return on R&D spending. He found that a dollar spent on R&D returned eight times more than a dollar spent on new machinery. A new machine helps you do old work better; it delivers incremental improvement. R&D leads to innovation—whole new products and services that presumably are of a higher value than the ones they replace.

Competing with Information

One of information's most powerful advantages is its ability to wipe out inventory. The battle of information versus inventory is an age-old business rivalry, a perpetual game of one-upmanship, like the badinage of Shakespeare's Beatrice and Benedick or the children's game of rock-paper-scissors. The giant department store with thousands of items in stock versus the boutique with a carefully chosen selection, personal service, and knowledgeable staff. The category killer versus

---

* Companies are, however, having a hard time holding on to those gains in the form of profits—a problem and an opportunity that are addressed in the discussion of the "information wars" in Chapter 9.

the discount store. The encyclopedia that contains something about everything versus the monograph that contains precisely what you want. (For service companies, the role of information's antagonist is played by assets like truck fleets or bank deposits.) This competition has been fought on the basis of cost and availability: Do you have what I want when I want it at the price I want to pay? For most of business history, inventory beat information, largely because information could never be precise enough. Companies covered up for what they didn't know by keeping extra stock on hand.

How powerful can it be to use information in place of inventory? Powerful enough to bring the world's biggest companies to their knees—for the substitution of knowledge for inventory, land, and other physical capital is how the Japanese automobile industry clobbered Detroit. Lacking both money and space, the Japanese turned away from capital-intensive, U.S.-style automaking and invented an information-intensive industry. Crowded Japan didn't have room for gigantic factories; cash-strapped Japanese companies couldn't afford to tie up trillions of yen in in-process inventory. The solution: Instead of holding parts just in case, summon them to arrive just in time. The technology behind Toyota's manufacturing genius is called *kanban*. The vaunted kanban system is a little piece of paper, like an index card, attached to a bin of parts. When the bin gets low, the worker on the assembly line clips the card to a string like a moving clothesline, and the card zips back, signaling "more parts, please." That's all *kanban* is—except that the lines of communication go as far back as possible, even deep into Toyota's supplier network, and, as a result, no one carries any more inventory than absolutely necessary. Real-time, accurate *information* takes its place.

In today's wired world of commerce, information beats inventory much more often. The plummeting cost of information and its associated technology, dropping faster than Wile E. Coyote, has changed the economics of organizations. Companies can deploy it in huge quantities, sort and resort it *ad infinitum*, transport it at warp speed, and substitute knowledge for goods. According to David Hale, the chief economist of Zurich Kemper Financial Services, "new computerized control systems . . . have produced a structural downward adjustment in [companies'] required levels of stocks." The ratio of inventories to goods consumed varies with the business cycle—rising as unsold goods pile up at the start of a recession, falling as recovery takes hold, then slowly rising again—but the trend is unmistakably downward.

Victories of information over inventory are transforming business after business. In the oldest of industries, farming, knowledge is doing work that grain elevators and acreage did. Says Seth Lloyd, a professor of mechanical engineering at MIT: "A nineteenth-century farmer who wished to provide a cushion against the failure of his wheat crop would plant some fields of corn; today's farmer sells options—bits of information on pieces of paper that represent transactions on a mercantile exchange—to provide a guaranteed income in case the crop fails." At Pioneer Hi-Bred International, scientists breed special strains of corn for disease resistance, high yield, or specific attributes like oil content. A decade ago such work ate up hundreds of acres of farmland and consumed untold numbers of man-hours. These days agricultural chemists can create new hybrids by manipulating the plant's DNA directly at a laboratory bench. Apart from the cost savings, Pioneer Hi-Bred expects to knock two years off the seven- to ten-year time it takes to develop a new hybrid. With more resources available, the company now can devote its efforts to producing a proliferating line of specialized products—breeding strains rich in cornstarch for industrial users or in specific oils for food processors. The upshot, says research vice president Rick McConnell: "Corn is no longer a commodity."

As the usefulness of information, information technology, and information work grows, businesses find more ways to substitute them for expensive investments in physical assets—not just inventories, but also factories and warehouses. By using high-speed data communications networks to track production, stock, and orders, GE Lighting has since 1987 closed twenty-six of thirty-four U.S. warehouses and replaced twenty-five customer service centers with one new, high-tech operation. In effect, those buildings and stockpiles—physical assets—have been replaced by networks and databases—intellectual assets. In eastern Belgium, a few stones' throws from the Dutch border, stands an Owens Corning factory that makes fiberglass insulation. The business is a seasonal and cyclical one, strongly influenced by the amount of residential and commercial construction, but the manufacturing process runs most efficiently if the plant can make continuous, long runs of the same product. In combination, seasonality and process led Owens Corning to build big stocks of inventory—boards and bags of fiberglass stored in a gigantic warehouse and sometimes in open air.

"We need a bigger warehouse," a plant manager told me. He's not going to get it, Rich Karcher, the chief financial officer of Owens Corning Europe, vows: "We've got to substitute information for inventory." By matching raw-material stocks more precisely to production plans, and linking incoming orders directly to purchasing and manufacturing schedules, Karcher estimates that the plant can cut its raw-material and finished goods inventory enough to obviate the need for more warehousing forever.

The substitution of information for inventory has begun to reinvent retailing. In Hallmark Cards stores, an electronic kiosk can print a card just for you. You can go into a record store and have a cassette custom-made. IBM and Blockbuster Video have the technology to make CDs on the spot, downloaded from a server somewhere. For now, music companies are not willing to make a deal, but it is coming—a teenager will walk into Tower Records, ask for the new Alanis Morrisette CD, and the clerk will manufacture it while she waits. A high-speed data line will replace the inventory.

It is only a matter of time before books are made the same way. Cathy Walt, a consultant, moonlights teaching a course in the anthropology of organizations at Rutgers University's business school. Rather than use a textbook, she selects articles from professional journals and newspapers, chapters from books, and other material. She takes these to her local Kinko's copy shop, which negotiates permission fees with the copyright holders. Kinko's scans the material into a computer, prints it and binds it, using high-resolution printers that produce a page that's as good-looking as this one. There's no dust jacket, and the binding is merely utilitarian, but it's good enough for Walt and her students. And there's no inventory—not a single copy too few, not one too many. Technology will not have to get much better before a person can walk into Barnes & Noble and find a machine that looks like a cross between a copier and a jukebox. Select a book. Stick in a credit card. Go to the coffee bar. A few minutes after you and your cappuccino find a table, a clerk will come over and hand you a perfectly decent-looking—maybe even a very good-looking—paperbound copy of John Grisham's latest thriller, still warm from the printer. Publishers and booksellers will have a chance to reduce the drag on the industry from the huge weight of inventory—more than a third of books shipped by publishers return unsold.

Some retailers have dematerialized entirely. Already, especially in the Christmas shopping season, each day's mail brings a stack of virtual department stores. CUC International, the electronic shoppers club, has no inventory whatsoever. It has a catalog, that's all, a list of, say, dozens of available clock radios. A customer calls the company's 800 number, or logs onto Compuserve or America Online, and places an order; CUC passes it on (taking a commission), and the order is shipped from the manufacturer. The CEO, Walter Forbes, says: "This is virtual reality inventory. We stock nothing, but we sell everything."

The triumph of information over inventory is even visible in banking:

> The banks are made of marble,
> With a guard at every door,
> And the vaults are stuffed with silver
> That the worker sweated for.

So went a rousing 1950's folk anthem. Today, the bank branch office, with its marble walls, steel bars, imposing safe, and big inventory of bills and coins, has become an automatic teller next to the Coke machine at the front of the supermarket, with a small inventory of bills. Even that has begun to shrink to a small box the size of an ordinary book, a scanner for a credit or debit card, with no bills at all, just a spurt of electrons that takes money from a shopper's bank account and pays it to the A&P. Once again, information (the *idea* of money) replaces physical goods (the greenbacks themselves).

"If you had to do the banking industry over again, you wouldn't use bricks and mortar," says Neal P. Miller, manager of Fidelity Investments' New Millennium Fund. You'd certainly use a lot less of them. Between December 1993 and October 1995, Wells Fargo & Company, the nation's ninth biggest bank, which got into banking by acting as a storage depot for '49ers gold nuggets, reduced the number of its traditional, 7,500-square-foot branches from 624 to 537, on its way down to perhaps 400. For every traditional branch it is closing, however, Wells Fargo is setting up, in California supermarkets, a full-service "minibranch" of 400 square feet—less than one fifteenth the size of the old branches—and it is installing an additional 500 manned kiosks of 36 square feet.

There's a simple but powerful lesson to be drawn from this catalog of the ways in which knowledge companies use information to beat back inventory: every bin of parts, every pallet of raw material, every uncollected bill, every piece of paper in transit from one person's in-box to another ties up time and money to no useful purpose. It's "working capital" to an accountant—and driving it out is one of the first ways in which investments in information and knowledge can boost corporate performance.

Information Takes on an Economic Life of Its Own

Nicholas Negroponte, the visionary director of the Media Lab at the Massachusetts Institute of Technology, writes that the world of atoms—tangible, physical reality—is giving way to a world of bits—ethereal electronic impulses. In this cyberspacey future, PCs become vending machines to which people turn for everything from making love to buying stock in an initial public offering. Both of those happen now, but so does much that contradicts the somewhat frightening image of a nation of people sitting alone in dim rooms before glowing computer screens. Catalog merchants like Lands' End have opened real stores; revitalized downtown districts like Baltimore's harbor district, New York's Times Square, and the Third Street Promenade in Santa Monica, California, are crowded with people made of very real atoms. Dematerialization isn't the whole story. The knowledge company and economy are more subtle and much more interesting than dematerialization alone. In the knowledge company, information begins to take on a reality of its own, separate from physical goods; it becomes, paradoxically, as tangible a reality as the material stuff we're used to. Understanding the materialization of the immaterial takes some explanation—but it's essential to learning how to compete with knowledge.

In the old corporation, information was very much connected to the physical flow of things—taped or stapled to it, usually. If you wanted to buy a shirt, you went to a store, picked one out, and paid for it, using cash, a check drawn on a local bank, or your store charge account, whose records were kept upstairs in the credit office. The shirt and the information about the shirt, including the exchange of money, were all in the same place. My first job—not counting mowing lawns, shoveling snow, and handling a friend's newspaper route when he was away at camp—was summer work as a stockboy in a men's clothing store in Chicago's Loop. I opened cartons of trousers, jackets, and suits, each of which contained a sheaf of paper describing the contents; then I consulted a price list, stuck price tags on the merchandise, and hung the stuff on racks; thus festooned with the information that described it, the clothing waited its turn to go down to the selling floor. In factories, meanwhile—this is abstract, but it's neat—machines embodied all the knowledge necessary for them to do their jobs. Each machine was a specialist: It knew how to cut and sew a buttonhole, how to stamp out a piece of metal of exactly this or that shape, how to drill a hole precisely so wide and so deep. The machine was in the same place as the knowledge it needed to carry out its task—one could say it knew its own instructions.

In the new economy, information flow and physical flow frequently diverge. If you want a shirt, you might look at a catalog, use a telephone to send your voice through an electronic network, and recite the number of a credit-card to a clerk who is probably in Omaha, the center of the telemarketing industry; he or she checks the card's validity via another network, then uses a third electronic network to dispatch instructions to the company's warehouse—which is probably not in Omaha—to send the shirt to you. The shirt and the bill travel separately to your home. You pay your bill not to the merchant but to the credit-card company, which collects its payment not in cash but during a dead-of-night electronic transfer of entirely disembodied funds from your bank to its bank, then on to the merchant. At no time have the shirt, the information about it, or the transaction been in the same place. Even if you buy the shirt in a store using a Visa or Master-Card, you and the shirt will return home by a completely different route from the path the transaction will follow. In the factory, meanwhile, where once stood many machines that knew what to do, there now pose a few "smart" machines that are in fact sublimely ignorant. Computer-controlled flexible manufacturing systems sport hundreds of drills and other tools and have an almost infinite capacity to vary the work they do, but someone or something else has to tell them what that is. The machine is not the same as the knowledge of how to do a task. Without a programmer—or another computer—to instruct them, it is lost.

Information was once a shadow, and little more: a price tag on a suit, a notation in a ledger. Deriving from physical reality, sometimes thrown before it, sometimes following behind, information was always inseparable from it; useful not for its own sake but because of what it revealed about whatever cast it; dependent for its very existence—if a shadow can be said to exist at all—on the body that made it.

The shadow has come unstuck, like Peter Pan's, caught when the window snapped shut on it. It is a defining fact about organizations in the Information Age: Knowledge and information take on their own reality, which can be detached from the physical movement of goods and services. From this divergence come at least two important implications. First, knowledge and the assets that create and distribute it can be managed, just as physical and financial assets can be. Indeed, intellectual and physical-financial assets can be managed separately from one another; they can be managed together; they can be managed in relation to one another. Second: If knowledge is the greatest source of wealth, then individuals, companies, and nations should invest in the assets that produce and process knowledge. Those assets are not necessarily high-tech gizmos, and those investments should not all be high-tech investments. In the previous section I deliberately chose traditional industries like farming, retailing, and banking to show how much more value those companies can bring to their stockholders and customers through knowledge.

Old habits of mind die hard. Because physical flows and the flow of information used to mingle in one indivisible stream, it is easy to confuse them. Failing to understand the difference can cost an organization dearly. A few years ago, one of the largest publishers in the United States, whose principal business was textbooks, acquired a smaller company, which chiefly published fiction and nonfiction sold in retail bookstores—"trade" books. Soon after the acquisition, arrangements were made to consolidate the two warehouses. Handling the books was no problem: The acquiring company's warehouse had plenty of shelves and loading docks; more people would be hired. But more computers were also needed to handle order-entry and billing— the flow of information; the question was how many. To answer it, the acquiring company looked at the trade publisher's records to see how many books it had shipped in previous years. It then added data-processing capacity based on its own experience of how much was needed to bill and ship that many books.

"How many books?" was the wrong question, however. The company had confused managing inventory with managing information. The right, unasked question was, "How many *orders and invoices* do you process?" The acquiring, textbook company shipped mostly large orders—hundreds of copies of a text per order. The trade publisher shipped mostly small quantities—thirty or fifty books in assorted titles—cutting many more invoices than the acquiring company realized. By the time the resulting information traffic-jam was sorted out, the new division had lost most of a quarter's worth of sales.

Understanding that one can manage the shadow, the information flow, can be an enormous source of efficiency and profit. With modern computer networks, it is no longer necessary to tape or staple the information to the product or service: Each can be handled on its own. This is how reengineering began. Before it was demonized, reengineering, the radical redesign of business processes in pursuit of gigantic performance improvements, became so popular that in 1995 U.S. companies paid more for reengineering consulting services than the nation spent to import that other productivity-enhancer, coffee. The insight that gave reengineering its primary source of value was that strands of information, when they are disentangled from the movement of products and services, can be managed much more efficiently than when the two are bound up with one another.

The End of Assets

The knowledge company travels light. When information has replaced stockpiles of inventory and when it has left its material body and taken on a business life of its own, a company ultimately becomes a different *kind* of creature. A traditional company is a collection of physical assets, bought and owned by capitalists who are responsible for maintaining them, and who hire people to operate them. A knowledge company is different in many ways. As we'll see in the next chapter and in Part Two, not only are the key assets of a knowledge company intangible, it's not clear who owns them or is responsible for caring for them.

Indeed, a knowledge company might not own much in the way of traditional assets at all. Just as information replaces working capital, so intellectual assets replace physical ones. A knowledge company's financial structure can be so different from that of an industrial company that it is incomprehensible in traditional terms. Comparing Microsoft to IBM helps show how. The lives of the two companies, of course, have long intertwined. IBM, the talismanic corporation of the fifties, sixties, and seventies, chose Microsoft's disk operating system (hence MS-DOS) to run its personal computers in 1983, making it possible for Gates's company to become the touchstone company of that decade and this one. So powerful has Microsoft become that it is easy to forget that Big Blue has sales more than fifteen times greater than those of the wee usurper—just IBM's software business generates more sales than all of Microsoft. And of course, IBM, with its famous one-word motto THINK, its galaxy of Nobel-prizewinning scientists, and 3,768 patents granted to its employees from 1993 to 1995 alone, is no slouch when it comes to corporate brainpower.

But Tom Watson's old company was built on a different model from the one that Gates and Paul Allen used to make Microsoft. A look at the two companies' books shows astonishing differences. Despite IBM's much greater sales, Microsoft is the more valuable company: As of November 1996, IBM's total market capitalization was about $70.7 billion; Microsoft's total capitalization was $85.5 billion. But the assets underlying that capital were entirely different. At the beginning of 1996, IBM owned, net of depreciation, $16.6 billion worth of property, plant, and equipment; Microsoft's net fixed assets totaled just $930 million. Put another way, every $100 socked into IBM buys $23 worth of fixed assets, while the same $100 investment in Microsoft buys fixed assets worth just over a dollar.

Clearly, an investor who acquires shares of Microsoft is not buying assets in any traditional sense; for that matter, he is not purchasing much in the way of assets if he buys IBM or Merck or General Electric. A dollar invested in a corporation buys something different from the same dollar invested in the same corporation a few years ago. Margaret Blair of the Brookings Institution has calculated the relationship between tangible assets (property, plant, and equipment) and total market value for every U.S. manufacturing and mining company in the Compustat database. In 1982, she found, those assets accounted for 62.3 percent of the companies' market value; ten years later, they made up only 37.9 percent of the value of the whole. And these were industrials.

Some enormously successful enterprises have almost no tangible assets whatsoever. One can argue, for example, that Visa International, though it processes financial transactions worth a third of a trillion dollars a year, doesn't exist. Visa is a membership organization, an alliance of banks and other financial institutions. Each member company exclusively owns that portion of the Visa business—i.e., the portfolio of credit-card holders—it has created. Founder Dee Hock calls it "an inside-out holding company in that it does not hold but is held by its functioning parts." For years, shareholders of Electronic Data Systems (EDS) did not own its assets, though the stock traded on the New York exchange. Everything EDS owned belonged to General Motors until GM spun it off in 1996. EDS's shareholders owned merely GM's revocable assurance that some portion of EDS's earnings would be paid to them as dividends.*

It is characteristic for knowledge companies to strip their balance sheets of fixed assets. Headquarters moves into rented space, banks securitize mortgages, manufacturers let Ryder trucks lug their freight rather than own their own fleets; vertical integration cedes to the virtual organization. The knowledge company doesn't care about owning assets. In fact, the fewer assets the better; so long as it has intellectual capital, the company can get the revenues without the burden and expense of managing and paying for assets. Companies like Union Pacific ostensibly run railroads but really operate information systems, directing freight cars (probably leased from someone else) over their tracks. Banks and other financial service companies

---

* It's another measure of the falling importance of physical assets that most companies pay far more for information than they do for equity. It is not surprising that organizations like law firms and think tanks spend a lot for information and not much for physical assets. As Karl-Erik Sveiby points out in his book *Managing Knowhow,* "knowhow companies" don't need much in the way of physical or financial capital. But in fact *almost all* companies, including heavy industry, pay more for information than they do to attract capital. Paul A. Strassman, author of *The Business Value of Computers,* has compared the annual cost of equity capital for nearly 3,000 U.S. companies with the same companies' information expenses, using their sales, general, and administrative costs as a reasonable approximation. More than 90 percent of the companies—the few exceptions being steel, mining, transportation, and real estate businesses—spent more for information. The median company paid nearly five times more; one shop, a consulting firm, had a 32-to-1 ratio. Strassman concludes: "The capital-based industrial economy has been superseded by the managerial-dominant information economy." (Strassman's calculations can be found on the World Wide Web at http://www.strassman.com.)

have become less concerned with the amount of financial capital under their control. Says Dennis Beresford, chairman of the Financial Standards Accounting Board, "When I started auditing banks in 1970, everybody was pushing to enhance the size of their balance sheets. These days they're doing just the opposite." They're going after revenues, whether from loans (interest-rate spreads) or, increasingly, from fees. A third of large banks' revenues derive from noninterest sources, such as data processing, sales of securitized assets like mortgages, and service fees; these produced less than a quarter of big-bank revenue in 1982. Chances are, the mortgage on your home is no longer owned by the bank that wrote it; instead it was lumped together with others into a "mortgage-backed security" that the bank sold to investors and which trades like any other stock or bond.

Lenny Mendonca, a McKinsey & Co. consultant, puts it this way: "The game of financial intermediation"—accepting money from Peter and investing it with Paul—"is no longer won by having the intermediated assets on your balance sheet." Traditionally, insurance companies owned enormous portfolios of assets—real estate, bonds, stocks, etc.—and used the return on those assets to pay policyholders. Today, the assets produced by the hottest insurance products—variable life and annuities—belong to policyholders, usually in the form of mutual funds; instead of owning them, the insurance company manages them for a fee, and what counts is premium income. The Equitable Companies administers third-party assets worth more than twice as much as the company's own hoard.

Making allowances for thousands of exceptions, one could say that businesses are moving to one side or the other of a dividing line: Asset-owners versus asset-renters. Although one hesitates to apply the logic of intellectual capitalism to businesses whose employees majored in carbohydrate packing, sports franchises have, by luck or wit, become nimble Information Age businesses, renting the fixed assets they need and outsourcing whatever isn't a core competence. Only five of the twenty-eight Major League baseball teams, and just three of the National Football League's thirty clubs, own their own stadiums. Would George Steinbrenner threaten to move the Yankees from the Bronx if he carried the House that Ruth Built on his books? Only if he could put it to good use—selling it to someone, or converting it into apartments, which is what the citizens of medieval Arles did with the Roman arena in that French city, and what became of the land in

Brooklyn where Ebbets Field once stood. In their eagerness to attract sports teams with taxpayer-built stadiums, local and state governments have handed them free tickets out of town. Knowledge companies don't want assets.

As fiduciaries for their owners' assets, managers must understand this phenomenon. It's vital to competing, especially in industries that cannot escape owning assets. Here's the rule of thumb: The more differentiated and proprietary the work, the more likely you should own the assets it requires. Microsoft, whose sacred cow is code, owns no factories; Intel, whose mantra is manufacturing, builds its own. Says Adrian Slywotzky, a consultant whose book *Value Migration* discusses how changing competitive conditions affect business models: "For a lot of asset-intensive businesses, like real estate, chemicals, or steel, making money will be tougher" because they have so much money tied up in their physical assets.

But not impossible. As we have seen, almost all organizations are knowledge-intensive. Even an asset-heavy utility company like Electricité de France sells its expertise—its knowledge of how to run a network—by helping to build plants and manage power companies in Argentina, China, Ivory Coast, Portugal, Sweden, Ukraine, and elsewhere. Because knowledge and knowledge assets now have a reality of their own, the management of intellectual capital is available and valuable to any organization. Most organizations have barely begun to pursue its benefits. They've replaced inventory with information and they've substituted knowledge for fixed assets, but these are the anticipated, planned, cost-cutting gains from innovation—the first-order effects of the Information Age. Says Richard Collin, CEO of a French software company called Trivium: "Today, we are thinking in terms of using knowledge to improve productivity in our old businesses—how to do the same with less. Tomorrow, we will think of competition— how to do more in new businesses." As we shall learn in Part Two, the lineaments of tomorrow can be seen in several organizations that have taken seriously the management of their most valuable assets, their intellectual capital.

CHAPTER 3

The Knowledge Worker

I THINK I CAN.
—WATTY PIPER

A dozen or so men and women are seated around a table in a conference room, neatly but casually dressed in blue jeans, chinos, T-shirts and polo shirts. They have canted their chairs to face one end of the room, where a woman stands before a pair of easels on which pads of oversized paper have been clipped. It's time for the weekly meeting.

Over the next hour, several pages of the flip charts will be filled with statistics and notes as the group wrestles with the challenge of improving their company's production of electrical arresters. These are surge protectors that guard power stations and transmission lines against lightning strikes; the smallest are about the size of a hockey puck, the largest as big as a telephone booth. One of the men has pushed his chair a couple of feet back from the table; occasionally he smirks in a nervous way that instantly betrays what lies behind his superior attitude: He doesn't feel up to dealing with this stuff, so he will pretend it's beneath him.

Numbers go up on the flip charts. The group is coming up about 11 percent short of one of its goals—it is in charge of assembling disks, which are made in elsewhere in the plant, into completed arresters, and it has missed a few delivery dates. They need to know why. After a discussion of possible causes—each one listed on the charts—it's clear that the biggest problem is that too many incoming disks have to be sent back to be reworked. There's some technical discussion of the precise nature of the fault in the disks, then it's time to decide what to do. One option: Stockpile more disks, but why tie up money in inventory? The group decides first to have a joint meeting with the people in charge of disk-making to see if together they can work out changes in the process so that fewer faulty disks are made in the first place.

Actually, the words are in Spanish: *falta de discos; processo de produccion.* This is a General Electric factory in Bayamón, Puerto Rico, an industrial suburb of San Juan. To someone familiar with GE, seeing its jargon in another language is a surprise, like running into a friend who has bought big red-framed eyeglasses: There's a momentary pause before you recognize that *Promesas Compledas* must be "Promises Kept," GE-speak for meeting the delivery schedule you and your customer agreed to. Measuring the percentage of promises kept is one way GE tracks operating performance. There's another same-but-different aspect to the meeting. Although the people in the room are reporting and analyzing data, discussing how to coordinate the work of one department with the needs of another, setting goals for improving the plant's efficiency, and fleshing out ideas for ways to change the manufacturing process, none of them is a manager. It could hardly be otherwise. The facility employs 125 hourly workers and just 8 salaried "advisers," plus a plant manager. That's it: three layers, no supervisors, no staff—about half the number of managers a traditional factory would employ. Knowledge work—the work of planning, supervising, scheduling, and managing—has become part of the job description of the hourly workers.

Bayamón is not just a "flat" organization with an "empowered" workforce. It is a perpetual-learning machine, dedicated to turning blue-collar workers into knowledge workers. Employees change jobs every six months, rotating through the factory's four main work areas.

After they have done a full circuit, everyone on the floor not only knows the job he is doing, but also knows how it depends on the workers upstream and how it affects the next person in line. The reward for learning is a triple-scoop compensation plan that pays for skill, knowledge, and business performance. The first time around the plant, workers get a twenty-five-cent-an-hour pay raise at each rotation; thereafter they can nearly double their pay by "declaring a major," so to speak, and learning a subject like machine maintenance or quality control, taught by arrangement with a local community college. More pay comes from passing courses in English, business practices, and other subjects. Toss in bonuses—$225 a quarter or more— for meeting plantwide performance goals and having perfect attendance. Promotions and layoffs are decided by what people know, not by seniority.

From Hands to Minds

The notions of a "knowledge economy" and a "knowledge company" have a bit of the abstract about them, but there's nothing abstract about knowledge work. It's what you do—and, if you're old enough, you know how different it is from what you did. Information is, probably, the most important raw material you need to do your job. That used to be true for only a few people; now it is true for most, and those who are not knowledge workers are not as well rewarded as they were. Also left out are people who, though they handled information, did routine, unthinking work. High in what used to be the Pan Am Building in midtown Manhattan, dozens of workers once sat in rows at steel desks, sorting and counting used airline tickets and matching them up with travel agents' records to make sure that the agents paid the airline what they should. Pan Am is gone, and so is the job: Used tickets are checked and matched by automated systems, and what little clerical labor is required is performed in low-wage countries like the Dominican Republic.

It's not particularly surprising that those office sweatshop jobs were automated mostly out of existence; it is astonishing, in retrospect, that some of the most expensive real estate in the world was ever given over to them. What befell those ticket-sorting jobs has, of course, happened to other easy targets for automation: The number of telephone operators, for example, fell from 244,000 in 1983 to 165,000 in 1994. ATMs have begun to replace bank tellers. The number of secretaries is slowly dropping, and telephone callers say that they would rather leave a message in someone's voice mailbox than have a secretary take it down on a pink "While You Were Out" slip.

More and more people spend their working day in the realm of information and ideas. Overall, according to calculations by Stephen R. Barley, professor of industrial engineering and industrial management at Stanford University, the share of the American labor force whose jobs primarily involve working with things (farmworkers, operators and laborers, craftspeople) or delivering nonprofessional services (hotel and restaurant workers, distribution workers, retail clerks, domestic servants, barbers and beauticians, health aides, etc.) will have fallen by more than half by the turn of the century, from 83 percent in 1900 to an estimated 41 percent; those who work chiefly with information (in sales, managerial and administrative, professional and technical, or clerical jobs), were 17 percent of the workforce in 1900 and will be 59 percent as the new century dawns.

Other analysts have cut the pie in different ways, but it always tastes the same. A four-piece division by Dennis Swyt of the U.S. National Bureau of Standards looks like this:

YEAR	PRODUCTION WORKERS	PERSONAL SERVICE	MANAGERIAL & ADMINISTRATIVE	TECHNICAL & PROFESSIONAL
1900	73.4%	9.0%	13.3%	4.3%
1940	57.2	11.7	23.6	7.5
1980	34.2	13.3	36.1	16.1

Secretary of Labor Robert B. Reich, in his 1991 book *The Work of Nations*, described three broad job categories: Routine production services (including factory labor and supervisory jobs, back-office clerical work, and the like), accounting for a declining quarter of American jobs; in-person services, a growing 30 percent; and the elite, "symbolic analysts"—lawyers, consultants, engineers and designers, advertising executives, professors, etc., who perform "problem solving, problem-identifying, and strategic-brokering activities" and comprise about 20 percent of the labor force. (He left out miners and farmers as being too few to worry about and, because the focus of his book was global competition, also ignored government workers, including elementary and secondary schoolteachers, who are essentially unaffected by it.)

The flavor is unmistakable: An ever-growing percentage of people are "knowledge workers": Information and knowledge are both the raw material of their labor and its product. The heterogeneity of statistics about the economy's "service sector"—a lumpy mass that includes data about businesses ranging from janitorial services to neurosurgery—has masked the Information Age transformation of the workforce. At the height of the United States' near-panic about Japanese competition in manufacturing, worrywarts saw the service sector's rising share of the labor force and keened that America was becoming a nation of burger-flippers.

Some burger; some flip. What's really happening is an explosion of well-paid knowledge-worker jobs. The growth in service sector employment has been in mutual fund companies, accounting services, health care, computer software, and the like; the number of food-preparers, a category that includes the synecdochic fry cook, has in fact been falling. Executive, administrative, and managerial jobs are growing in number; "pink-collar" administrative support jobs are declining. Knowledge-intensive companies—those that have 40 percent or more knowledge workers—account for 28 percent of total U.S. employment, but in the last half decade they produced fully 43 percent of new employment growth. The major exception—a high-knowledge industry that lost more jobs than Hansel did bread crumbs—was computer manufacturing, but that exception actually proves the rule: Most job losses in computer-making came because manufacturers eliminated industrial workers (by outsourcing and moving factories offshore) and increased their force of knowledge workers, such as programmers, designers, and consultants.

It's not only that more people do knowledge work; also increasing is the knowledge *content* of all work, whether it's agricultural, blue collar, clerical, or professional. A physician today, armed with antibiotics, magnetic-resonance imagers, and microsurgical techniques, brings far more knowledge to his work than his pre-World-War-II predecessors, whose principal tools were boiling water and a kindly manner. Like the farmer before him, the factory worker—stripped to the waist, his heroic torso ruddy in the satanic light of a blast furnace—is becoming an artifact of a bygone age, carefully preserved on

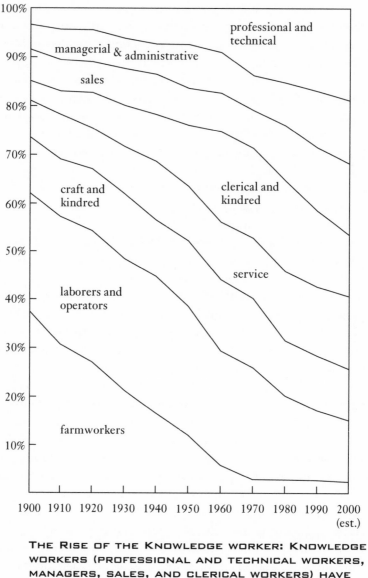

THE RISE OF THE KNOWLEDGE WORKER: KNOWLEDGE
WORKERS (PROFESSIONAL AND TECHNICAL WORKERS,
MANAGERS, SALES, AND CLERICAL WORKERS) HAVE
STEADILY INCREASED THEIR SHARE OF THE
LABOR FORCE.
Source: Stephen R. Barley

WPA murals. Now she is likely to work in an air-conditioned control
room, watching a set of screens and dials, emerging from time to time

to visit the robots under her command or to go to a meeting where she and colleagues pore over histograms, Pareto charts, fish-bone diagrams, and other tools of statistical analysis to see what new ways they can find to cut time and waste out of the manufacturing process.

According to Kiichi Mochizuki, a former executive at a Japanese steel company who heads the Pacific Institute, a New York City research group: "These days, with computerized factories and digitally controlled machines, mathematics are very important for factory operations. When you talk about skill—the word 'skill' is wrong: It implies manual dexterity to carve the wood or hit something with a hammer. Now skill is mental rather than manual." Witness the GE factory workers in Bayamón, whose jobs involve more brain than brawn. In 1972, two thirds of the employees of Corning, Inc., chiefly used their hands and worked with things; today, two thirds chiefly use their minds and work with concepts, data, and information. Automobile assembly workers who once had to heft a part and bolt it in place now must know how to operate the robots that do the lifting. The intellectual component of their work has, by contrast, increased. They do their own troubleshooting and much more managerial work; only half as many supervisors patrol automobile assembly-plant floors as did at the start of the 1990s, a number that is expected to fall by half again before the decade ends. Ten years ago, among production workers in general, the majority—57 percent—were operators, fabricators, and laborers; the rest were higher-skilled precision production and craft workers. Today the percentages are reversed: 55 percent are precision workers, 45 percent operators and laborers.

Not surprisingly, manufacturers are hiring better educated workers to perform these knowledge-intensive jobs. Before 1947, Ford's personnel department didn't even bother to note how much education its employees had. Today, between a third and two fifths of carmakers' new hires have at least some post–high school education, a number twice as high as it was less than a decade ago.

Office work has been similarly transformed. Computers, tireless, unimaginably fast computers, strip away the mechanical, repetitive, soul-destroying elements of work—the re-adding of spreadsheets, the retyping of letters. In 1973, a friend of my mother-in-law, a middle-aged woman who worked as a secretary in a two-person office, received an electric typewriter for Christmas from her boss. It was so much easier than her old manual, she happily complained, that she gained five pounds. Now secretaries say that electronic mail saves them between one and two hours a day of waiting for the computer to print envelopes and letters for mailings, hanging around fax and photocopying machines, or preparing packages for the FedEx pickup—and each of *those* was a significant time-and-scutwork saver.

One result: fewer secretaries.

More significant result: They aren't secretaries anymore. Rather than re-adding spreadsheets, they're helping to analyze them; rather than retyping letters, they are doing research; rather than setting up meetings, they are arranging conferences. They've drained the typing pool and put in a gym.

The Rising Price of Brains

Markets are pitiless. They reward whatever creates value and ignore or punish whatever does not. It's nothing personal. The Invisible Hand is unseeing as well as unseen: It simply moves, and moves on, neither knowing nor caring whether it has delivered a pat on the back or a blow to the jaw. It moves more slowly in labor markets than in others. In a matter of minutes, investors in the stock market might take billions of dollars from AT&T and hand it over to IBM, but families don't quickly uproot themselves to pursue a new opportunity in another town, auto mechanics don't learn computer programming over long weekends, and companies hesitate—at least briefly—before turning longtime employees loose or hiring new ones. Governments, understandably, are more likely to try to slow down the labor market than they are to intervene in other markets, to protect their citizens from its worst punishment and to tax the recipients of its greatest rewards.

Still, the Invisible Hand moves labor markets, too. If knowledge is the greatest source of economic value, one would expect to see labor markets reward people who work with their brains and slap around those who do not. In 1995, writer Susan Sheehan drew a moving portrait of an Iowa couple. The wife was an aide at a nursing home, bathing, dressing, and feeding the residents, putting them to bed at day's end. Her husband did heavy lifting, too, for a company that set up barricades and signs at construction sites and piled sandbags around them to hold them against the wind. Together they earned just over $31,000 a year and were sinking into debt. Several years before, he alone had earned about that much at a factory that made carwashes, but he'd lost that job and others like it had become rare. A high school graduate, he once enrolled in a vocational-technical school, but quit because his math was weak; several years before, she had been unable to type well enough to keep a job as a data-entry clerk and had accepted a demotion to file clerk. Now in their forties, they felt doomed to earning $7.00-an-hour incomes for the rest of their lives. The couple, Sheehan wrote, "once considered themselves middle class."

It is not their fault that they are victims of expectations peculiar to one time and place, nor do they merit any less sympathy for the fact. For most of history in most of the world, their occupations—personal service and laborer—have been the stuff of working-class, not middle-class, status. The extraordinary economic hegemony of the United States after World War II allowed the country's employers to offer middle-class lives to almost everyone who was white and worked. As Europe recovered after the war and Asia began to boom, that worm inevitably turned. But global competition is not why Sheehan's Iowa couple is suffering: Nursing home aides and highway-construction workers don't compete with Germans or Malaysians. Nor, however, do they participate in the information economy, which is where the labor market now bestows its rewards; their sojourn in the middle class was brief and they have rejoined the working class.

Much has been said and written about rising income inequality in the United States and other industrialized nations and the travails of the people who once formed the backbone of their economies. You can argue that income inequality is not rising, but you would be wrong; it is rising now, at the start of the Information Revolution, as it did at the start of the Industrial Revolution. You can argue that it is of no moral, political, or economic consequence; you would be wrong again, but that subject is beyond the scope of this book. Rising income inequality has been blamed on the Japanese, cheap Third World labor, free trade agreements, corporate greed, and changes in tax and welfare policies. You can marshall statistics to support any of these arguments; you can also tear them apart.

Income inequality is rising because these are no longer industrial economies, and their labor markets have not yet caught up. The one set of numbers no one has been able to argue away shows that educated people command a greater pay premium than they used to. While the pitiless forces of the market have been reducing the rewards for physical labor, those same forces have been handing out greater rewards to knowledge work. Since 1969, when the decadence of the Industrial Age first became apparent, the "educational pay premium" has increased for both men and women in every industry. Since 1979, only one group of U.S. men has made gains in real weekly earnings: college graduates. That year, male college graduates commanded income 49 percent greater than men with just high school diplomas; fourteen years later, in 1993, the education premium was 80 percent. It is significant that college-educated workers' wage premium has grown despite the fact that supply has increased, too, as the percentage of the workforce that attended college rises.

The education premium proves the growing role of knowledge in creating value and wealth. An economist at the University of California at San Diego, James Rauch, has shown that for every year of additional education in a city's workforce, productivity goes up about 2.8 percent. In other words, if the average worker in, say, Houston has ten years of schooling and the average worker in Atlanta has eleven years, output per worker in Atlanta will be nearly 3 percent higher. Some of the difference might be ascribed to a smart worker's being able to work more efficiently; it's more likely that a smart workforce does altogether different work that has greater higher knowledge content—lawyering or software writing versus printing or freight forwarding. Though computers have been blamed for income loss among nonmanagement factory and office workers, the opposite is true: The more computers are used in an organization, the higher the pay of its employees. According to Gary Burtless, a senior fellow of the Brookings Institution in Washington, D.C.:

> Among economists, the leading explanation for increased wage inequality is changes in the technology of production. Such innovations as the personal computer or new forms of business organization have favored workers with greater skill and reduced the value of unskilled labor.

Otherwise, why go to school? In Sweden's formerly socialist society, public policy held that it was unfair to reward blue-collar workers less well than their bosses, and pay scales were set accordingly. Consequently, learning didn't pay, too few Swedes bothered to get a post-secondary education, and a "brain drain" occurred as a disproportionate number of the best-schooled Swedes sought work outside the country. The flip side: When educated workers get bigger paychecks, fewer people stay uneducated. Four out of five American adults are high school graduates, up from two out of three just fifteen years ago. The percentage of men who have spent at least four years in college has grown from 20 in 1980 to 25 in 1994, the percentage of women from 13 to 20. In 1993, for the first time ever, more young Germans enrolled in their nation's universities than entered its "dual education" system of apprenticeships designed to train people for industrial jobs. Within the ranks of the college-bound, competition for admission to the institutions considered to be best has jumped. Harvard College, for instance, received 18,190 applications to join the class of 2000, 11 for every place it could offer. Five years before, the ratio of applications to places was eight to one.

Bottom Line: The End of Management as We Know It

What do you do?

The rise of the knowledge worker fundamentally alters the nature of work and the agenda of management. Managers are custodians; they protect and care for the assets of a corporation; when the assets are intellectual, the manager's job changes. Knowledge work doesn't happen the way mechanical labor did. The work of hands and clerks was mostly and rightly set up according to the division of labor described in Adam Smith's pin factory: Narrowly defined jobs carefully arrayed, the workers measured and rewarded by some numerical scorecard—how many bumpers the assembly-line workers bolted on, how many tickets the office workers sorted and matched, how much wood the woodchucks chucked. Supervisors, middle managers, and general managers looked over their charges' shoulders, collected data about their output, and passed it up to their superiors in ever-greater degrees of aggregation. Managers' work was defined in the acronym POEM: Plan, Organize, Execute, Measure. Top executives mainly talked about financial goals—return on equity, earnings per share, and so on. Management-by-the-numbers reached an epitome—or a nadir—in Harold Geneen's notorious operations reviews at ITT in the 1960s and 1970s, where trembling business-unit managers of the farflung conglomerate appeared to be grilled by bosses whose knowledge of the empire they ruled extended no further than the printouts stacked in front of them at the enormous table where they sat. One company in the top 50 of the *Fortune* 500 was so single-minded in pursuit of a 20 percent return on equity that all its top executives were given underwear boldly imprinted "ROE 20%."

What has come to be known as Taylorism—after Frederick Winslow Taylor, the industrial engineer who founded Scientific Management at the turn of the century—not only worked, but for many decades worked brilliantly. The essence of Taylorism isn't just drudgery, constant repetition, and narrow job descriptions. The genius of the man was to urge that management apply knowledge as well as the lash: Take complex work, apply brainpower to it, and find ways to do it simpler, faster, better. It is fashionable to dump on Taylor, but important to remember that Scientific Management was a great leap forward, not just in terms of productivity but also in terms of the dignity of labor. Henry Ford's assembly line is a prime example of Taylorism, and it was a wonder of the universe at the time.

But Taylorism has its limits, as Henry Ford's descendants learned. The only brainpower Taylor used was managerial brainpower. Taylorism is "Father Knows Best" management. Hundreds of years ago, people studying the nature of intelligence figured out that the brain is the seat of reason. But what directs the brain? they wondered, and they imagined a little man inside, called a homunculus. But wait, someone asked: Where did *he* get the knowledge? Maybe from a still smaller man, and one yet smaller, till finally you reached some eensyweensy pea-sized something that was the fount of all wisdom. It's silly biology. And, at least as far as knowledge work is concerned, it's silly organizational theory, with these nested Russian dolls, and, tiniest and smartest of all, the fount of all knowledge, the CEO.

Knowledge work is utterly different. It has a professional flavor. Professionals are measured not by the tasks they perform but by the results they achieve. A lawyer is not evaluated on the number of words in her closing argument but on how well chosen and effective they are, not on the number of footnotes in her brief but on whether it makes a winning argument. The expertise to which a lawyer is most likely to defer is that of another member of her profession, not that of a boss. Indeed, she doesn't have a boss telling her how to do her job—she has a client, a customer, who expects her to plan and organize her own work. When work is about knowledge, the professional model of organizational design inevitably begins to supersede the bureaucratic.

The explosion of scientific and technical knowledge, the rapid diffusion and fast-growing power of information technology, knowledge's increasing share of corporate value-added, the rise of the knowledge worker—all these work together, each simultaneously chicken and egg, horse and cart, cause and effect, to force new kinds of organizational design and new managerial methods and substance. Says Stanford professor Stephen Barley:

> As firms hire increasing numbers of professionals, as professions spawn specialties, and as new technologies create work that requires esoteric knowledge, expertise becomes more balkanized and firms begin to resemble confederacies of occupations rather than sleek pyramids of control . . . When those in authority no longer comprehend the work of their subordinates, chains of command should cease to be viable for coordination.

The trend away from standardized mass production toward specialized knowledge work makes command-and-control management less necessary—a good thing, too, because it's also less feasible. "Smarter Than My Boss" says a button on the bulletin board in my office. You probably are; you were probably hired precisely because you know things your boss doesn't know. Knowledge workers, alone or in teams, plan, organize, and execute many aspects of their own work. Much of the measurement—tallying sales, counting hours worked, taking inventory, approving invoices, et cetera ad infinitum—is done automatically by computer. No wonder middle managers have been disappearing from the labor force faster than popcorn from a bowl.

If the job of managers is no longer to tell people what to do and make them do it, or to gather, transmit, and process information, then what is their job? Part of the answer is apparent in the enormous demand for books and tapes and seminars on leadership, as opposed to management. It is also apparent in the goals executives set and in the rhetoric they use. Companies are in business to make money, and ultimately their success or failure is expressed in financial terms, but the language of management is increasingly nonfinancial. The rallying cry is no longer "shareholder value" but "values." In his best-selling book, *Leadership Is an Art*, Herman Miller CEO Max DePree wrote of a "covenant"—not a contract—between company and employee as the basis for superior management. If "values" and "vision" and "empowerment" and "teamwork" and "facilitating" and "coaching" sometimes sound like so much mush-mouthed mishmash—which they sometimes are—that's a reflection of the fact that managers are groping toward a language and a means for managing knowledge, knowledge work, and knowledge-intensive companies. Financial accounting provided such tools and measurements for industrial capitalism; intellectual capitalism desperately needs the practical language we will give it in the second part of this book, or it will be mired in a quicksand of meaningless verbal goo.

In the middle of the last century, Karl Marx noted that the worker of his day, unlike the craftsman and the small farmer of previous generations, no longer owned the tools of his trade or the product of his labor. In Marx's terms, he was "alienated" and "estranged" from his work. Marx was wrong about many things, but not about this. In the factory system both the tools and the output belonged to the boss, the capitalist. Like the parts in the bins alongside the assembly line, Taylorized workers were interchangeable. Management could replace one worker with another with little or no impact on production. The man worked for the machine.

Now, the machine works for the man. The rise of computers, far from dehumanizing people, is forcing machinery to adapt to our idiosyncratic humanity. Picture Frederick Taylor, the man with the stopwatch, doing time-and-motion studies of your great-grandfather the bricklayer. Fast-forward to today: Andersen Consulting has a "usability lab" designed to uncover problems in the software it writes. In the portable version of the lab, the firm comes to your office, aims a camera at your computer and one at you, and records your keystrokes. A consultant watches, taking notes as you fumble, curse, or hit the help key. It looks like Taylor with a Camcorder, but for one crucial difference: Taylor stepped forward to tell the worker how to become more like a machine; the Andersen consultant goes back to tell the engineer how to make the machine more humane.

Not that we are all destined for lives as itinerant knowledge workers, a-wandering with laptops on our backs. Many jobs still and always will require big, expensive machines bought by someone else. But in the age of intellectual capital, the most valuable parts of those jobs have become the most essentially human tasks: sensing, judging, creating, building relationships. Far from being alienated from the tools of his trade and the fruit of his labor, the knowledge worker carries them between his ears.

PART TWO

Intellectual Capital

CONTENT

LET US NOW SUPPOSE THAT IN THE MIND OF EACH
MAN THERE IS AN AVIARY OF ALL SORTS OF BIRDS—
SOME FLOCKING TOGETHER APART FROM THE REST,
OTHERS IN SMALL GROUPS, OTHERS SOLITARY, FLYING
ANYWHERE AND EVERYWHERE . . . WE MAY SUPPOSE
THAT THE BIRDS ARE KINDS OF KNOWLEDGE, AND
THAT WHEN WE WERE CHILDREN, THIS RECEPTACLE
WAS EMPTY; WHENEVER A MAN HAS GOTTEN AND
DETAINED IN THE ENCLOSURE A KIND OF KNOWLEDGE,
HE MAY BE SAID TO HAVE LEARNED OR DISCOVERED
THE THING WHICH IS THE SUBJECT OF THE
KNOWLEDGE; AND THIS IS TO KNOW.
—PLATO

CHAPTER 4

The Hidden Gold

IT'S HID IN MIGHTY PARTICULAR PLACES, HUCK—SOMETIMES ON
ISLANDS, SOMETIMES IN ROTTEN CHESTS UNDER THE END OF A
LIMB OF AN OLD DEAD TREE, JUST WHERE THE SHADOW FALLS
AT MIDNIGHT; BUT MOSTLY UNDER THE FLOOR IN HA'NTED
HOUSES . . . IT LAYS THERE A LONG TIME AND GETS RUSTY;
AND BY AND BY SOMEBODY FINDS AN OLD YELLOW PAPER THAT
TELLS HOW TO FIND [IT]—A PAPER THAT'S GOT TO BE CIPHERED
OVER ABOUT A WEEK BECAUSE IT'S MOSTLY SIGNS
AND HY'ROGLYPHICS.
—MARK TWAIN

W hen the stock market values companies at three, four, or ten times the book value of their assets, it's telling a simple but profound truth: The hard assets of a knowledge company contribute far less to the value of its ultimate product (or service) than the intangible assets—the talents of its people, the efficacy of its management systems, the character of its relationships to its customers—that together are its intellectual capital. Everything discussed in Part One—the dominance of information in the value chain, investment in the capital equipment of the Knowledge Age, the substitution of knowledge for physical materials and assets, the move by labor markets to reward knowledge work—tells us that someone who invests in a company is buying a set of talents, capabilities, skills, and ideas—intellectual capital, not physical capital. You don't buy Microsoft because of its software factories; the company doesn't own any. You buy its ability to write code, set standards for personal-computing software, exploit the value of its name, and forge alliances with other companies. Merck did not become, for seven consecutive years, the most-admired company in *Fortune*'s annual survey of corporate reputations because it can make pills, but because its scientists can discover medicines. Dr. P. Roy Vagelos, CEO of Merck during its run atop the most-admired-companies list, said: "A low-value product can be made by anyone anywhere. When you have knowledge no one else has access to—that's dynamite. We guard our research even more carefully than our financial assets."

Today, when knowledge has become the primary raw material and result of economic activity, organizational intelligence—smart people working in smart ways—has moved from a supporting role to a starring one. For the people who allocate money to corporations (that is, investors) and people who allocate money within them (that is, managers) and the people who allocate their lives to them (that is, employees), intellectual capital has become so vital that it's fair to say that an organization that is not managing knowledge is not paying attention to business.

There's only one problem: Trying to identify and manage knowledge assets is like trying to fish barehanded. It can be done—the word for it is "to guddle"—but the object of the effort is damnably elusive.

Before companies can make the most of their ideas, their leaders need to understand how and why intellectual assets have gone unmanaged, and to realize the tremendous costs of this negligence—the money wasted, the opportunities squandered. We'll see those things in this chapter; then, in the next, we'll define and identify intellectual assets in such a way that leaders can do something to enhance and exploit them.

Accountants Can't Count Intellectual Capital

One reason organizations don't manage knowledge is that it almost always comes wrapped in some tangible form—in the paper of a book, in the magnetic tape of an audiocassette, in the body of a speaker, in the stones of a historical monument. We manage the forms rather than the substance, which is like a viticulturist paying more attention to the bottle than to the wine. It's easier, after all, to count the bottles than to describe the wine, and in the old economy of "congealed resources," it was also a reasonable thing to do: Accounting for the forms—the costs of material and labor—captured most of the value of the product. But in the economy of "congealed knowledge," it doesn't come close. How can it when, for example, the same information can be presented in many different forms, each of which has a different cost structure? You can see the same movie in a theater, on TV, or on videotape, read the same article in the *New York Times* on paper or on America Online, scan it into a computer and fax it to Uncle William in Adelaide or e-mail it to Aunt Adelaide in Williamstown. Moreover, the digitization of everything often removes the wrapper entirely. It no longer makes sense to manage the production of intangible goods and services solely by measuring and managing the process of putting wrapping paper and a ribbon on them.

Yet most corporations do exactly that. They are run like old industrial companies. People who allocate resources—managers, the board, investors—get plenty of information about physical and financial assets. They can tell you how much money a company has in the bank, how large a credit line it has, the price of its stock, the value of its land and buildings; they can and do measure its use of working capital, inventories, and the like. They can tell you how many lathes are grinding away on the floor of the factory in Findlay, Ohio, when they were bought, and how many of them should be replaced soon. But knowledge—the greatest source of value and competitive advantage—must fend for itself. Who has it? Where is it? What's in the files in the basement? How should it be managed? Says Tom Davenport, a consultant turned professor of business at the University of Texas at Austin: "In most organizations, while many people use, generate, or distribute information, the only real managers of information behavior are lawyers," who are chiefly concerned with protecting trademarks, patents, and secrets.

The management of intellectual capital is like a newly discovered, still-uncharted ocean, and few executives understand its dimensions or how to navigate it. They may know a bit about codified intellectual assets like patents and copyrights. They may have an inkling of the value of others, such as brand equity. They may intuit that training and the experience gained on the learning curve belong somehow in their asset base. But talent is intellectual capital too. The value of a lab, for instance, includes its scientists' ability to make new discoveries in the future. Can you put a price tag on that? How much could you get if you sold the R&D that doesn't bear fruit you can use, but that someone else might want? How do you value intangibles like design, service, and customizing, which distinguish winners from losers? The chief financial officer can tell you how big the company's payroll is, but cannot tell you the replacement cost of employees' skills, much less whether they are appreciating or depreciating. The human resources director may know how much the company spends on formal training, but doesn't know how much learning resulted from it.

Armies of clerks and banks of computers track physical and financial assets, but those accounting systems cannot cope with brainpower. The first accounting textbook was published in 1494 by a mathematically minded Venetian monk named Luca Pacioli. Pacioli's *Summa de arithmetica, geometrica, proportioni et proportionalita* is famous (among accountants) for showing how to use double-entry bookkeeping. For accounting, double-entry bookkeeping was as big a deal as the Arabs' invention of zero was for mathematics. The modern corporation would not be manageable, or even possible, without a system of debits and credits that gives a coherent picture of the many different streams of goods and money that flow through an enterprise.

Says David Wilson, a CPA and partner at Ernst & Young, a Big-Six accounting and consulting firm: "It has been 500 years since Pacioli published his seminal work on accounting and we have seen virtually no innovation in the practice of accounting—just more rules—none of which has changed the framework of measurement." The balance sheet took its present form in 1868; the income statement dates from before World War II. It is a framework that fits the industrial enterprise, not the intelligent one, Robert K. Elliott pointed out in an important essay called "The Third Wave Breaks on the Shores of Accounting":

> It focuses on tangible assets, that is, the assets of the industrial revolution. These include inventory and fixed assets: for example, coal, iron, and steam engines. And these assets are stated at cost. Accordingly, we focus on *costs*, which is the *production* side, rather than the *value created*, which is the *customer* side.

Pacioli's scheme won't cut it anymore. In a knowledge-based company, says Judy Lewent, the highly regarded chief financial officer of Merck & Co., "the accounting system doesn't capture anything, really." One reason, according to Edmund Jenkins, an Arthur Andersen partner who chaired a task force of the American Institute of Certified Public Accountants that studied the need for new ways of accounting for corporate performance: "The components of cost in a product today are largely R&D, intellectual assets, and services. The old accounting system, which tells us the cost of material and labor, isn't applicable."

At bottom, accounting measures a company's accumulation and concentration of capital, and is based on costs—that is, it assumes that the cost of acquiring an asset fairly states (after some adjustments for items like depreciation) what that asset is worth. The model falls apart when the assets in question are intangible. As knowledge and its wrapper have become separated, the relationship between current value and historical costs has broken down. The cost of producing knowledge bears much less relationship to its value or price than the cost of producing, say, a ton of steel. In the Industrial Age an idea couldn't become valuable unless a measurable collection of physical assets was assembled around it to exploit it. Not so now. Unlike machinery or money, says Michael Brown, chief financial officer of Microsoft, "Ideas have power by themselves. They can accumulate without travelling through an institution, and then suddenly explode." Netscape, for example, concentrated an enormous amount of intellectual capital that assumed scarcely any physical or institutional form until, released into the market as an initial public offering in 1995, the capital manifested itself financially—to the tune of $2 billion.

Some organizations never did have wrappers to count, like law firms, consultants, advertising agencies. They couldn't count output in any meaningful way, but they needed to measure something, so they measured time: For internal purposes as well as for billing, they prepare detailed information about how much time their employees spend on client assignments. But time is simply a proxy for costs, and costs tell nothing about the value of what an enterprise produces, and tell managers only a small part of what they need to know to run the business. Cost data is of particularly limited value when intangibles can be sold in different forms—ticket to the symphony, CD, or radio broadcast.

Yet What's Uncounted Counts Plenty

One reason people give intellectual capital short shrift is that they can't see the brain gain—the returns on their investment. An investor who chose between buying stock in IBM or Microsoft solely on the basis of their financial statements would learn nothing about what makes the two companies valuable. At American Airlines, jetliners show up as assets. However, the information system that runs Sabre— the reservation service that is more profitable than the planes are—is almost entirely an intangible asset, and is nowhere to be seen on the balance sheet. Like electrons in a cloud chamber, knowledge assets leave only ghostly images in corporate ledgers.

Yet their economic power is as real as that of a split atom. The case of Cordiant, the advertising agency that used to be known as Saatchi & Saatchi, illustrates both the value of intellectual capital and the risks associated with not recognizing it. In December 1994, institutional investors, upset by what they viewed as the arrogance and fecklessness of Maurice Saatchi, forced the board of directors (which Saatchi chaired) to dismiss him. Protesting Saatchi's dismissal, several other executives left the company, too, and several large accounts—first Mars, the candy-maker, and later British Airways—defected. As far as the balance sheet was concerned, Saatchi's dismissal was a nonevent. Nevertheless, the stock of the company, which had been trading on the New York Stock Exchange at 8 ⁵/₈, immediately fell to 4. Among several ways of interpreting what happened at Saatchi & Saatchi, one stands out: The institutional shareholders thought they owned Saatchi & Saatchi. In fact, they owned less than half of it. Most of the value of the company was human capital, embodied in Maurice Saatchi and his coterie.

Seldom does a market ascribe value to intellectual assets—and often, then, it gets the number wrong. In 1976, Andrew Lloyd Webber, the composer/creator of the musicals *Cats, Evita, Phantom of the Opera*, and *Sunset Boulevard*, among others, formed The Really Useful Company, which held the rights to all his work. Whatever you think of Webber's music, The Really Useful Company's leader has written Really Successful Stuff.* In 1986, Webber took the company public. Its assets: the Palace Theatre in London, worth about £2 million, the rights to Webber's musicals and songs (chiefly *Cats*), a seven-year con-

---

* Two men were captured by terrorists, accused of being spies. After a perfunctory trial, they were found guilty and sentenced to be shot. On the day appointed for their execution, the terrorists' leader offered each man a final wish. Said one: "Before I die, I'd like to listen one last time to the collected works of Andrew Lloyd Webber—every note, everything." Said the other: "Shoot me first."

tract with Webber, and an insurance policy on his life (he was thirty-seven). The deal was done; the total value of all the shares, including a sizable chunk Webber retained, was £35.2 million. Four years later, Webber bought it back. Based on what he paid for the shares he didn't already own, the value of the company was now £77.4 million—a figure derived chiefly from calculations by investment bankers who used established ways to evaluate intellectual property like copyrights and patents.* A year later, Webber sold 30 percent of the company to the record company PolyGram. The price: £78 million, more than the entire operation was supposedly worth a year before. Webber's *Sunset Boulevard* had opened in the meantime, but that did not turn out to be the main reason the company more than tripled in value. Rather, the City's best analysts had grievously underestimated the revenue and hence the worth of the old copyrights—intellectual assets for which formulas exist, tried but not always true.

When a company is bought for more than its book value (the equity portion of its balance sheet), that premium usually consists of intellectual assets—anticipated revenues from patents, customer relationships, brand equity, etc., plus a premium for obtaining management control. Since the rules of accounting won't permit paying something for nothing, *faute de mieux*, the bean counters simply subtract the book value from the purchase price and call the difference "good will," an essentially meaningless term. Take a look at what companies pay to acquire others, however, and you will often see that "good will" accounts for more than half the purchase price.

A case can be made against putting measurements of intellectual capital onto company books (see Appendix), but there's no excuse for ignoring them. The price of ignorance is enormous. In a well-documented study of how managers and investors allocate resources, Harvard Business School's Michael Porter found that capital "is more likely to be dedicated to physical assets than to intangible assets whose returns are more difficult to measure. For most companies, investments in plant and equipment with easy-to-measure cash flows are more confidently valued and justified than investments in

---

* Essentially, these involve forecasting future earnings from the intellectual property in question, then calculating the net present value of those future earnings. A description of how to calculate net present value is in the Appendix on p. 222.

R&D, training, or other forms where the returns are more difficult to quantify."

By the same token, companies that have begun digging into their knowledge assets have discovered that they are at the mouth of a gold mine. Dow Chemical Corp. found its rich seam of gold almost by accident. The company had spring cleaning in mind in 1993 when the company created a new job, director of intellectual asset management. The idea was to turn a passive function—central record-keeping for Dow's 29,000 in-force patents—into active management of the opportunities patents represent by cleaning up the portfolio and seeing what additional licensing revenue might be obtained from them.

Says Gordon Petrash, who holds the job: "Patents aren't the only intellectual assets—there's art and know-how—but they're the easiest place to start." Easiest doesn't mean easy. Petrash found that Dow exploited fewer than half its patents. Worse, most were orphans: No business unit was responsible for commercializing or licensing them. Surprised, Petrash checked with other companies and found that most have at least as high a percentage of unused, unattended patents— some worth potential millions but all costing money. (Just as the owner of an empty building still owes property tax and has to keep the plumbing and the roof fixed, so it is with intangible assets: Keeping an invention's patents in force over their lifetime costs some $250,000 in legal bills, filing fees, taxes, and so on.) Just from working with business units to create and weed patent portfolios, Petrash's group saved more than $1 million in maintenance costs in its first 18 months.*

The value of the gold that was hidden inside Dow is stupendous.

---

* Petrash developed a simple but effective six-step process for managing intellectual property:

1. Begin with strategy: Define the role of knowledge in each business or business unit. New products might be the number-one priority in one division; for another, it might be brick-and-mortar spending to achieve manufacturing economies of scale, or money to open offices in Poland and Brazil.

2. Assess competitors' strategies and patent portfolios.

3. Classify your portfolio: What do you have, what do you use, and—crucially—who in the business should be responsible for it?

4. Evaluate the cost and value of your intellectual properties, and decide whether to keep, sell, or abandon them. Dow keeps a scorecard that classifies all patents and pending patents according to whether they are currently in use (by Dow or under license), of potential business use, or of no interest to the company. The numbers are always changing, but in the fall of 1995 they showed the com-

Over ten years, Petrash figures, Dow will save about $50 million in tax, filing, and other maintenance costs. Even better: By bringing valuable but unused patents out from the corporate attic, he estimates that the company will increase its annual revenue from licensing patents from $25 million (the 1994 total) to about $125 million by the year 2000. And these, remember, are the savings and revenues just from attending to Dow's most obvious intangible assets, the codified know-how represented by patents. The long-range goal is to extend the work of knowledge management into less defined, and more valuable areas of intellectual capital—"art and know-how," trade secrets and technical expertise. That, Petrash asserts, is worth billions.

He's not alone. Charles Handy, a fellow at the London Business School and foresighted author of *The Age of Unreason*, estimates that the intellectual assets of a corporation are usually worth three or four times tangible book value. Leif Edvinsson, director of intellectual capital for Skandia AFS, the giant Swedish financial services company, thinks that is conservative: He calculated that for most organizations the ratio of the value of intellectual capital to the value of physical and financial capital is between five-to-one and sixteen-to-one. The inevitable metaphor is the iceberg. Above the surface, the financial and physical resources, glittering in the sun, visible, sometimes even awesome. Beneath, unseen, something vastly larger, whose importance everyone recognizes but whose contours no one knows. A recent poll of executives from eighty mostly large corporations—companies like Amoco, Chemical Bank, Kodak, Hewlett Packard, and Pillsbury—showed that four out of five believed managing the knowledge of their organizations should be an essential or important part of business strategy—but only 15 percent felt they did it well.

No executive would leave his cash or factory space idle, yet if

---

pany was currently using about 36 percent of its patents, thought 50 percent were potentially useful, and had no interest in the remaining 14 percent.

5. Invest: Based on what you learned about your knowledge assets, identify gaps you must fill to exploit knowledge or holes you should plug to fend off rivals, and either direct R&D there or look for technology to acquire.

6. Assemble your new knowledge portfolio and repeat the process ad infinitum.

It's nothing fancy. But, says Petrash, "We don't find anybody else doing the whole package," adding, "The business guys understand how to do this with their hard assets. We help them do the same with intellectual assets."

CEOs are asked how much of the knowledge in their companies is used, they typically say, "About 20 percent." That is the observation of Betty Zucker, who studies knowledge management at the Gottlieb Duttweiler Foundation, a Swiss think tank. Says Zucker: "Imagine the implications for a company if it could get that number up just to 30 percent."

To do that requires more than anecdotes, estimates, or polls. By definition the intangible is hard to grasp. It must be rigorously defined in ways that make it palpable and useful, that create understanding and have a bias toward action. To find the hidden gold, one must have a map.

CHAPTER 5

The Treasure Map

KNOWLEDGE IS OF TWO KINDS. WE KNOW A SUBJECT
OURSELVES, OR WE KNOW WHERE WE CAN FIND INFORMATION
UPON IT.
—SAMUEL JOHNSON

If you're so smart, why aren't you rich? It's been called "the American question" by some economists. I was in high school the first time I remember hearing it: The story went around the halls that a student had defiantly thrown it in the face of a teacher during an argument over a grade, asking, "If you're so smart, why are you a teacher? Teachers don't make any money." (The teacher reportedly answered, "If you were smarter, you would realize there is more to life than money.") Many years later, I heard it from Herb Kelleher, the very smart CEO of Southwest Airlines. In Dallas speaking to a number of executives about the value of intellectual capital, I'd quoted Walter Wriston, who had retired as CEO of Citicorp but was still on its board, who argued that Citicorp's assets were understated; he said that the sophisticated software that ran the bank's retail-banking system, especially its automatic teller machines, should really be counted among its assets.

At the time, Citicorp was in trouble. Profits were niggardly, the stock was trading at about $10 a share, and, worst, the bank's financial assets had been so depleted by bad loans that it was under watch by federal regulators. Behind the cloud from the True menthol cigarettes he smoked, Kelleher seemed to be wondering if Wriston's concern for intangible assets might have something to do with the fact that the bank was so short of the other kind. "If those boys in New York are so smart," he asked, "why aren't they making any money?"

It was a good question. It's one thing to aver that intelligence is an organization's most important asset. It's quite another to turn that insight into plans and strategies that lead to better performance. Intellectual capital can be as ephemeral as the Holy Grail, the elusive talisman that only the pure could discover, which was the object of the quests of the Knights of the Round Table. In Arthurian legend, only Sir Galahad was finally allowed to gaze directly into the Grail's divine mysteries, and when he did, he renounced the material world and was borne aloft on angels' wings. That won't do for a business executive, who needs to make the mysteries of organizational brainpower serve material purposes indeed.

To do that requires not just a definition of intellectual capital but a description that executives can use to plan how to invest in and manage knowledge assets. We'll provide that in this chapter, in three steps. First, we need a working definition—something that describes what we're looking for when we look for intellectual assets, what they are and do. Second, we need to explore a pair of problems that can easily thwart the treasure-hunter: How misconceptions about the difference between kinds of information can become red herrings, and how much of an organization's intellectual capital resides in hard-to-see tacit knowledge. To escape from these problems, we need, third, to know where in a business to look for knowledge assets.

A Working Definition

A phrase we have used previously—the sum of an organization's patents, processes, employees' skills, technologies, information about customers and suppliers, and old-fashioned experience—is an illustration, not a definition. Others have offered definitions too vague to be translated into the agendas and actions of managers and employees: "an individual's accumulated knowledge and know-how [that] is the source of innovation and regeneration"; "ability, skill, and expertise . . . embedded in human brains." Closer is language offered by Hugh MacDonald, house futurologist at ICL, the big British computer maker owned by Fujitsu: "knowledge that exists in an organization that can be used to create differential advantage"—in other words, the sum of everything everybody in a company knows that gives it a competitive edge. But that tells more about what intellectual capital does than about what it is. Leaders and managers need something beyond the notion of "smarts" that will, as professor David Klein and consultant Laurence Prusak say, permit them "to account for intellectual capital more formally, to nurture its development more deliberately, and to invest it more wisely."

Klein's and Prusak's definition of intellectual capital is a good start: "Intellectual material that has been formalized, captured, and leveraged to produce a higher-valued asset." One virtue of their definition is its distinction between "intellectual material" and capital. An address on a Post-it note, a report fallen behind a credenza, a brainstorm while commuting to work, a piece of urgent news learned by a sales representative who can't get to a phone—all of these are intellectual material, but none is capital. An untethered idea or a mere piece of information—John Doe's address, say—isn't an asset, any more than a pile of bricks is a factory.

Intelligence becomes an asset when some useful order is created out of free-floating brainpower—that is, when it is given coherent form (a mailing list, a database, an agenda for a meeting, a description of a process); when it is captured in a way that allows it to be described, shared, and exploited; and when it can be deployed to do something that could not be done if it remained scattered around like so many coins in a gutter. Intellectual capital is packaged useful knowledge.

It's also good that Klein's and Prusak's definition reminds us that valuable intellectual assets can be found in mundane places as well as exalted ones. Economically valuable ideas don't have to be erudite or complicated or highly technological. Says Paul M. Romer of the University of California at Berkeley, the leading exponent among economists of the value of ideas: "Ideas are the instructions that let us combine limited physical resources in arrangements that are ever more valuable." Most employees will never encounter anything that's on the cutting edge of science. They are trying to do their jobs better. That's as important an aspect of intellectual capital management as anything else. GE's chairman Jack Welch cautions leaders not to become so enamored of "big I" Ideas that they ignore the "small i" ideas. Says Welch: "We get 6% and 7% productivity increases routinely now, mostly because of 'small i' ideas . . . An idea is not necessarily a biotech idea. That's the wrong view of what an idea is. An idea is an error-free billing system. An idea is taking a process that used to require six days to do and getting it done in one day. Everyone can contribute. Every single person."

The idea of formalized, captured, and leveraged knowledge is easy to understand when the intellectual material in question is a patentable invention or a sheaf of economic data that needs to be digested, or when real or arbitrary deadlines provide obvious boundaries for knowledge. You created formalized, captured, and leveraged knowledge every time you wrote a term paper in college. The editors of the *New York Times* put a thick package of knowledge on a million doorsteps every morning; if some of it is revised or corrected the next morning, we understand that deadlines make newspapers a rough first draft of history. But Klein's and Prusak's definition loses some clarity when it's applied to large or uncertain agglomerations of knowledge assets—those of a whole business or a field of study, for example, or the contents of a person's brain. Packaging "softer" kinds of intellectual material, or knowledge for which no familiar constraining vessel exists, has bedeviled thinkers about knowledge management, just as journalists have struggled, with only passing success so far, to adapt their knowledge-making factories—buildings where caffeine is converted into ink—to the paperless, twenty-four-hours-a-day world of the Internet.

Problems in Packaging "Soft" Knowledge

When the package or the intellectual materials in question are hard to specify, two problems emerge. The first is one of classification: What kinds of material qualify to be included, and what should be left out? What's an asset, and what's noise? The second is a problem of recognition: Lots of intellectual capital is unexpressed, tacit knowledge—

such as, for example, the background expertise and relationships a salesman builds up over many years covering a territory. How does one find that?

CLASSIFCATION

The classification problem crops up everywhere, but especially when systems engineers talk about "data warehouses" and "knowledge management architecture." Sooner or later, usually sooner, someone points out that information is not all of equal value, and proposes classifying it. There's *data:* The temperature is 77 degrees. There's *information*, a context into which the data can be put: That's hot for this time of year. There's *knowledge*, a conclusion drawn from the data and information: We should postpone the ski trip, or global warming is a bigger problem than we thought. Inevitably, someone adds a fourth category, *wisdom:* Everybody talks about the weather, but nobody does anything about it. The techies, if it's techies having this conversation, then begin wrestling with the packaging problems this hierarchy of knowledge presents: How can we turn corporate smarts into a knowledge management process and system, an intellectual capital asset that provides the data and information people need to become knowledgeable, but is not cumbersome and will not overwhelm them with trivia?

Can't be done, is the short answer. (We'll describe what can be done in subsequent chapters.) The idea that knowledge can be slotted into a data-to-wisdom hierarchy is bogus, for the simple reason that one man's knowledge is another man's data. For example, a lifetime of newspapers, magazines, conversations, and experience may give a voter political beliefs that she considers to be knowledge—even wisdom. But what's knowledge to her is mere data to the poll taker hired by a politician running for reelection. Conversely, that politician's long-incubated and hard-won expertise in, say, environmental policy is just one bit of data in the voter's evaluation of his performance in office.

Like beauty, knowledge exists in the eye of the beholder. Knowing the probably minuscule changes in the price of a company's stock just before or after it posts a quarterly dividend is of such trivial import to most investors that they consider it no better than data, and probably noise; but it's cornerstone knowledge to the "quants" at Fletcher Capital Management and a few other companies, who bet and make their fortunes by trying to exploit just such tiny changes.

There's a vital lesson here: *Knowledge assets, like money or equipment, exist and are worth cultivating only in the context of strategy.* You cannot define and manage intellectual assets unless you know what you are trying to do with them. Says Dutch consultant Rob van der Spek, who specializes in knowledge management issues:

> People in companies know intuitively what the difference is between data and knowledge. The problem begins when you start speaking about knowledge carriers and start addressing the management issues which are related to these carriers. Many of these discussions came out of vested interests of people working in domains which are already focussed upon the management of these carriers such as human resource management ("knowledge can only be in the minds of people"), document management & librarians ("knowledge is in documents"), information system management ("knowledge management is information management with the word information changed to knowledge"), knowledge engineering ("knowledge is something which can be captured in computer applications"). We have chosen to work only on the basis of "real" problems, perceived by the people, written down in terms of quality, costs, transaction time or job satisfaction and bypassing any discussions about knowledge, data . . . This approach starts at first with the identification of the types of problems you would like to solve within organizations (or opportunities you would like to focus on).

Yet it's important to separate trivial and transitory information from important intellectual assets, especially in an era of numbingly rapid change. Half of what a freshman engineering student learns is obsolete by the time she graduates, people say; the obsolescence of electronics knowledge is so fast that techies use the phrase "Internet years" the way children say "dog years." Liam Fahey, a professor of business at Babson College and a stalwart of the Strategic Leadership Forum, likes to pose the following question: How long will it take before half the knowledge you need in your job is obsolete? If he poses it to a group, a third of the audience members usually say that the half-life of their knowledge is less than two years, another third that it's less than five years.

They're wrong. Certainly intellectual assets, like any others, depreciate over time, some faster than others, but Fahey's audiences are confusing data with knowledge. In balance-sheet terms, they have jumbled raw material and inventory with capital assets—confused intellectual *working capital* with *intellectual capital.* In order to analyze intellectual capital, we need to separate the two. Intellectual working capital, workaday information—the price of a stock, the name and phone number of XYZ Corp.'s purchasing executive, the number of gaskets in the warehouse, a nation's merchandise trade balance—changes all the time. A worker might need precise, up-to-date information at any given moment, but not necessarily at this moment. What he does need, at every moment, is a way to get the data he might need at any moment. And he needs a more enduring body of knowledge—the various contexts in which the data become meaningful: trends in the industry, what influences purchasing decisions at XYZ Corp., where to get good gaskets cheaply and fast, why merchandise trade balances do or do not matter. These too change—depreciate—but less quickly.

Forget about arbitrary distinctions among data, information, knowledge, wisdom; that's a tar baby. The stuff we're looking for, intellectual capital, takes just two forms. First, there's *the semipermanent body of knowledge*, the expertise, that grows up around a task, a person, or an organization. These might be communications or leadership skills, understanding the biochemistry of viruses, knowing what customers are really paying for when they come to your company and how to price it (its "value proposition," in consultantese), familiarity with an organization's processes, values, and culture ("the way we do things around here"). The second kind of knowledge assets are *tools that augment the body of knowledge*, either by bringing in facts, data, information—call them what you will—or by delivering expertise and augmentation to others who need them when they need them, that is, leveraging them. Phone numbers are not intellectual capital; phone books are.

RECOGNIZING TACIT KNOWLEDGE

A lot of "soft" knowledge eludes definition because it is tacit rather than explicit, and therefore hard to explain or even to see. Use of language is a good illustration of the difference. Native speakers of

French don't stop to think before saying: *"C'est la plume de ma tante."* The knowledge that *plume* and *tante* are feminine nouns has become automatic; but someone learning French in school may need to stop and think, or use a dictionary. Similarly, Westerners know that *Rogers* precedes *Rubin* in the phone book; but how does one use a phone book in a language like Japanese, which has no alphabet? How would one order *Hashimoto*, and *Kodama*, and *Kurasawa?**

The lesson of the perennial best-seller *What Color Is Your Parachute?* is that people know more than they realize—that over the years they develop huge repertoires of skills, information, and ways of working that they have internalized to the point of obliviousness. Identify them, name them, package them, and these hitherto tacit capabilities can be the basis of a new career.

As it is with individuals, so it is with organizations and groups, whether they are companies or street gangs. They brim with tacit knowledge: Intuitions, rules of thumb, mind-sets, unwritten rules of turf and territory, unconscious values. Some of it's trivial: Jones takes long martini lunches, so if you want his attention, get him in the morning. Some of it conflicts with explicit knowledge: The company says it encourages honest dissent, but everyone knows only brown-nosers get promoted. Some of it describes major business issues: In our industry, customers care chiefly about price and quality takes a backseat. Much of it exists in the uncodified talents of experts: Jones, even when he's less than sober, somehow manages to fix software glitches that no one else can. Tacit knowledge adds up to a lot. Says Hubert Saint-Onge, vice president of Canadian Imperial Bank of Commerce: "Out of these beliefs and assumptions, the organization adopts values, principles, and 'ways of doing things' which in turn determine how it makes decisions and shape the collective behavior of its members."

The great virtue of tacit knowledge is that it is automatic, requiring little or no time or thought. A typist whose knowledge of the keyboard is tacit is much faster than one who has to hunt and peck. Our

---

* Japanese uses a conventional phonetic order of syllables, rather than an order of letters. The order is A-I-U-E-O, Ka-Ki-Ku-Ke-Ko, Sa-Shi-Su-Se-So, Ta-Chi-Tsu-Te-To, Na-Ni-Nu-Ne-No, Ha-Hi-Hu-He-Ho, Ma-Mi-Mu-Me-Mo, Ya-Yi-Yu-Ye-Yo, Wa-Wi-Wu-We-Wo . . . Thus the words would be listed *Kurasawa, Kodama, Hashimoto.*

inebriated pal Jones can sort through possibilities and zero in on the cause of a crashed hard drive more quickly than someone who has to reinvent a dozen wheels along the way. On a larger scale, an organization that possesses an unexpressed and possibly inexpressible "feel" for the market will serve it deftly and seemingly effortlessly. If it is evaluating ideas for new products, for instance, it will need to spend little time and money on market research and it will have few internal arguments because everyone knows instinctively what the customer wants and how to mobilize to deliver it.

But every virtue has a set of reciprocal vices, and tacit knowledge has three: It can be wrong; it's hard to change; and it's difficult to communicate. Heaven help that deft organization if the market changes radically, or if it tries to transplant its instinctive feel for customers to, say, Indonesia. Because tacit knowledge is unexpressed, it's often unexamined; it can go wrong without one's being aware of the fact. The history of Total Quality Management shows how stubborn error can be. For decades American manufacturers knew without needing to be told that it was better to live with a few defects than to spend the enormous amounts of time and money that preventing them would require. (There was a countervailing conventional wisdom, not much heeded. I worked for a company whose production manager had a sign over his desk that read "Why is there always time to do it over, but never time to do it right?" That didn't stop him from making hasty mistakes; the sign was just his way of asserting they were someone else's fault.) Even when W. Edwards Deming proved that the cost of poor quality—inspections, rework, returns, etc.—greatly exceeds the cost of excellence, no one listened: "Everyone knew" otherwise. Deming had to go to Japan to find a receptive audience. When Japanese industrial success, based in considerable part on Deming's ideas, battered American industrialists, they scurried across the Pacific to learn the Japanese secret. Only then did they realize that what they knew implicitly was incorrect, and changing corporate mind-sets took years.

Tacit knowledge tends to be local as well as stubborn, because it is not found in manuals, books, databases, or files. It is oral. It is created and shared around the watercooler. Tacit knowledge spreads when people meet and tell stories, or if they undertake a systematic effort to nose it out and make it explicit. Says Saint-Onge: "E-mail and telecommuting are fine for handling explicit knowledge, but they can't transmit tacit knowledge. If you're on autopilot and the world changes, you're cooked."

Tacit knowledge needs to become explicit; what's unspoken must be said aloud. Otherwise it cannot be examined, improved, or shared. Over the course of several years, technicians in one division of AMP, the Pennsylvania-based maker of electrical and electronic devices, learned how to drill minuscule holes in ultra-thin plastic and metal rings to make connectors for fiber-optic cables. Its drillers became the best in the world; the precision of their work allowed AMP to make some connectors for half its competitors' cost. Yet technicians in another division of the company, which made connectors for copper wiring systems, knew zilch about the skill of their brethren. It wasn't until the company mapped its technology assets that AMP knew what it knew and was able to train the copper-connector group in the skills the fiber-optic group had developed.

It's a never-ending cycle: Identifying tacit knowledge; making it explicit so that it can be formalized, captured, and leveraged; encouraging the new knowledge to soak in and become tacit.

Thus someone trying to invest in or manage smarts—this intellectual material that needs to be formalized, captured, and leveraged to produce a higher-valued asset—has to solve two problems before he can identify what he's looking for. First is separating knowledge from noise, which can be done only by means of strategy. Intellectual capital doesn't exist without a purpose and point of view: My knowledge assets are not necessarily useful to you, nor are my company's. Citicorp's ATM software is certainly a valuable asset, but Herb Kelleher of Southwest Airlines wouldn't pay a sou for it. Second, much intellectual capital is tacit—and tacit knowledge cannot be sold no matter how many sous someone is willing to fork over. But even this squishy, soft stuff must somehow be identified and leveraged—put through the tacit-to-explicit-to-tacit cycle—if an organization hopes to use it better.

Where to Look for Intellectual Capital

Every organization houses valuable intellectual materials in the form of assets and resources, tacit and explicit perspectives and capabilities, data, information, knowledge, and maybe wisdom. However, you can't manage intellectual capital—you can't even find the soft forms of it—unless you can locate it in places in a company that are strategically important and where management can make a difference. The question then becomes: Where to look?

The answer is, in one or more of three places: Its people, its structures, and its customers. This is the elegant taxonomy of Hubert Saint-Onge of the Canadian Imperial Bank of Commerce, and Leif Edvinsson of Skandia. They divide intellectual capital into three parts, like Gaul: Human Capital, Structural Capital, and Customer Capital.

In the Skandia/CIBC model of intellectual capital, each of the three elements—human, structural, and customer capital—can be measured and targeted for investment. Each is intangible—each reflects the knowledge assets of a company—and yet each describes things that managers and investors can get their arms around. Moreover, once you are thinking in categories like human, structural, and customer capital, it becomes possible to ask the questions that allow you to identify tacit as well as explicit knowledge.

Saint-Onge, whose business card opaquely proclaims him "Vice President, Learning Organization and Leadership Development," is an earnest, bright-eyed enthusiast with a gift for abstract reasoning that does credit to the Cartesian roots of francophone education. He hangs his hat in human resources and is responsible for translating the often-fuzzy rhetoric of a learning organization into a business reality bankers can believe in. That mandate led him to Edvinsson, a Swede educated in finance at Berkeley, who in 1991 left a Swedish bank to become Director of Intellectual Capital of Skandia Assurance and Financial Services (AFS), Skandia's biggest and fastest-growing division. As befits a man who had to make up his newly invented job as he went along, Edvinsson is an unabashed experimenter, constantly seeking ways to "tangibilize hidden value" and new images by which to describe them. He compares them to the roots of a tree, the walls of a house, or a body's nervous system. Whatever the metaphor, he is certain that intellectual capital is the raw material from which financial results are made.

"Leif gave us the idea of structural capital," Saint-Onge says of their brainstorming sessions. "We gave him customer capital." To each of them, human capital went without saying—but not without examination. Simply saying that employees' brainpower is an intangible asset is meaningless. Several neurons in my head keep occupied remembering some snippets of Anglo-Saxon—*Hwæt, we Gar-Dena* . . . —that aren't worth squat to *Fortune*. Point of view, remember, matters: Thus human capital is "the capabilities of the individuals required to provide solutions to customers." That leaves my Anglo-Saxon out; it can also leave *me* out if my other capabilities are no longer needed to do the things customers will pay for.

The distinction between human and structural capital is fundamental to managing knowledge. *Human capital* matters because it is the source of innovation and renewal, whether from brainstorms in a lab or new leads in a sales rep's little black book. But smart individuals don't necessarily make for smart enterprises. Says Betty Zucker: "Universities are a collection of brilliant people, but not examples of collective brilliance. Because there is little knowledge flow, the university is not intelligent as a whole. On the other hand, the people who work at McDonald's have an average IQ, if that, but it's a very intelligent organization, able to provide the same quality cross-culturally. They modularized and standardized their knowledge." By contrast, three-star chef Paul Bocuse, a far more talented cook than anyone at McDonald's, failed when he tried to open franchises.

Sharing and transporting knowledge—leveraging it—requires structural intellectual assets, such as information systems, laboratories, competitive and market intelligence, knowledge of market channels, and management focus, which turn individual know-how into the property of a group. Like human capital, structural capital exists only in the context of a point of view, a strategy, a destination, a purpose. Thus it is "the organizational capabilities of the organization to meet market requirements."

Structural capital is what turns a monk who can do elegant calligraphy into the smiling star of a Xerox television commercial, who can make many copies of a document. Augmenter and megaphone, it packages human capital and permits it to be used again and again to create value, just as a die can stamp out part after part. As Sid Caesar put it: "The guy who invented the first wheel was an idiot. The guy who invented the other three, *he* was a genius." Compiling human knowledge into structural intellectual capital helped Skandia AFS move quickly to take advantage of the worldwide trend toward deregulation of insurance and other financial services. In one project, Edvinsson worked alongside technologists and actuaries to cut the time involved in opening an office in a new country from seven years to seven months. They did it by identifying techniques and technology that could be transplanted anywhere. While AFS's product line differs from place to place, the process of recording payments need not, for example; as one Skandia executive put it, "The financial event is the same from Bogotá to Uppsala." From this work AFS created what it calls a "prototype concept"—a collection of software applications, manuals, and other structured know-how that can easily be customized to take account of local laws or support any line of financial products. The company has used similar knowledge-transfer strategies to encourage cross-border sales, offering products developed in one country to customers in another. Those sales now account for about 15 percent of Skandia AFS's premium income.

Customer capital is the value of an organization's relationships with the people with whom it does business. Saint-Onge defines it as "the depth (penetration), width (coverage) and attachment (loyalty) of our franchise"; Edvinsson adds, "It's the likelihood that our customers will keep doing business with us." It could be broadened to include the value of relationships with suppliers—call it "relationship capital"? Whether the relationship is upstream or downstream, its economics and dynamics are the same.

It is here, in relationships with customers, that intellectual capital turns into money—though it should be emphasized that customer capital cannot be expressed solely in dollar terms, even if that is its ultimate manifestation. Because customer capital resides on the banks of the revenue stream, it is more often measured—and counted—than human and structural intellectual assets. Brand equity, for example, is a form of customer capital for which well-established valuation methods exist. It's done by calculating the premium customers are willing to pay for a branded product versus a generic one—say, Kellogg's Corn Flakes versus a supermarket label—then using cost-of-capital and return-on-capital figures to calculate the value of the asset (the brand's reputation) that produces that premium. The Coca-Cola brand name, the world's most valuable, is worth about $39 billion.

But the intangible attachment of customers shows up in many non-financial ways, as Coca-Cola learned when it tried to change the formula for its core product. Customer capital shows up in complaint letters, renewal rates, cross-selling, referrals, the speed with which your phone calls are returned. Most important, it is manifest in learning, access, and trust. When an airline chooses between General Electric, Pratt & Whitney, and Rolls-Royce for engines to power a new plane, its decision is based on the quality of its relationship with each company as well as on price and technical specifications. The better that relationship, the more likely the buyer is to share its plans and expertise with the seller—that is, the more likely a company can learn with and from its customers and its suppliers. Shared knowledge is the ultimate form of customer capital.

The next chapters will look at human, structural, and customer capital in detail. Step-by-step instructions for managing them will differ for every organization, but I will discuss the dynamics and management principles of each, and show how companies have successfully invested in and exploited them. As we shall see, the ways in which they can be measured, managed, and enhanced are often nonfinancial; they are nevertheless obviously real, and a far cry from the fuzzy notion of "organizational intelligence" or "smarts."

Crucially, intellectual capital is not created from discrete wads of human, structural, and customer capital but from the *interplay* among them. Structural capital in the form of databases, computer networks, patents, and good management can augment the talent of an engineer; bad tools and bureaucrats can devalue it. Whatever customer affection and brand equity typewriter-maker Smith-Corona had lost their value when the people and systems of the company weren't able to keep up with technological change. When human capital, in the form of top-notch engineers and state-of-the-art technology, doesn't interact with customer capital, the result is called an Edsel. Like money in a mattress, says Hugh Macdonald, "intellectual capital is useless unless it moves. It's no good having some guy who is very wise and sits alone in a room."

But that's where you start: with people.

CHAPTER 6

Human Capital

JOHN HIGGINS: MOST OF MY EQUIPMENT DON'T COST ME A
    THING, WRITING IT OFF YEAR BY YEAR. WHAT'S IT CALLED,
    ARTHUR?

ARTHUR HIGGINS: DEPLETION AND DEPRECIATION.

JOHN: YEAH, THAT'S IT. MEANS IT'S RUNNIN' DOWN, DON'T
    WORK SO GOOD AS IT DID.

DR. PRAETORIUS: ONE THING ABOUT TEACHERS AND WRITERS
    AND SUCH. THEY HAVE LESS BOTHER WITH THEIR INCOME TAX
    THAN FARMERS AND OIL WELL OWNERS.

JOHN: THAT SO? WHY?

DR. PRAETORIUS: BECAUSE THEIR EQUIPMENT IS TALENT AND A
    HIGHLY DEVELOPED MIND, AND WHEN THEY RUN DOWN AND
    DON'T WORK SO GOOD AS THEY DID, THE DEPLETION AND
    DEPRECIATION CAN'T BE WRITTEN OFF THEIR INCOME TAX.

JOHN: SEE WHAT I MEAN? WHAT'S SO SMART ABOUT 'EM?

—JOSEPH L. MANKIEWICZ, *PEOPLE WILL TALK*

"The prettiest little factory you'd ever want to see"—That's how the owner, John Hazen White, describes the place. To get there, you leave Interstate 95 in Cranston, Rhode Island—a pretty little factory in *Cranston?*—and make a couple of left turns onto a shabby street whose convenience stores, gas stations, and shuttered factories stand as a testament to the deindustrialization of New England. After a few minutes, a low red-brick building appears on your left; from one corner of the building rises a square, four-story clock tower. For years window glass gave a hollow-eyed look to the round openings in the tower's decorated brickwork; now clockfaces, installed in 1994, beam there once again. This is Taco, Inc.—with a long *a*, Tay-co—a manufacturer of decidedly unglamorous pumps and valves, and it stands as a testament to the power of human capital.

Most of Taco's 450 employees work in this plant, and a few up the coast in Fall River, Massachusetts, Lizzie Borden's hometown. They are the usual New England mix: Irish and Italian and French-Canadian, and recently many Hispanic and Southeast Asian immigrants. As you enter the building a receptionist sits directly in front of you behind a sliding glass window. To your right a staircase leads up to the executive offices. Between them is a door bearing a sign: LEARNING CENTER.

In here, where there are classrooms, a computer lab, a library, and a conference room, and at nearby community colleges and universities, this small (1995 sales were between $80 and $90 million) privately held company provides employees an astonishing offering of educational opportunities—more than six dozen courses in all. A few are brief, standard stuff, such as orientation programs, fire and safety drills, introductions to Taco's products, Weight Watchers, and quit-smoking programs. But there's more.

A whole series of courses is clearly work-related: These are classes—some carry college credit—in blueprint reading, CNC machining, ISO 9000 auditing, statistical process control, Total Quality Management, manufacturing methods, customer service, telephone skills, employment law. Still there's more.

In June 1995, five Taco employees earned high school equivalency diplomas. Taco offers three levels of instruction in English as a second language, doubling the value of the courses by using them to introduce students to American history, teach them how to deal with their children's schools, and help them learn money-management skills. Dozens of employees have taken Conversational Spanish I and II, the better to communicate with non-English-speaking colleagues. There are courses in arithmetic, algebra, personal computing, speech—and art and gardening. Still there's more.

The governor of Rhode Island, the mayor of Providence, and other public officials have come to Taco to describe their work and answer questions. The chief justice of the state supreme court came to teach history. Seven employees have recently submitted applications for

U.S. citizenship. Employees' children have gone whale-watching with oceanographers from the University of Rhode Island, learned to play stringed instruments from members of the Rhode Island Philharmonic, and put on a musical play, having spent two weeks building sets, writing a script, and rehearsing.

The cost to employees: nothing, though art students pay for materials. The cost to Taco: a quarter of a million bucks to build the learning center, which was dedicated in late 1992; about $200,000 a year to operate it; and another $100,000 or so annually in extra wages and lost production. Employees are entitled to take one course at a time, and if it's work-related are paid for the time they spend in class.

"I don't have any idea why the hell it happened," John Hazen White says, "except I wanted to do it." Fit and lean, clear-eyed behind bifocals, the eighty-four-year-old White took over Taco in 1942 when his father—"the old man," White calls him—collapsed and died from a heart attack while trying to land a procurement contract from the War Department.

Like most owners of private companies, White—otherwise a picture of garrulity—clams up about profits, but it's clear that Taco has been good to him: Three Rhode Island universities—Brown, Johnson & Wales, and the University of Rhode Island—have received million-dollar gifts from him, and the state's Sea Scouts have, over the years, set sail in a fifty-four-foot schooner, a twenty-nine-foot cutter, and a forty-foot yawl he gave them.

This spending on training, schooling, and citizenship—is it the benign folly of an idealistic octogenarian, or a canny old man's investment in the future of a family business? "Does it come back to us? Of course it does," says White. He refuses, however, to put a monetary value on the return: "It comes back in the form of attitude. People feel they're playing in the game, not being kicked around in it."

If there's no quantifying the benefit from Taco's learning center, there's no gainsaying it, either. Taco makes circulators, pumps, heat exchangers, flow controls, and other items used in commercial and residential heating and air conditioning equipment. Says thirty-nine-year-old John White, Jr. (around the plant, he is "Johnny," his father "Mr. White"), Taco's executive vice president: "When I came into the business in 1982, half the industry was family-owned. I've watched them die like flies."

Taco itself got swatted in the 1990–92 recession, which hit construction, and therefore Taco, particularly hard. The company had no sales growth whatsoever from 1987 through 1991. Though it never lost money, profits were "kind of poopy," says Johnny White. Then in the spring of 1991, sales suddenly nosedived: If the first quarter's trend persisted, Taco's business would fall 20 percent. It might not be able to survive in New England, or stay in the family.

There were three options. One was to cut costs, move South to cheaper labor, and hope to ride out the storm; but the Whites had seen too many competitors that didn't survive that strategy. A second option: Bull through the recession, buying new machines, take losses, and bet on blasting out when recovery came. This was more risk than the Whites were willing to take. They chose a more modest but ultimately harder plan, to bet that human capital could do what financial capital couldn't. The first step was to bring costs under control, which meant dropping planned capital spending and, unhappily, laying off about a fifth of the factory workforce and three tenths of the office staff. That pill swallowed, the Whites began to execute the plan: Attack the in-process inventory that clogged the plant, thereby freeing up cash; reinvest that cash in the efficiency of the factory; and, when the recession lifted, use the recovery's new sales to fund big-ticket equipment so as to increase capacity without adding back staff.

If the first improvements could not depend on money from the capital budget, the resource for generating them would have to be human capital. Johnny White says: "We made a commitment that we would not displace people with machines—the layoff was survival, not displacement—and said, 'Now let's fix the place.' "

There was lots to do. Seeking the ideas and approval of hourly workers every step of the way, Taco went after the inventory. One at a time, beginning with the worst logjams, work processes were reorganized. Suppliers were told to make smaller, more frequent deliveries. Where once there were lines of workers each doing a small operation on a part (with cratefuls of incoming and outgoing pieces at each station), there began to appear cells and clusters of workers all performing several operations and drawing on smaller boxes of parts. Work stations were moved to shorten the trips forklift operators made to the storage bay. None of it was fancy, but it didn't have to be. Says Johnny White: "The difference between the way the plant looked four years ago and a nineteenth-century factory was that back then women wore high-button shoes."

Success hung on employees' informed and full-hearted willingness to offer ideas, kibitz, and learn new tasks—that is, on human capital's wringing gains out of physical capital. The Learning Center thus became central to the bargain Taco made with employees, as Johnny White describes it: "You step to the plate and improve your work skills; we'll provide the tools to do that." Informed by courses on TQM and manufacturing methods and empowered by the financial and citizenship skills they learned, Taco's employees saw that their ideas could make a difference. As the economy turned around, Taco stuck to its end of the deal—bringing in new equipment, but not automating people out of their jobs. Every dollar Taco paid for machines came out of reduced inventory costs. No, it isn't the prettiest factory you'd ever want to see, but from photographs taken in 1991 it's hard to imagine the well-lit, clean, spacious building of today.

From the low point in the spring of 1991 to the summer of 1995, sales doubled. The number of employees—and their names, for Taco enjoys a turnover rate of less than 1 percent—remained unchanged. Prices scarcely budged. That's a compound annual rate of increase in labor productivity of about 20 percent, a stunning gain, almost entirely attributable to people rather than machinery or technology.

Taco gets these powerful results for less than $700 per employee per year, about what it usually gives in holiday bonuses and profit sharing. Sure, its patrician owner is partly animated by a sense of noblesse oblige, but the senior White is motivated as much by self-interest. When he was growing up, back in the twenties and thirties, his mother hoped he would follow her father, an Episcopal bishop in Indiana, into the priesthood. He disappointed her. "I decided to be a teacher," the old man says. "There's no saint in me."

There is a huge economic and management literature about human capital. Surveying it would overstretch my competence and exhaust your patience. Nor will this chapter catalog best practices in human resources management.* The economic value of human capital doesn't need to be proved: Taco's story is just one of many that dem-

* *The Human Resources Financial Report*, published annually by the Saratoga Institute, 12950 Saratoga Avenue, Saratoga, CA 95070, is a good source of these. It's expensive.

onstrate it. We must do three things in this chapter, though. The first is to strip the sentiment from the subject. We all spout goop about the importance of the human asset; the fact is, some employees are indeed immensely valuable assets but others are merely costs, and grumpy ones at that. We have to find out which is which.

Second, we'll look at how organizations can increase their human capital. Finally, we'll look at one of the condundrums of human capital: It's a corporate asset, but people cannot be owned. How, then, can managers make sure that their organizations benefit from increases in human capital?

Our Most Important Asset—Really

Ideas are free. They are also an abundant, probably an infinite, resource. Any parent who has left a two-year-old alone for a few minutes knows that coming up with ideas is an innately human trait that requires no special training or education; it's the organized development of constructive ideas that is a management challenge.

Ideas are also immensely valuable—more valuable than we usually realize. According to Yale University's Robert Shiller, 72.1 percent of U.S. household wealth consists of human capital, which he defines as the present value of expected lifetime wages; we saw in Chapter 3 that training and education powerfully affect wages.

We're used to thinking of employees in terms of their pay—their cost. But what is their value? How much is a job really worth? Imagine a person earning $100,000 a year, who's likely to get a 5 percent raise at Christmas. Think of her career as an asset, an investment that throws off $100,000 in dividends, plus enough capital appreciation that next year it throws off $105,000. Tomorrow on her way to a meeting at the office in Samarra, she is hit by the proverbial truck. She wants to leave her heirs an asset worth what her career is worth. What's the number? At this writing, the interest rate on thirty-year Treasury bonds is about 6.5 percent—so to get $100,000 she'd need about $1.54 million of them. But her career is worth more: Because of that 5 percent raise, next year she'd need bonds worth $76,000 more, about $1.62 million. This year's total return—cash dividends plus capital gains—isn't $100,000, but $176,000. Protecting the equity in a career is a lot more important than protecting the equity in a house.

Imagine, then, the value of the human capital represented by all the employees of a company. In the aftermath of AT&T's notorious 1996 announcement that it would reduce its workforce by 40,000 people, consultant Tom DeMarco estimated that the massive downsizing amounted to a $4 billion to $8 billion human capital write-off—equivalent to wiping out more than a third of the company's stock of property, plant, and equipment.

There's lots of evidence of the value of this asset to organizations. It amounts to this: Smart workers work smarter. Meet Robert Zemsky, professor of education at the University of Pennsylvania and co-director of the National Center on the Educational Quality of the Workforce (EQW). Working with the Census Bureau, EQW's Zemsky, Lisa Lynch (an economist at the Fletcher business school at Tufts University) and Peter Cappelli (professor of management at Wharton) have been studying the relationship between education and productivity at more than 3,100 U.S. workplaces. In a report issued in 1995, which controlled for factors like age of equipment, industry, and establishment size, EQW showed that, on average, a 10 percent increase in workforce education level led to an 8.6 percent gain in total factor productivity. By comparison, a 10 percent rise in capital stock—that is, the value of equipment—increased productivity just 3.4 percent.* Put another way: The marginal value of investing in human capital is about three times greater than the value of investing in machinery.

Why, then, do companies manage it so haphazardly? A principal reason, I believe, is that they have a hard time distinguishing between the cost of *paying* people and the value of *investing* in them.

* Total factor productivity (Zemsky's number) cannot be compared directly to labor productivity (the number I could infer from what Taco told me), though both measure efficiency. Labor productivity measures output (widgets or dollars) per unit of labor (hours, dollars, or number of employees). Total factor productivity is output divided by all costs—labor, raw materials, and capital equipment. That's a better measure, but even the U.S. Government mostly relies on labor productivity numbers, because they're more readily available.

Identifying Which Human Capital Generates Wealth

Human capital is, to quote Yeats out of context, the place where all the ladders start: the wellspring of innovation, the home page of insight. If intellectual capital is a tree (one of Leif Edvinsson's metaphors), then human beings are the sap—in some companies, the saps—that make it grow. Money talks, but it does not think; machines perform, often better than any human being can, but do not invent. Every reasonably sized company has some sort of form managers fill out before buying new equipment: a request for capital expenditures that asks for a calculation of a return on the investment. While there's sometimes, ahem, creative writing on those forms, it is nothing compared to the inventiveness that would be needed to complete an identical form calculating the return on investment in a new employee, especially one who is expected to think.

The point bears emphasizing: *Routine, low-skill work, even if it's done manually, does not generate or employ human capital for the organization.* Often the work involved in such jobs can be automated, which is why these are the jobs most at risk nowadays; when it cannot be automated, the worker, contributing and picking up little in the way of skill, can easily be replaced if he leaves—he is a hired hand, not a hired mind.

I'm not saying that such workers lack skill or talent. They might have jeroboams of brains, but it is private stock; the employer doesn't get any. Pull a first novel off the shelf at a bookstore, and read the author's biography on the jacket: John Doe, it says, a graduate of the University of Chicago, has sheared sheep in Montana, tended bar in Fort Worth, loaded cargo on the docks of Baltimore, and worked as an orderly in a Rangoon mental hospital. If the listening skills he learned as a bartender made him a better worker in Rangoon, that was happenstance; he has been picking up human capital to put in his novel, not to offer to his employers.

Our point of view must be organizational, not individual: The question for companies is how to acquire as much human capital as they can use profitably. If the primary purpose of human capital is innovation—whether of new products and services, or of improvements in business processes—then human capital is formed and deployed when more of the time and talent of the people who work in a company is devoted to activities that result in innovation. Human capital grows two ways: when the organization uses more of what people know, and when more people know more stuff that is useful to the organization.

USING MORE OF WHAT PEOPLE KNOW

Unleashing the human capital already resident in the organization requires minimizing mindless tasks, meaningless paperwork, unproductive infighting. The Taylorized workplace squandered human assets in such activities. Frank Ostroff, a fellow at Perot Systems, recalls how he first realized the extent of the waste when as a college student he took a summer job at a tire-making factory in Ohio: "We'd spend eight hours a day doing something completely mindless like applying glue to rubber to tire after tire, the same thing all day long. And then these same people would go home and spend their evenings and weekends rebuilding entire cars from scratch or running volunteer organizations." The company got eight hours' work from those people, but no benefit from their minds.

In the Information Age, no one can afford to use human capital so inefficiently. With competition fierce, says GE's chairman Jack Welch: "The only ideas that count are the A ideas. There is no second place. That means we have to get everybody in the organization involved. If you do that right, the best ideas will rise to the top." GE's Work-Out program—a never-ending series of town meetings in which employees propose changes in work processes and bosses are required to approve or reject them on the spot—is one proven way to begin the process of getting at the ideas of more people.*

For more than a decade business leaders have been taught, to the point of being hectored, the virtues of bureaucracy-busting, teamwork, coaching, etc. Here's all you really have to know about the subject:

---

* For more on Work-Out, see my piece, "GE Keeps Those Ideas Coming," *Fortune*, August 12, 1991, p. 40 ff; or see Noel Tichy and Stratford Sherman, *Control Your Destiny or Someone Else Will* (New York: Currency Doubleday, 1993).

Programs like Work-Out succeed because they provide safe places where people can share ideas about work without getting shut down by bosses and bureaucrats. To use more of what people know, companies need to create opportunities for private knowledge to be made public and tacit knowledge to be made explicit. In the next chapter we'll discuss how some companies are setting up electronic networks and other knowledge-sharing systems. But people in every company already have informal networks and forums—mentoring relationships, Friday-night poker games, etc.—where tips are exchanged and ideas generated. At their best these are "communities of practice," an especially powerful kind of learning forum we'll discuss later in this chapter.

GETTING MORE PEOPLE TO KNOW MORE STUFF THAT IS USEFUL TO THE ORGANIZATION

Leaders need to focus and amass talent where it is needed, whether by hiring or by teaching. As always with intellectual capital, the link to strategy is essential. Kodak, for example, a great company built on the silver-halide chemistry that underlies the photography business, is struggling to build the human capital it needs to succeed as the electronic processing of digital images threatens to erode the chemistry-based business. As the 1990s began, task forces all over Kodak were busy trying to find ways to use digital imaging in its product line. The effort led nowhere, though the company in a decade had invested $5 billion in digital-photography R&D. In 1992, Kodak with great fanfare rolled out its Photo CD, a $20 service that allowed shutterbugs to scan pictures onto a compact disc that could then be mailed to Grandma, who could see them on her TV, provided she had a $400-to-$800 device (or a Mac) to plug into it—not a likely success. Kodak's problem was one of scale and focus: The small groups were imprisoned in the divisional boxes that created them; the boundaries made it difficult for the groups to collaborate or share their knowledge—at one point there were twenty-three different groups working to develop digital scanners. Kodak had a few teams of snipers; it needed a massed corps.

Recognizing the problem when he became CEO in 1993, Kodak's George Fisher dismantled the departmental task forces, putting most of them into one department, a new digital and applied imaging division. Its sales (of such products as "smart" film that stores shutter speed and other data to allow better photo processing and a CopyPrint station, now set up in many photo stores, that uses digital technology to make on-the-spot enlargements of ordinary prints) totaled $500 million in 1994, and are expected to reach $1 billion in 1996. There's a valuable lesson in Kodak's early experience with digital imaging: *Human capital is easily dissipated. It needs to be massed and concentrated.* That means that organizational intelligence, like any asset, must be cultivated in the context of action: Random hiring of Ph.D.s won't cut it. What are you going to do with them? Human capital needs its structural and customer siblings to make a difference.

Kodak faces the unusually daunting task of investing for a future for which there is not yet a market to sell to or learn from—while at the same time protecting its lucrative silver-halide franchise. Few companies face the likelihood that their entire business might become based on a completely different science. For most, the challenge, less difficult but no less important, is to find and enhance those talents that truly are assets—for not all skills are created equal. Any task, process, or business relies on three different kinds:

1. *Commodity skills:* abilities that are not specific to any particular business, are readily obtained, and are more or less equally valuable to any number of businesses. Typing and a cheerful telephone manner are commodity skills; so are some highly technical abilities, such as air-conditioner maintenance or benefits administration.

2. *Leveraged skills:* knowledge that, while not specific to a particular company, is more valuable to it than to others. Most big companies need programmers, but Andersen Consulting, IBM Consulting, and EDS can leverage the skill because they sell it to many different customers, whereas programmers for, say, Bank of America or General Motors can add value only to their employers. Similarly, a law firm can get more value from an attorney than a corporation can, which is why partners at the firm your company uses probably earn more than the in-house counsel who hires them. Leveraged skills tend to be industry-specific, but not company-specific.

3. *Proprietary skills:* the company-specific talents around which an organization builds a business. Proprietary knowledge, as it deepens, becomes a selling point: McKinsey is *the* strategy consulting firm, the

University of Chicago has *the* economics department, Ritz-Carlton is *the* expert in hotel management. Some proprietary skills become codified in patents, copyrights, and other intellectual property, but much more comes from the concentration of expertise and experience that answers the question, "What have we got that they ain't got?"

Look at your company's or your department's workforce and, roughly, parcel out the people into the four quadrants of this grid.

DIFFICULT TO REPLACE, LOW VALUE ADDED	DIFFICULT TO REPLACE, HIGH VALUE ADDED
EASY TO REPLACE, LOW VALUE ADDED	EASY TO REPLACE, HIGH VALUE ADDED

Unskilled and semiskilled labor go in the lower-left quadrant: The organization may need such people—maybe a lot of them—but its success doesn't depend on them *as individuals:* One job-holder is pretty much as good as another, one want-ad will bring dozens of qualified replacements, training time is short. Above them, in the upper left, go people who have learned a complicated set of ropes but don't pull the strings, such as skilled factory workers, experienced secretaries, or people who hold staff jobs such as quality assurance, auditing, or corporate communications. They may be hard to replace and doing important work, but it's not work customers care about. An advertising agency, for instance, might lose clients if its billing department constantly messes up, but it wins them on the basis of creative services. Lower-right workers do stuff that customers value highly, but as individuals they're fungible. Many people with leveraged skills go into this quadrant: A book needs a great jacket, for example, but there are lots of superb designers. Finally, in the upper-right quadrant go the stars: people who play irreplaceable roles in the organization and who are damn near irreplaceable as individuals. Some are perched high in the company tree; most aren't. They might be research chemists, top sales reps, project managers, movie stars. One group at Hewlett-Packard estimates that incoming engineers need more than two full years before they become full-fledged contributors to their team; hard to replace, indeed, and an expensive investment.

A company's human capital is in the upper-right quadrant, embodied in the people whose talent and experience create the products and services that are the reason customers come to it and not to a competitor. That's an asset. The rest—the other three quadrants—is merely labor cost. (Incidentally, placing yourself on the grid is a useful way to evaluate your job security or to analyze whether you would find yourself closer to the upper-right quadrant in a new position in the company or with a different employer.) The greater the human-capital intensity of a business—that is, the greater its percentage of high-value-added work performed by hard-to-replace people—the more it can charge for its services and the less vulnerable it is to competitors, because it will be even more difficult for rivals to match those skills than it is for the first company to replace them. Smart organizations, then, will spend and invest as little as possible in work that customers do not value and whose workers' skills are easy to replace, automating what they can; employee retention doesn't much matter to fast-food joints, for example.

DIFFICULT TO REPLACE, LOW VALUE ADDED INFORMATE →	DIFFICULT TO REPLACE, HIGH VALUE ADDED CAPITALIZE
EASY TO REPLACE, LOW VALUE ADDED AUTOMATE	EASY TO REPLACE, HIGH VALUE ADDED DIFFERENTIATE OR OUTSOURCE

Those in the upper-left quadrant present a trickier management challenge: You need them, but you wish you didn't because your customers don't value them. The goal here, in Shoshana Zuboff's inelegant but useful coinage, is to *informate* their work: that is, change it to add more information value, so that it starts to benefit customers. Take, for example, the way many corporate staff functions have been transformed. At GE, the corporate audit staff—once a fearsome cadre of traveling checkers—turned itself into in-house consultants. Auditors, youngsters picked for their high potential, used to come from finance backgrounds; now half are operations or information systems experts. When she first joined the group fifteen years ago, says former audit staff head Teresa LeGrand: "The first thing I did [when visiting one of GE's business units] was count the $5,000 in the petty cash box. Today we look at the $5 million in inventory on the floor, searching for process improvements that will bring it down." The auditors have become competitive assets, not just inspectors. The same things happen when quality assurance prevents errors instead of just catching them, or when the accounts-payable department arranges for electronic data interchange that not only gets the bills paid but increases customer satisfaction.

Those fungible worthies in the lower-right quadrant present a choice. You can outsource the work. According to an Arthur Andersen survey of more than 300 chief financial officers, two out of five companies outsource shipping. More than a third outsource information systems: one out of every twelve dollars spent by corporate America on information technology flows through an outsourcing contract. According to Roy Smith, vice president of Microelectronics and Computer Technology Corp., three out of ten large U.S. industrial companies outsource more than half their manufacturing.

By outsourcing, a company is liberated from the need to invest in expertise that isn't proprietary. For EDS, which manages information systems for client companies, expertise in the relevant information technologies is the basis of comparative advantage: It *pays* to be world class. For companies like Xerox, an EDS client, it *costs*. A lot. It ties up resources that would be better sunk into sources of expertise that are profit centers—imaging and copying technologies—rather than cost centers. That's especially true in a fast-changing environment. With so many demands on your attention and your pocketbook, you want to put your money where you will make money. You want to invest to outpace the pack, not just to keep up with it.

The alternative to outsourcing is differentiation—finding ways to turn generic knowledge into something your company is uniquely able to exploit, or can exploit in unique ways. Whenever a company advertises itself as selling "solutions," it's trying to differentiate high-value commodity knowledge. Knowing how to make desktop computers, for example, is no longer the proprietary talent of a few companies but a cutthroat, low-margin business. Customers mix and match Compaq, Gateway, Hewlett-Packard, IBM, and other machines in client-server networks—some computer resellers even cobble computers together from different manufacturers' components. The proprietary human capital resides in designing and manufacturing key components (such as Intel's and Motorola's microprocessor know-how) and in configuring desktop computers, servers, and mainframes into custom-designed networks. Every major computer-maker has gone into the consulting and systems-integration business because that's where the proprietary knowledge is.

How to Build Human Capital: The Role of Community

When the CEO says "people are our most important asset," he's speaking of the folks in the upper-right quadrant of our chart: people who know how to serve customers in ways that give the company an edge. Considering human capital in these terms sheds new light on how to build it, and on the process of capitalizing individual knowledge to create an organizational asset. In particular, it tells you that training, in the traditional sense, is a waste of money. Workers at Taco and the GE power protection plant in Puerto Rico are not "trained." They are offered opportunities to learn skills they can use—at work or after hours—to benefit their careers or their lives. As John Hazen White put it: "People feel they're playing in the game, not being kicked around in it."

By defining human capital in terms of what people must know to serve customers and benefit themselves, Canadian Imperial Bank of Commerce has devised a brand-new approach to employee development. It's a model of how to build useful human capital, rather than simply stuffing trainees into classrooms as if they were anchovies in a jar. Working from CIBC's new Leadership Centre, a 125-room residential campus an hour north of downtown Toronto, Hubert Saint-

Onge and his colleagues developed what they call competency models. These describe the abilities *that customers expect* from the people they deal with at the bank: familiarity with its product line, a knowledge of accounting, selling skills, expertise in credit analysis—about four dozen in all. Obviously, the range and depth of knowledge expected of a teller differ from what a branch manager or loan officer should know, so the competency models were turned into "competency maps" that, in effect, display the skills people need to move along career paths.

Then CIBC abolished training. If that sounds bass-ackward, consider: Most training programs are pitched too high or too low, are delivered in classrooms to an audience that needed the information last month or won't need it for two years, and cost the earth. Says Saint-Onge: "Most companies can't tell you how much they spend on training. It took us six months to decipher—$30 million a year! And one penny out of a hundred hits the mark." Says John Seely Brown, director of Xerox's Palo Alto Research Center: "The false correlation of learning with training or education is one of the most common and costly errors in corporate management today."

Instead the bank puts the monkey on employees' backs: Armed with their competency maps, employees are responsible for learning what they don't yet know or enhancing what they do—to perform their current jobs, not to prep for the job on the ladder's next rung. The idea is for employees to close the gaps between what they can do now and what customers expect them to be able to do. They have access to books and software at the Learning Room at each branch; managers are instructed to let them shadow colleagues to learn from them; if necessary, they can take courses. But the initiative is theirs, the scheduling is theirs, and, because employees learn things they need now, both they and the company can measure achievement rather than participation—an output, not a cost; a skill attained, not a seat warmed. Department heads can aggregate individuals' records to track, for example, how fast their crew is learning, or whether it is weak in any particular area—data that provide a far better picture of human capital development than the amount of time or money spent in training. The CIBC program simultaneously defines the core competencies of the company and shows individuals how they can grow in the knowledge that the bank needs.

The relationship between individual learning and an organization's human capital—not just its stock of knowledge but its capacity to innovate—involves groups even more than it does individuals. It makes sense that a corporate asset should be social in origin.

Think about a document you signed on your first day at work and stuck in a long-since-lost file. In it, you promised not to reveal company secrets and agreed that the fruits of your labors—ideas, intellectual property, whatever—belong to your employer, not to you. It probably contained language like this:

> In consideration of my employment by Random Rightsizing, Inc., I hereby assign to the company all inventions or innovations conceived or developed by me during my employment, and agree not to use or disclose any confidential information I may receive as a result of my employment by the company . . .

Swiping secrets is odious to both law and etiquette, and that's a legally enforceable document. It is also hornswoggle. First, you swap proprietary information all the time; in fact, the company probably wouldn't prosper unless you did. Second, the real genesis and true ownership of ideas and know-how aren't corporate. Nor personal, for that matter. They belong to something that is coming to be known as a "community of practice."

If the term "community of practice" wasn't invented at the Institute for Research on Learning, that's where it's most often bandied about. IRL, in Palo Alto, California, was founded in 1987 as a sort of eleemosynary spinoff of Xerox's Palo Alto Research Center. Its mission—to study how people learn—makes it a center for basic research for the Information Age. The fundamental finding in IRL's work is that learning is a social activity: However romantic the image of the scholar bent over his desk in a pool of lamplight, learning happens in groups.

That's an insight with huge—and problematic—implications for managers. Not every group is a learning place. You can't take a dozen people at random, give them a pot of coffee and a box of doughnuts, and expect them to learn something. Groups that learn, communities of practice, have special characteristics. They emerge of their own accord: Three, four, twenty, maybe thirty people find themselves drawn to one another by a force that's both social and professional; they collaborate directly, use one another as sounding boards, teach

each other, strike out together to explore new subject matter. You cannot create communities like this by fiat, but they are easy to destroy. They are among the most important structures of any organization where thinking matters; but they are, almost inevitably, subversive of its formal structures and strictures.

Communities of practice are the shop floor of human capital, the place where the stuff gets made. Brook Manville, a consultant at McKinsey & Co., defines a community of practice thus: "A group of professionals, informally bound to one another through exposure to a common class of problems, common pursuit of solutions, and thereby themselves embodying a store of knowledge." Most of us belong to more than one, and not just on the job: The management team; the engineers, some in your company and some not, trying to cram more circuits onto a wafer of silicon; the church choir. Different communities might have concerns that overlap. Trying to solve a problem for his church choir—how could they mark the day's hymns without damaging the hymnals by dog-earing or paper-clipping pages?—led tenor Arthur Fry to conceive the product that became Post-it notes, developed by a community of adhesives experts at 3M.

IRL's Etienne Wenger points to several traits that define communities of practice and distinguish them from other groups. First, they have history—they develop over time, indeed "you can define them in terms of the learning they do over time." Second, a community of practice has an enterprise, but not an agenda; that is, it forms around a value-adding something-we're-all-doing. It could be a gang seeking to carve a place for itself on the streets, or a district sales office wanting to be the best doggone district office in the company; it could be people who don't work side by side but share a mission, like antitrust lawyers, Alcoholics Anonymous groups, or (an example described by John Seely Brown of Xerox PARC) copier repairers who exchange tips at the watercooler. Third, the enterprise involves learning; as a result, over time communities of practice develop customs, culture—as Wenger puts it, "a way of dealing with the world they share."

Perhaps most intriguing, communities of practice are responsible only to themselves. No one owns them. They're like professional societies. People join and stay because they have something to learn and something to contribute. The work they do is the joint and several property of the group—"cosa nostra," our thing.

These traits give communities of practice a distinct place in the ecology of the informal organization. Project groups and teams have a charter and report to a higher authority: Even if they have no box on an organization chart, they have an agenda, a deadline, accountability, a membership list. A community of practice is voluntary, longer-lived, and has no specific "deliverable" such as a report or a new product. Affinity groups and clubs—the salesmen who play poker every Friday night—are about fellowship rather than work. Grapevines and other networks may support your work, but are not central to it.

Like Poe's purloined letter, communities of practice are so obviously present in our daily lives that we don't usually notice them. When we do, however, the implications are anything but quotidian. Communities of practice perform two main jobs of human capital formation: knowledge transfer and innovation. James Euchner, a vice president in Nynex's research and development department, began thinking about them when he was puzzling over why some groups at Nynex were quick to adopt new technologies, others not. For example, some groups needed, on average, seventeen days to set up data services for customers. Euchner hired an anthropologist to learn why they took so long. She found that different departments involved in the process never communicated informally and, as a result, didn't understand one another's roles and needs and couldn't solve problems together. When she and Euchner put the workers together in the same room, they created an environment that allowed informal groups to form around various tasks, which soon grew into a full-fledged community of practice. Result: a mutual sense of purpose and a sharing of ideas that cut the time to provision data services to just three days.

Euchner found himself face to face with a challenge communities of practice pose: Organizational learning depends on these often invisible groups, but they're virtually immune to management in a conventional sense—indeed, managing them can kill them. A study by three academics—Ronald Purser of Loyola University in Chicago and William Pasmore and Ramkrishnan Tenkasi of Cleveland's Case Western Reserve University—shows why. The professors followed two product-development projects in the same big American manufacturer. One, a major upgrade of a key technology, was rigorously managed and relied on big fortnightly meetings to keep everybody up to speed; the other, a radical innovation, was scarcely managed at all: The professors called it "self-organizing . . . informal . . . egalitarian."

The former slogged; the latter soared; the main reason, Purser et al. found, was that the formal structure of the first group erected barriers to learning. Chief among them: failure to use already-available knowledge, withholding important knowledge because of mistrust or conflicts between groups, holding discussions from which key people were missing, failure to take heed of important information from other divisions or the business environment, and divergent values between groups. Essentially, the formal structure of the first group prevented people from talking; the second group, like GE's Work-Out meetings, was full of places where people felt free to speak up.

If they can't manage communities of practice, managers can nevertheless help them. How?

Recognize them and their importance. They're relatively easy to spot within a department or business unit, like those copier repairers; harder to see are communities that cross lines. Look for jobs that exist in different functions, business units, or geographic areas, suggests George Pór, head of a Santa Cruz, California, firm called Community Intelligence Labs, who has helped Intel and Dow Chemical support communities of practice. Plant or office managers, sales reps, metallurgists, MIS weenies—from Abilene to Aberdeen, these have common enterprises; all probably do some knowledge sharing; they would benefit from closer contact.

In Silicon Valley, National Semiconductor has encouraged communities of practice by giving them semiofficial status. It set up a Communities of Practice Council, in which half a dozen communities are currently members, among them a group of technologists who focus on designing computer chips for communications signal processing, another exploring wireless computing, a third specializing in design for manufacturing. These are all critical technologies for many different lines of business at National Semiconductor—so it's vital that expertise isn't bottled up inside one business unit. The Communities of Practice Council helps them by offering technical support (such as designing internal Web pages) and lobbying for funds to, for example, fly an outside expert to company headquarters to speak to a group. Though they don't show up on the org chart, these professional associations are recognized as important by top management; one has even taken on responsibility for reviewing all microchip designs developed by different business units.

Give them the resources they need. Communities of practice don't need much in the way of resources: Let them build an intranet, use the conference room from time to time, put an occasional get-together on the expense account, bring in a speaker. Company communications systems are usually laid out along existing departmental lines—and thus are inimical to brainstorming, floating trial balloons, and other informal means of sharing problems and ideas. Brevetting people to work for a time in another business unit or department can also help. For the company, there are major benefits from connecting people who may otherwise unknowingly duplicate each others' efforts or walk away from projects that are too big to undertake single-handed.

National Semiconductor began supporting communities of practice because of the need to retain key people. In 1991, the company was in deep trouble: Its memory-chip manufacturing business had become a low-margin game that it could not win. To support development of higher-margin businesses, new CEO Gil Amelio (who has since moved on to Apple Computer) reorganized the company according to product lines, but also imposed significant layoffs. There was a nasty unintended consequence: Some people were let go who were not key people for any one product line, but had important expertise in skills and technology that *all* the product lines depended on.* Engineers began to band together to try to protect these hidden key people, and in the process created the communities of practice that management has since embraced. Says Skip Hovsmith, who directs National's mobile-computing research, "We needed a way to

---

* These people have a name: Rudi. Rudis were named by Patricia Seeman when she worked at Swiss pharmaceutical company Hoffman-LaRoche. (She now is a consultant at Ernst & Young.) As part of a project to help the company shorten the time required to get regulatory approval for new drugs, Seeman put together an intracorporate database-cum-Yellow Pages that showed, for example, who knew the most about the kinds of clinical trials American authorities wanted to see, who knew about German requirements, etc. As she asked people what they knew and what they did, she encountered several—the first was a man named Rudi—who answered simply, "I sort of help people out." The Rudis, it transpired, were guides to the whereabouts of essential corporate knowledge. They nevertheless did not appear to *do* anything, which put them at great risk from cost-cutters. Says Seeman: "The Rudis are the gray mice, whom senior management never notices—people who not only know something, but take the time to share and are very good storytellers." (Interview, April 17, 1996).

transfer our allegiance from the product line to the engineering practice. Communities of practice are the bridge."

Fertilize the soil, but stay away from actual husbandry. Says Valdis Krebs, a Los Angeles consultant who helps businesses solve organizational design problems by mapping networks to reveal how work really gets done: "Fund them too much, and you'll start to want deliverables. You won't get what you want. You'll get what the community wants to deliver." That's because these groups are motivated by their enterprise—this thing we're all learning about. For them, boundaries exist to be crossed, just as mountains exist to be climbed. Information wants to be free.

That's the subversive part. Stanford professor Stephen Barley puts it: "As communities of practice proliferate, occupational principles begin to compete with administrative principles." A person's responsibilities to the communities of which he is a member sometimes conflict with each other, and with the rules and interests of the company he works for. Watch a bunch of scientists at a convention: They swap secrets like street vendors opening their jackets to flash contraband Rolexes. In the late 1980s, Eric von Hippel, a professor at the Sloan School of Management at MIT, studied how manufacturing process engineers in the steel minimill industry traded proprietary information even with direct competitors. With so much to learn in their relatively young business, the steelmakers—from companies like Nucor and Chaparal Steel—evidently figured that sharing secrets was a fair price for progress. Says Von Hippel: "It happens everywhere. The standard corporate view is you're giving away the store, but the fact is, if others are cooperating and you decide not to, you fall behind."

How to Own Human Capital

You hang your hat at Citicorp, Disney, or Whirlpool. The question is, where is your heart? Increasingly, workers offer their first, deepest loyalty to their professions and communities of practice rather than to their employers. In these days of free-agency, athletes think of their value in terms of being linebackers or shortstops, rather than being

Bears or Cubs. For obvious reasons, the same is true of knowledge workers, a fact that underscores the fundamental conundrum of human capital: *People can be rented, but not owned.*

Valuable, hard-to-replace knowledge, the key to competitive advantage, is forged in communities of practice, but they and the human capital they create are no respecters of shareholder value. The leader's challenge, then: How can human capital be turned to proprietary advantage? Some knowledge can, of course, be owned outright and protected by intellectual-property laws. As we will see in the next chapters, some can be codified as structural capital.

Ceding "ownership" of human capital to a corporation, however, has to be voluntary. The short, but not simple way to do this: Create a sense of cross ownership between employee and company. Says management thinker Charles Handy: "I believe that corporations should be *membership communities* [my italics] because I believe corporations are not things, they are the people who run them. In order to hold people inside the corporation, we can't really talk about them being employees anymore. To hold people to the corporation, there has to be some kind of continuity and some sense of belonging."

A paradox lies at the heart of the Information Age organization: At the same time that employers have weakened the ties of job security and loyalty, they more than ever depend on human capital; for their part, knowledge workers, because they bring to their work not only their bodies but their minds—even their souls—are far more loyal to their work (though not to their employer) than those tire-makers whose first love was for the hobbies that waited for them at home. Compounding the problem is the fact that the most valuable knowledge workers are also best able to leave their employers, taking their talent and their work with them. Say Kathryn Rudie Harrigan and Gaurav Dalmia:

> Knowledge workers . . . are likely to split their loyalty between their profession and peers on one hand, and their employing organization on the other. They stay committed to particular firms as long as those firms provide them with the needed resources for working on interesting projects. If this isn't forthcoming, knowledge workers will swiftly trade up to bigger sandboxes . . . To be effective, knowledge workers need to bond with their employing firms.

Bonding . . . sandboxes . . . If it sounds like Dr. Spock, don't worry. Organizations can help create bonds of ownership, resolving the paradox, in both implicit and explicit ways that are thoroughly adult. The implicit way is to recognize and foster the growth of intellectual communities in areas that are central to their competitive advantage—that is, in those hard-to-replace, high-value activities in the upper-right quadrant of the chart discussed above. A vibrant learning community socializes human capital, which gives the company an ownership stake in it; if Sally leaves, three other people know most of what she knows—and though Sally has left the company, she is probably still part of the community. Remember, chances are that key employees are *already*, consciously or not, members of such communities. They are chemists (currently working for Du Pont), managers (whose paycheck says General Electric), human resources professionals (once at Procter & Gamble, now with Intel, thinking of going on their own as consultants). If the heart of that community is in your shop, they will want to stay there. But if their primary source of professional satisfaction is learning about cheese, you won't keep them if you offer only the chance to build a better mousetrap.

We discussed above some of the ways companies can foster the growth of communities of practice: giving them semiofficial status, making resources available, creating trans-organizational communication systems, moving employees around among business units to meet others doing related work.

Clearly there is risk in supporting these groups, which operate by their own logic, which is driven by their learning enterprise rather than the enterprise's profit and loss statement. The biggest risk, however, is not that they will blurt company secrets or wander off into irrelevant intellectual byways but that the heavy hand of management will choke them. Learning communities cannot be contiguous with the boundaries of the corporation, business unit, or department; nor should they be. Says Nynex's Jim Euchner: "Boundaries don't just keep information in. They keep it out, too." If some proprietary information leaks, so what? If the community is centered in the company and has grown around its highest-value work, then the company will get more advantage from it than peripheral members will. Von Hipple's study of information-sharing in the steel industry revealed that people made sure they got as much information as they gave and were unlikely to share information with rivals who appeared to have little to offer in return. Moreover, they were punctilious about guarding truly vital competitive knowledge. As Von Hipple puts it: "Famous chefs trade recipes—'But not my mousse! I will never give away this secret!' "

There are also explicit ways to forge the company-employee bond that allows companies to capitalize human assets—namely, to treat employees like the capitalists they are. Human capital represents a major portion of the total value of some companies. Says shareholder activist Robert A. B. Monks: "I would never invest one nickel of passive capital in a service firm where the value-added is done by people who go out the door at 5 P.M. I don't know how to put a fair value on the proposition." That's an idea-packed comment. A "passive" investment position, that is, just buying stock—but what about an active one? "Go out the door"—but what if you can find ways to make sure that those assets don't go out the door, either by giving them a real ownership stake, or by seeing to it that the company truly owns a piece of the brains of those people?

It's no accident that employee stock ownership has risen with the emergence of the Information Age, and is more prevalent in knowledge-intensive businesses than in traditional companies. Nor should it be surprising that incentive-pay plans have become much more popular. In 1993, MIT's Erik Brynjolfsson wrote: "According to the American Productivity and Quality Center, over half of all employers have implemented an incentive pay plan within the past five years. A shift to the use of incentive pay when employees have information not available to their employers makes sense . . . the employer can get the employee to choose actions that will make them both better off only by giving him a share of the profits and losses that result from his actions." Human capitalists are investors.

Henry Ford owned the means of production of his automobiles. He also owned the output—the car—until a customer bought it, at which point Ford had no further claim on it. The production and output of knowledge work, however, do not belong only to the company that employs the knowledge worker. Says Michael Brown, the chief financial officer of Microsoft: "Fifteen or twenty years ago, a person was either an employee or he was unemployed. Now, look around: People are owners, managers, and employees—sometimes all three in the same hour." When I write an article in *Fortune*, the magazine owns the copyright for the words I use—but *Fortune* doesn't have exclusive ownership of the underlying knowledge. I still have it. *Fortune* has it. And if you read it, you have it too. In other words, when knowledge is the chief resource and result—the input and output, the raw material and finished product—ownership of that knowledge becomes fuzzy, shared: The worker is part-owner, the capitalist is part-owner, and the customer is part-owner.

Paradoxically, it is by recognizing "virtual employee ownership" in systems of compensation and governance that companies can protect their own interest in their intellectual assets.* In this world of employee capitalism, the traditional functions of human resources management—with its emphasis on training, benefits administration, and treating employees equitably (but not considering employees as contributors of equity)—have little to say. For HR to play a real role in developing and managing human capital, it, like any other discipline, must invest in company-specific, high-value expertise in areas such as defining the boundaries and skills of core competence, improving executive development, promoting cross-fertilization among high-potential managers and experts in vital technologies, and developing compensation systems—including stock ownership—that reward improvement in the processes and disciplines that are part of the company's intellectual capital.

The accelerating popularity of stock options and employee stock ownership plans are obvious ways in which corporations can hold on to human capital by linking it to financial capital. According to Microsoft's Michael Brown, "employee ownership is a profound example of how the information age has changed the nature of the corporation." Microsoft has never needed other people's money. When Bill Gates and Paul Allen founded the company in 1975, they bor-

---

* Of course, companies reward human capital by paying higher wages to experienced employees. Generalizing from labor-market studies by Robert C. Topel, who examined pay differentials—usually salary reductions—when long-term workers were laid off and took new jobs at different companies, Brookings Institution economist Margaret M. Blair estimates that "as much as 14% of total wages and benefits paid to employees of corporations in the United States may represent a return to firm-specific human capital." If so, Blair figures, the wage premium paid for human capital might equal two thirds or more of pretax corporate profits. When human capital earns a return only in the form of wages, however, neither the employee nor the employer sees its relationship to wealth creation. The employee sees the income as an entitlement; the employer sees its best workers as a costly expense rather than as a valuable source of wealth.

rowed a little, but it's been pay-as-you-go ever since: $60 billion in market capitalization, all generated by internal cash flow; the company has never had a dime in long-term debt.

Why, then, did Gates and Allen bother to incorporate in the first place, which they did in 1981? And having incorporated, why did they decide to take the company public in 1986, if they didn't need to raise capital? Part of the reason was to limit liability—not even Bill Gates can risk taking on America's tort lawyers. But that wasn't the major factor. Says Brown: "For pure information age companies, the principal barrier to entry is the ability to concentrate intellectual property. When these companies go public, they don't do it to raise proceeds to build plants. They do it to monetize the value of their employee ownership programs. Microsoft was originally incorporated to create a vehicle to share ownership, not to ramp up production. And the principal reason we went public was to monetize the value."

Let's play that back. Gates and Allen formed a corporation not to raise money but because they needed a vehicle to share ownership. With whom? With their employees. Why? Because they had created the company's key property—line upon line of software code—and owned its most important asset for the future—the knowledge of how to write more code. Forming a corporation and taking it public gave employees a financial incentive to keep their assets working for Microsoft, rather than take them elsewhere.

Even traditional companies, which depend on huge factories and need to reward the shareholders who put up the money to acquire them, can take a leaf from the books of Microsoft and companies like them. General Electric now gives stock options to 22,000 employees, versus just 200 in the 1980s; but stock ownership isn't the only way to compensate employees for the fact that they own part of the company even if they own no shares. Manufacturing workers in the European building materials group of Owens Corning, which makes fiberglass insulation, now receive a substantial portion of their compensation in the form of "gainsharing," according to which they are paid extra if the company meets certain targets. What's significant about the program is that all the goals—safety, low absenteeism, efficient use of raw materials, etc.—are items under the influence of the employees themselves, rather than company-wide profit goals employees cannot directly affect; similarly, sales and marketing employees have a gainsharing program tied to activities they, too, can control.

The gainsharing bonus thus becomes, in effect, a dividend paid to employees for investing human capital. It is a recognition of the fact, as Peter Drucker says, that "the true investment in the knowledge society is not in machines and tools but in the knowledge of the knowledge worker . . . The industrial worker needed the capitalist infinitely more than the capitalist needed the industrial worker . . . In the knowledge society the most probable assumption for organizations—and certainly the assumption on which they have to conduct their affairs—is that they need knowledge workers far more than knowledge workers need them."

Yet the organization has a legitimate claim on the human beings it employs and the human capital they create. To this point, Robert K. Elliott, vice chairman of KPMG Peat Marwick, says something marvelously simple: If every person were able to capture the full value of his services, there would be no corporations. What makes the corporation possible is the fact that it pays its staff—in aggregate—less than what they are worth. Or, to put the point more kindly: When people work together, they create something that is worth more than the sum of their individual efforts. The difference is profit, return to capital. Take away that surplus, no company: Indeed, where individuals are able to capture for themselves almost all the value of their human capital, they often become independent contractors. For most of us, though, there is some economic value that is created by our being part of an organization, a reason why the work we do is more valuable when we do it with a group than when we go it alone. That value belongs to the organization. In a similar way, there is intellectual value that is more than human capital, and that belongs to shareholders. It is structural capital.

CHAPTER 7

Structural Capital I

KNOWLEDGE MANAGEMENT

TELL ME THE BRAND OF WHISKEY THAT GRANT DRINKS. I WOULD
LIKE TO SEND A BARREL OF IT TO MY OTHER GENERALS.
—ABRAHAM LINCOLN

A story is told—I have no idea if it is true—about Abbott Lawrence Lowell, president of Harvard University from 1909 to 1933. It goes like this: One day a visitor asked him, "How is it, Mr. Lowell, that so much knowledge is concentrated here on the banks of the Charles River?" Lowell purportedly replied: "It's very simple. Every year, we admit to the college the most brilliant young men in America"—in those days, they were all men, and almost all American—"and when they graduate four years later, they are entirely ignorant. So they must have left their knowledge here." That, in caricature, is the challenge facing managers: How do they turn the candlepower of their people into the wattage of the corporation, rather than into something that goes out at 5 P.M.?

Human capital, the sap flowing beneath the bark of a tree, produces innovation and growth, but that growth ring becomes solid wood, part of the structure of the tree. What leaders need to do—and this chapter will show how to do—is contain and retain knowledge, so that it becomes company property. That's structural capital. Simply put, it is knowledge that doesn't go home at night. The distinction between human and structural capital had been talked about in Sweden for a couple of years before it was picked up by Leif Edvinsson of Skandia AFS. I first heard it in December 1992. Edvinsson, a ginger-haired man with down-turning eyes, was speaking in one of those anonymous ballrooms whose cut-glass chandeliers and wall sconces pay ersatz homage to the elegance of a far different time and place. But this was Tysons Corner, Virginia, which only a generation ago was a sleepy rural crossroads but now is the heart of the edge-city technopolis outside Washington, D.C., the third most important technology center in America. Gathered at round tables in the ballroom were a group of men and women who had come to explore new ways to measure and manage performance in the Knowledge Era. Edvinsson's audience, mostly from human resources or with backgrounds in organizational development, expected a hymn to the glories of employee brainpower, and he seemed to be obliging them as he told them that human capital is the source of innovation in a company. Then he went on: "The structural capital is more important." The temperature in the room dropped.

Yet he's right, at least as far as management is concerned: It is the job of management to build corporate assets. Most companies are filled with smarts, but too much of it resides in the computer whiz who speaks a mile a minute in no known language, in the brash account manager who racks up great numbers but has alienated everyone, or in files moved to the basement. Or it's retired and gone fishing. Even the smartest people in the world need a mechanism to assemble, package, promote, and distribute the fruits of their thinking. Says Peter Drucker: "Only the organization can provide the basic continuity that knowledge workers need in order to be effective. Only the organization can convert the specialized knowledge of the knowledge worker into performance." Like a blast furnace that converts iron and coke into steel, the organization concentrates, processes, and reifies knowledge work. The entrepreneur and the inventor are pure human capital; the business person is something else. Thus Thomas Edison, when he founded the company that became General Electric, turned his human capital into something structural.

Structural capital belongs to the organization as a whole. It can be reproduced and shared. Some of what comes into the category of structural capital is entitled to legal rights of ownership: technologies, inventions, data, publications, and processes can be patented, copyrighted, or shielded by trade-secret laws: You can sell them, and you can sue anybody who takes them without permission. Some of it is cutting-edge science, but only some. Few products that Clorox makes, for example, are high-tech wonders—we're talking about bleach, charcoal, kitty litter, salad dressing, etc.—but to make them in uniform quality around the world Clorox depends on more than 8,000 manufacturing standards documents that specify machine settings, grades and quantities of raw material, testing procedures, and so on. But also among the elements of structural capital are strategy and culture, structures and systems, organizational routines and procedures—assets that are often far more extensive and valuable than the codified ones.

The Case for Managing Structural Capital

Imagine a factory inside whose walls is everything necessary to make a product—machines, component parts, other raw materials, safety glasses and hard hats, testing equipment, forklifts, the works. But suppose this stuff is heaped and scattered about the building without rhyme or reason. Parts are never counted or sorted; every time a worker has to bolt the gearbox onto the product, he must leave his post and search for ten minutes before he finds the box of bolts and three minutes more before he finds the right one; bins overflow with random jumbles of spare parts and components; the testing equipment is a city block from where the finished product comes off the line—if "line" is the word, for the plant's arrangement seems more like a plate of linguine than a line. Half-finished examples of discontinued products lie all over the building, and navigating a forklift through the mess is like driving in Manhattan on the last shopping day before Christmas. Trash is never collected. Instead, every few months a bulldozer drives through the plant, pushing out the door whatever lies in its path.

I have described your teenager's bedroom, I know, but I have also described your company's management of knowledge, and mine. In a two-week period in 1995, thirty-nine messages went up on the *Fortune* editorial staff's QuickMail bulletin board. Nine were "Does anyone know . . . ?" questions. A typical posting began: "Anyone out there have an expert or two to throw my way?" Six more were "Does anybody have?" questions, half concerning a missing reference book. (The miscreant put it back.) Thus fifteen of the thirty-nine messages (38 percent) were requests for information that already reposed, God knows where, in the group—a minidatum that doesn't begin to tally how often in that fortnight my colleagues and I sent private e-mail questions, queried the library, stopped one another in the hall, rummaged through files, or otherwise scavenged for knowledge that the organization already possessed. I'd guess that each of us spends the equivalent of two or three weeks a year searching for information that others have already.

There writ small is the case for managing the accumulated knowledge of individual employees in order to transmute it into a corporate asset. Writ large, the case goes like this:

> Systematic management of intellectual capital creates growth in shareholder value. This is accomplished, among other things, through the continuous recycling and creative utilization of shared knowledge and experience. This, in turn, requires the structuring and packaging of competencies with the help of technology, process descriptions, manuals, networks, and so on, to ensure that the competence will remain with the company when the employees go home. Once packaged, these become a part of the company's structural capital—or more precisely, its organizational capital. This creates the conditions for the rapid sharing of knowledge and sustained, collective knowledge growth . . . Lead times between learning and knowledge sharing are shortened systematically. Human capital will also become more productive through structured, easily accessible and intelligent work processes.

Rapid knowledge sharing, collective knowledge growth, shortened lead times, more productive people—these are the reasons for managing structural capital. Physical material is inspected, warehoused, barcoded, and audited; intellectual material, though it is far more important, is scattered, hard to find, and liable to disappear without a trace. Says Paul Pederson, a partner at Price Waterhouse Consulting: "In the heat of marketing, consultants will promise that the firm has, say, established knowledge of world-class standards for logistics. And the firm does have it—but it's in your office, or my briefcase, or with some guys out in California, or dispersed in all three places." Just as customers in the old economy expected uniform excellence in manufactured products, today's customer demands a consistently high standard of expertise from you. Says Charles Paulk, chief information officer of Andersen Consulting: "When one of our consultants shows up, the client should get the best of the firm, not just the best of that consultant."

The key to managing the structures of corporate knowledge is to remember that organizational capital is, first and foremost, *capital*. Like all capital, it can be looked at in terms of *stocks* and *flows*. As Fritz Machlup put it, "At any moment of time, there is a stock of knowledge; during any period of time, there is a flow of knowledge." We'll look at each in turn, to see what lessons in knowledge management companies have learned by dealing with them. Managing structural capital is not especially difficult or strange—but it is new, and there is much to be learned from seeing how progressive companies do it.

Building Knowledge Stocks

If the subject of intellectual capital ever spawns a business fad, it will be under the guise of "knowledge management," because there's money to be made selling software, systems, and consulting services with the touted goal of allowing every person in an organization to be able to lay his hands on the collected know-how, experience, and wisdom of all his colleagues. Indeed, some companies have invested millions of dollars to pull their corporate intellectual capital together, map it, and make it easy to use—assembling and classifying their stocks of structural capital. One manifestation is described by Carol Anne Ogdin, founder of a Santa Clara, California, consulting firm called Deep Woods Technology: " 'Knowledge databases' are cropping up all over inside corporations we work with." These go far beyond handbooks and e-mail: They are major strategic initiatives, headed by senior executives who expect to change the way their companies operate. A look at these knowledge databases shows what's at stake and what's possible—and some of the ways that technology can support very practical plans for building knowledge stocks.

I've cited consultants because the big consulting firms led the way in turbocharged knowledge stockpiling—a surprise, since consultants are famous for diagnosing scratched corneas in their clients' peepers despite cataracts in their own. In the last few years, Andersen set up its Knowledge Xchange; Booz Allen & Hamilton developed KOL— Knowledge On-Line; Ernst & Young created a Center for Business Knowledge, KPMG Peat Marwick a Knowledge Manager, Price Waterhouse something called Knowledge View; the list goes on, and to it can be added dozens, at least, of smallish companies, consulting firms and software designers, who will, for a price, clean up your teenager's room.

To see how these work, take a look at Booz Allen's Knowledge On-Line. KOL, up and running since early 1995, is supposed to save Boozers from spending long and costly hours repeating each other's work and also to make it easy to tap the firm's experts and ideas regardless of geography or specialty. Thus a consultant in Indonesia helping an oil company improve customer service might want to crib from colleagues in Caracas or Houston, or adapt work a New Yorker did for a bank.

As long as he's got his laptop and a phone line, he can log onto KOL. One icon that appears on the screen is slugged "Experts/Résumés/History"; click on it and type a name, and up pops a colleague's résumé; or type "customer service," and the system will deliver a stack of résumés of consultants who know the subject. Another icon is tagged simply "Knowledge." Behind it are a number of databases. These contain thousands of documents, crossfiled by industry and topics such as reengineering, marketing, and change management. Our man in Jakarta can download benchmarking studies that Booz Allen colleagues have prepared on the oil industry, find abstracts of journal and magazine articles, or copy a presentation, prepared for a client in another industry, that contains an especially good checklist of things to look for when reengineering customer service. KOL also has bulletin boards, discussion forums, and training courses—a refresher on how to analyze costs, for example.

The other consulting firms' knowledge databases work more or less the same way, with different emphases depending on the underlying technology and the firm's specialties. (For example, Andersen

Consulting, which has a large management information systems practice, has loaded its Knowledge Xchange with prefabricated modules of software code that programmers can plug into applications they are writing.) Many knowledge databases have been installed on Lotus Notes; others use the Netscape software that dominates the World Wide Web on the Internet—"intranets," they're called.

All of them are ambitious attempts to pull scattered information and wisdom together to convert it into organizational knowledge. Cheap and powerful information technology has given new impetus to the dream of creating what amount to living libraries containing an entire stock of corporate knowledge. Of course that is flawed: Utopias always are. But the benefits are obvious. (We'll get to the less-obvious perils later.) First, a growing body of evidence shows that there are huge financial rewards for investment in knowledge management technology. According to Charles Paulk of Andersen Consulting, his company's knowledge database saves the firm millions a year in FedEx bills alone. A 1994 study of sixty-four companies, government agencies, and nonprofit organizations using Lotus Notes found that, even using conservative assumptions, the average organization earned a three-year return on its investment of 179 percent, much of it attributable to reduced cost and time of internal communications and improved tracking and administration of projects.

Second, knowledge databases make it easier to tap into colleagues' knowledge. One Friday in August 1995, for instance, Andersen's Peter Westcott, based in Chicago, needed to learn about something called FDDI, which is a blueprint for designing a fiber-optic data network. By Tuesday his question, posted on an Andersen Xchange bulletin board, had replies from colleagues in three states and Great Britain: Westcott had cast his net wider and hauled it back fuller, faster, and cheaper than he could have before—and with no need to make photocopies, fill out Federal Express waybills, or play phone tag. Best of all, his question created a piece of intellectual capital: a file that from now on is there for any Andersen consultant who needs the same information.

Knowledge databases also help companies work globally. Indeed, meeting the needs of customers with global operations of their own was a big reason several of the consulting firms set up knowledge databases in the first place. Big global customers wanted expertise delivered even to the most remote locations instantly, and they didn't want the advice they received in Chile to be inconsistent with or ignorant of new practices being put in place in Malaysia.

Another compelling reason to make a formal effort to map corporate brainpower: coping with growth and staff turnover. Price Waterhouse Consulting, where revenues have been rising more than 30 percent a year, expects to double its staff in five years. The faster newcomers can learn what the institution knows, the faster they can contribute to it. The firm also will lose its share of people. A company with a 10 percent annual turnover rate, which is better than average, will lose half its experienced workers in just five years, even if its total headcount stays the same. Every one of the departed will take knowledge worth retaining, and each new hire will bring in some knowledge worth sharing. "This," says Price Waterhouse's Pederson, "is why it's so important to capture the knowledge."

What Knowledge to Stock

What kinds of structural capital belong in knowledge databases? The list could be endless, and of course differs from company to company—an ad agency might want a big collection of demographic data that would be of little use to a freight forwarder, which, however, would want global customs information. There are, however, three items that by themselves justify the investment in building knowledge databases.

CORPORATE YELLOW PAGES

Knowledge grows so fast that any attempt to codify it all is ridiculous; but the identities of in-house experts change slowly. Someone in your company knows whether the contract with XYZ Corp. does or does not cover repair services or whether a certain electrical switch causes problems in countries that have 220-volt current. But who? Who speaks Arabic? Knows fluorocarbons? Led the project team that installed the phone system at headquarters? It takes far too much time to answer everyday questions like these. Companies rely on grapevines of certain slowness and uncertain reliability. You spend hours looking for a document, give it up as lost, and months later discover that the man in the next office wrote it. It should be so easy to construct a corporate Yellow Pages that it's remarkable how few companies have done it. Carol Anne Ogdin thinks the in-house Yellow Pages is the "killer app" of knowledge management technology, and it's easy to see why: A simple system that connects inquirers to experts saves time, reduces error and guesswork, and prevents the reinvention of countless wheels. "Not giant indexes," warns Arian Ward of Hughes Space and Communications, the world's leading maker of commercial communications satellites, because specific information changes too quickly for that, but "maps that show where the knowledge of the enterprise is located—in whose heads, for example."

LESSONS LEARNED

Knowledge work is custom work. Like many services, it tends to be created when and where it is sold. Even manufacturers of basic products have steadily transformed themselves from an economics of mass production to one of customization. (See Chapter 9.) But that doesn't mean each project has to begin from scratch.

A key way to increase structural capital is to bank lessons learned—in effect, checklists of what went right and wrong, together with guidelines for others undertaking similar projects. That's been the essence of the work Ward has done as head of business engineering at Hughes Space and Communications. Satellites are not only made to order but are also enormously complex, expensive, and unforgiving. (It's easier to send a crew to repair a power station on the Orinoco than a satellite in orbit.) Business is tough too, with fewer military contracts and more competitors. Consequently, says Ward, "it's very, very important to leverage what we learn so we can do the job better and faster next time." The problem—indeed, the habit—is what Ward calls "losing the recipe."

Knowledge hard won by engineers who designed a satellite two years ago might be unknown to a team attacking similar problems today; or the new group, knowing the solution but not the research that led to it, might not see its applicability or trust the work. Says Ward, who combines the open-shirt, laid-back style of Southern California with the cut-the-crap directness of his profession: "That's the way engineers are. If they didn't do the work themselves, they're convinced that it was done wrong or that they can do it better." The result: "islands of knowledge," similar to the "islands of automation" familiar to anyone who has ever been frustrated by the inability of incompatible computer systems to exchange data.

A big step in bridging the islands, in Ward's view, is to realize that knowledge takes at least two forms. The first is rules-based, where following procedures yields the one correct answer to a specific problem. Rules can often be automated, whether by a simple spell-checker or by a fancy expert-system software that produces, say, the best circuitry design for a signal processor. Most knowledge is less structured: The answer varies with the context; it takes the form of wisdom, experience, and stories, not rules. To capture, leverage, and capitalize this softer, often tacit knowledge, Hughes has begun building its own "knowledge highway." It began by connecting existing "lessons learned" databases, using groupware such as Lotus Notes; this, for example, gives designers of new satellites better access to reports of defects found in previous ones and alerts them to regulatory issues earlier than before. Hughes has documented cases where the use of lessons-learned files prevented rework and saved time; Ward also measures success with a tally of "repeated mistakes," a number that has been falling gratifyingly as engineers learn from one another. Like the modules of computer code on Andersen Consulting's Knowledge Xchange or Skandia's prefabricated prototype processes for opening new branch offices (see Chapter 5), the Hughes lessons learned databases create stockpiles of proven, usable knowledge.

COMPETITOR INTELLIGENCE

Suppose it's your first day as general manager of the thingamajig division of Universal Widget. How do you begin? Call a staff meeting, of course. And what do you ask for first? No, not the Sweet 'n Low and the Cremora. First you ask for the major customer files and the competitor files. You know what happens next. The meeting over, you follow the sales director to get the files from the locked drawer in his desk. He straightens up and offers the folders to you. As your hands close around them, he hesitates a moment, then says: "I can't promise that these are all 100 percent complete or up-to-date." It happens every time.

It's astonishing how badly companies organize knowledge about their suppliers, customers, and competitors. Nobody knows how much business you do with the world's biggest computer company, because each division store its records on its own computer and the systems cannot talk to one another; then, after you spend tens of millions of dollars to make the systems compatible, you still cannot total up the information because on some records the company is called IBM, on others it's I.B.M., and on still others it's International Business Machines.

In 1995, one of Monsanto's chemical businesses lost a big order to a competitor. Postmortem, folks at St. Louis headquarters learned that a sales rep halfway around the globe and in a different business unit had heard scuttlebutt about the impending sale, but time zones and the ordinary exigencies of organizational boundaries kept the knowledge hidden till it was too late to act on it. Now a program called "Knowledge Management Architecture" links hundreds of Monsanto's sales people who share news and gossip on a Lotus Notes database that is also used by major-account managers and in-house competitor-intelligence analysts. The program is modeled on work done by Ceregen, Monsanto's biotechnology unit. Ceregen's on-line competitor-and-customer database, to which all 600 employees have access, includes continuously updated company profiles and news from commercial and public sources and wire services; call reports from sales people; attendees' notes from conferences and conventions; an in-house directory of experts; news about Food and Drug Administration regulations; and other items, all cross-indexed by company, technology, and in other ways. In a fast-moving field like biotechnology, merely having current information in one place is a big advantage. Says Bipin Junnarker, the project director for KMA: "The focus shifts from 'How do I get the information I need?' to 'How do I exploit the information?' " The advantages of managing competitor and major-accounts knowledge are so persuasive that they alone can justify the investment for many companies.

Every company needs answers to the questions "What do we know?" and "Where is the knowledge?" The emphasis, however, is likely to be different, and so is the vocabulary. Forget for a moment highfalutin language about intellectual capital. To make the case for managing knowledge assets, says Richard Baumbusch, former executive director of USWest Communications, the core telephone business of that Baby Bell, "the pivotal insight was finding a language that engages operations managers." That meant a rhetoric—and a reality—of results. Agrees Harry Lasker, co-chairman of Renaissance Solutions, a Lincoln, Massachusetts, consulting company: "It's dysfunctional to take knowledge management out of a performance context. You should not map the knowledge of your organization if you cannot link it to the strategy or the performance that pushes the strategy." That's why real-world applications like a Yellow Pages, lessons-learned databases, and competitor intelligence are so important.

The perfect knowledge base—with every expert's name, every corporate policy, every needed fact just a few mouse-clicks away—will never exist. But it's a charming idea, in the sense that it has the power to mesmerize. The company's accumulated knowledge, just a few mouse-clicks away . . .

The problem is, you can do that already. As playwright John Guare observed:

> I read somewhere that everybody on this planet is separated by only six other people. Six degrees of separation. Between us and everybody else on this planet. The president of the United States. A gondolier in Venice. Fill in the names . . . [But] you have to find the right six people to make the connection.

To be sure, using high-speed microprocessors, intranets, and whizzy search-engines, you can automate, spiff up, hyperlink, and turbocharge the apparatus. You can preserve what might otherwise deteriorate, catalog what might otherwise disappear. But the sixty-four-bit question remains: If you build it, will they come? Will they bother to make the connection, and can they find what they are looking for? Before we address those questions, we need to look not just at stocks of structural capital, but also at flows.

Speeding Up Knowledge Flows

In addition to mapping and deepening expertise, the explicit management of structural capital can increase productivity. There are big gains to be won, as consultant David Skyrme argues, if "we learn to manage the 'mechanics' of knowledge, just as in the industrial era we

have (almost) learned how to manage the 'mechanics of production.' "
For example, Hewlett-Packard created an electronic network to manage and distribute knowledge to keep up with customers' demands for
speedy service on a global scale.

H-P's customer response network supports 1,900 technical support
staff, mostly engineers, whose job is to keep customers' computer
systems up and running. These systems are the customers' central
nervous systems: If they go down, they must be fixed fast. When a
client reports a problem, the call (or electronic message) goes automatically to one of four H-P hubs around the world, depending on the
time of day. Operators get a description of the problem and its ur-
gency, typing the information into a database and zapping the file to
one of twenty-seven centers where it might be picked up by a team
specializing in, say, operating system foul-ups. The database is shared
by all the centers and is "live"—that is, whenever an employee works
in a file, it is instantly updated, so every center has identical information about each job at all times. If the first center can't solve a problem
quickly, it follows the sun: At 6 P.M. in California, for example, the
action shifts to Australia, to be picked up by a crew a third of a world
away. The file, of course, is already there. No managers are involved
in moving the work around the net; if they were, the process could not
be seamless.

The structural capital in this case is the network itself—the path-
way along which knowledge moves. There are social forms of structural capital, too, every bit as real and effective as electronic circuitry—for example, unearthing and sharing best practices.

Abraham Lincoln pioneered sharing best practices when, told that
Ulysses S. Grant was overfond of liquor, he supposedly retorted: "Tell
me the brand of whiskey that Grant drinks. I would like to send a
barrel of it to my other generals." Dick Baumbusch took the same
approach at USWest. "Are some of your people better performers
than others?" he asks managers, who of course agree. Then: "Would
you like others to become as good?" Baumbusch worked with repair-
men in one territory to identify the best among them and learn their
secrets by following them around or bringing them together to talk.
Knowledge thus identified can be replicated and shared. The means of
doing that, Baumbusch believes, should vary: It might be training or
audiotapes for one group, kaffee klatches for another, high-tech databases for a third. At Xerox, which long ago realized that watercooler

conversation was one of the most important ways in which service representatives taught each other, tech reps' cars have been equipped with two-way radios, which allows them to spend more time with customers while still hanging out at a wireless watercooler where knowledge can be swapped. The technology is not important, though it seems self-evident that information technology can help manage information: What is, is the explicit effort to find useful knowledge, bottle it, and pass it around.

The next step is to integrate best practices into operations. The old way to do this was through manuals, training, and supervisors—cumbersome, unreliable, and expensive methods. Technology does the job faster and better. That's how Cigna Corp., the big Philadelphia insurance company, used structural capital to augment the talent of its people, in the process dramatically improving its performance. Cigna uses decision-support software to make sure its underwriters know and follow its best practices for pricing insurance policies. The Philadelphia insurer's property and casualty division was a miserable performer—in 1993 its active portfolio of U.S. P&C business lost $251 million. But that loss became an $87 million profit in the twelve months that ended September 30, 1995, and a $160 million profit a year after that. Cost-cutting, layoffs, and a reengineering effort led by Gemini Consulting played big parts in the turnaround, but weren't the whole story. Reengineering improves efficiency—like cleaning up your desk or, if you're really ambitious, my desk; but if, for example, you're underwriting bad risks as Cigna was, it doesn't help to be more efficient, any more than it helps a pilot to gain speed if he is losing altitude at the same time. Excellence comes from making more knowledgeable choices. Says Harry Lasker of Renaissance Solutions, which worked with Gemini and Cigna: "We found significant latent know-how in the organization. There were experts, but not a good means of extracting and publishing that know-how."

In underwriting, Cigna gave home-office managers the additional job of building and maintaining a knowledge base—basically a collection of checklists, rules of thumb, formal guidelines for risk assessment, and names of experts. It was installed into the same software that every underwriter uses to process applications. A nursing home in California wants insurance? The custom-built software tells where the nearest geological fault line is and how dangerous the company's experts consider it to be; it gives Cigna's formulas for assessing factors like staff training or sprinkler systems; and so on. When new information comes in—expert analysis, feedback from the claims department, or insights from the underwriters themselves—the manager/knowledge editor evaluates it and, if he thinks it's good, changes the database. Result: Every underwriter instantly incorporates the new best practice. Claims processors and agents have similar setups. The cost of all this? "Very little," Lasker avers. "They were collecting all the information anyway, but it just went into the files."

Unlike a pump on an assembly line, knowledge work rarely moves steadily forward. It's an open-ended series of to-and-fro collaborations and commitments—but even though it's less structured, structural capital can improve the flow of knowledge. In advertising agencies, for example, preparing an ad for a client is a disorderly, unpredictable process in which the client, the account rep, and the creative people might put an ad through dozens of big and little changes before it's done. The process must be tracked, but traffic management becomes a nightmare if every change—can we make it aqua instead of turquoise?—means a new set of forms. Paperwork, necessary but annoying, is a form of knowledge management whose procedures date from a time when objects were more important than information.

At Young & Rubicam, chief information officer Nicholas Rudd realized that the old system—"representing the movement of material with paper"—didn't describe the work. Worse, it was hard to know which of many versions of an ad was the current one, difficult to keep track of who was assigned to the project. Y&R's solution: a Lotus Notes database with "workflow" software. It's organized around four predictable and essential steps: requests for action (Chuck wants an ad), agreement (Bill, Kay, and Bob agree to do it), performance (they write the ad), and approval. Because Notes automatically updates all the files connected to a server, everyone involved in a project could instantly find where it was and which version of an ad was the "live" one. The physical movement of copy, sketches, and layouts is as erratic as ever—it has to be, in collaborative creative work. But by designing its traffic system around these predictable and essential steps, Y&R was able to take enormous amounts of often-bewildering paperwork out of the system while keeping better track of the status of projects. Three months after a pilot of the new traffic system began, participants reported that overtime had dropped from 27 to 13 percent and the number of jobs completed on budget had risen from 73 to 87 percent. In a stunning result, the number of people who complained that effort was often duplicated fell from 42 percent to zero.

In each of these cases—H-P's customer-response network, US-West's collection and distribution of best practices, Cigna's decision-support software, Y&R's traffic management—companies improved productivity adapting their organizational machinery, their structural capital, to increase the speed with which knowledge moved through the company. Three of the companies used information technology extensively, and the fourth, USWest, relies heavily on technology in other knowledge management applications, but "buy new software" isn't the moral of their stories. This is: Each of them recognized that the information and knowledge people use in their work is at least as important as any piece of equipment or truckload of material they use, and, like equipment or materials, can be managed more productively.

How to Escape the Old Trade-off: Speed Versus Expertise

Think of the words "structure" and "organization." What comes to mind? This, probably:

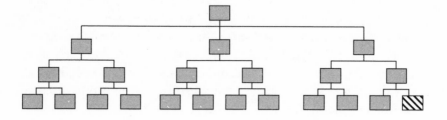

The grand old functional organization has so many critics that it is important to remember that it has many virtues. With its unambiguous lines of communication and control, the functional organization made clear who was responsible for what. The specialization of labor, and the organization of specialists into tightly supervised departments of finance, manufacturing, sales, etc., delivered a high degree of reliability. If the functional organization tended to become rigid and did not adapt well to change, those were not bad attributes for an economy of mass production, where competitive advantage and added value came from producing or delivering huge quantities of identical, inexpensive goods or services. Not inappropriately, customers are an afterthought in traditional organizational design: Only the sales force—represented above by the striped box—deals one-on-one with customers; the essence of its job is to rustle up buyers for what the company has already made.

Companies had good reasons for draining away corporate staff and several acre-feet of middle management, but there were babies in that bathwater: graybeards who'd seen it all, meddling staffers who occasionally—admit it—saved your hide; above all, layers of supervisors whose expertise and accountability for the work of their staff acted as a brake on wayward enthusiasm. For those contributions, companies paid a price in adaptability and speed. The process was costly and ·cumbersome (what experts call "a pain in the ass"). "The vertical processing of information"—up the chain of command, across, and down again—is "the slowest cycle in any organization," says Jim Manzi, who championed Lotus Notes when he was CEO of Lotus and now runs Nets Inc., a company that has created a virtual marketplace on the World Wide Web where business-to-business buyers and sellers can meet.

Knowledge should flow quickly and easily between functions. Says Robert Buckman, CEO of Buckman Laboratories, a Memphis-based specialty chemical company that does about a quarter of a billion dollars' worth of business in some eighty nations, "You can't go up to a guru and then back down, the way we used to. It's too slow; you lose relevant detail." In Buckman's business, like so many others, success comes these days from providing fast, customized solutions to particular customer needs. A paper mill, for example, won't just order carloads of chlorine for bleaching; instead, its experts and Buckman's will work together to concoct a chemical cocktail especially for the customer's equipment and product line.

When value is created in the field, your smartest people belong there, not tethered to their desks. They need both authority and knowledge. In hierarchies, rank defines power: A manager can okay deals up to $50,000, his boss to $100,000, her boss to $250,000 . . . That's obsolete. The question isn't how high the money gets; it's how high your customer's blood pressure gets. Says Harvard Business School professor Quinn Mills: "Does he need an answer immediately? Do you have to be able to be flexible? If so, you have to empower the person who talks to the customer." But empowerment without expertise is a prescription for disaster.

Just as information can substitute for inventory, so structural capital can stand in for organizational structures. First, automated processes that collect and distribute information, like H-P's customer response network or SAP, the hot enterprise-wide information management software system, can bypass the poky vertical flow of information. Second, communications networks, corporate Yellow Pages, and knowledge databases allow a company to put its best people on the front line *while still keeping their expertise available to the entire organization.* "This is the greatest revolution in the way of doing business we have seen in our lifetime," Bob Buckman says, and he foments it in the simplest possible way: a private forum on the Compuserve on-line service, open only to employees, where anyone can pose a question and anyone can offer an answer. A handful of sysops and technical experts monitor various subforums (mostly organized around the industries Buckman serves, such as pulp and paper, leather, and plastics), making sure that the best contributions are saved and publicized. The network and database replace the depth of knowledge a multitiered hierarchy offers with the breadth of knowledge that is the sum of employees' collective experience. Today, 40 percent of Buckman Laboratories' employees are out selling, and 72 percent are college graduates; the corresponding numbers in 1979 were 16 percent and 39 percent. The diaspora could not work without a means of efficient knowledge transfer from one farflung smartie to another.

Knowledge Management Needs Knowledge Managers

A factory won't start producing things on its own, and knowledge management will not happen without knowledge managers. Like any other organizational systems, methods, and departments, structures for managing knowledge must serve a clear strategic purpose. For example, McKinsey & Co., the consulting firm, began formally managing the knowledge of the firm before there was much in the way of technology to support the effort, amid falling demand for its bread-and-butter strategy consulting. That provoked a firm-wide reexamination of what customers wanted, and the realization that McKinsey needed to provide deep expertise in various industries and business functions. The firm had always prided itself on a collegial atmosphere, where the glory of the group took precedence over the prestige of individual consultants, and where knowledge, tips, and stories were freely shared; but that tradition reeled from the one-two punch of (1) clients' wanting more specific expertise, which resulted in more specialization in the firm and (2) the firm's own globalization, which made it more difficult to share knowledge. McKinsey's answer to the problem was a Rapid Response team. The heart of it resides at headquarters in New York, where a small staff of librarians and researchers fields questions from consultants. McKinsey partner Philip Brook Manville calls them "intelligent interrogators." Their job is three-fold: first to spend time talking to the inquiring consultant to understand the full dimensions of his question and to suggest possible ways to answer it; next to scour the firm's library (which contains internally produced research and write-ups of cases together with books, periodicals, and other data sources) much of which has been computerized to make searches faster; third to put the caller in touch with one or more of a few dozen colleagues who have volunteered to kibitz with co-workers and promised to reply right away, however busy their own schedules are. A volunteer system obviously won't work without company-wide agreement that it is a high strategic priority.

Indeed, structural capital, a distillate of human intelligence, relies on people being willing to share, and sharing is always voluntary (torture not being on the Approved List of Modern Management Techniques). Says Carol Anne Ogdin, imagining herself in an accounting firm where CPAs become partner based on their annual billings: "If I've found a particularly clever solution to a tax problem, it is not in my self-interest to post that solution to a knowledge database." Without a culture of teamwork and compensation and rewards that support it, a garden of knowledge will be as forlorn as a playground built next to a seniors-only condo.

And unless it's managed, it'll be as chaotic as a school yard at recess. An active knowledge management network tends to be a self-correcting system: Error degrades in sunlight. Neatness, however, is not among the benefits of networks. Error must be deleted as well as refuted; breakthrough new ideas need to be sought out and publicized as well as posted; processes and lessons-learned need to be documented and organizational memory organized. Someone, in other words, needs to be responsible for managing the content of organizational knowledge as well as its technology.

Enter a new kind of manager, the knowledge manager. Margaret Matthews, the "knowledge integrator" for Andersen Consulting's industrial products practice, which works with manufacturers of big or complex goods, is part librarian, part intellectual entrepreneur, and part cruise-ship social director. Matthews and her counterparts in other groups in the firm are responsible for keeping the database orderly, categorizing and formatting documents and chucking the obsolete; they're also charged with cajoling consultants to use the system, trolling for stuff to upload, and—crucially—identifying topics that ought to become research projects. She says, "We're trying to make knowledge management a professional discipline on a level like human resources and finance." They're not part of a separate staff group, however; they're located in the various "practice areas"—Andersen's equivalent of business units. Matthews, for example, reports directly to the head of the industrial products practice, which gives her firsthand knowledge of what the group knows and needs to know—a way to make sure that knowledge management is tied to business activity.

Above all, success in managing structural intellectual capital depends on leadership. I'm not a believer in elaborate systems of incentives and rewards for knowledge sharing; it seems to me that T-shirts and dinners-for-two and bonuses are more likely to encourage the widespread dissemination of trivia than the systematic enhancement of corporate brainpower. There is no greater incentive than a boss who believes. Says Bob Buckman: "I don't know of a single company where people aren't boss-watchers." If the boss happens to tell you that he saw something on an electronic forum that might help you with the problem you're working on, you'll no longer be a stranger to its precincts. If she makes it clear that she values sharing corporate knowledge, it will be shared. As Buckman puts it: "If you promote the people who do the best job of sharing, you don't need any other incentives."

Many leaders—whether it's because they're technophobes or because they rose to the top in a time when information was a scarce resource, most valuable when it was hoarded—preach the importance of organizational intelligence from the sidelines. Says Terry Neill, who heads Andersen Consulting's change management practice: "A lot of senior managers are mentally retired. They decide they don't have to learn how to use e-mail, and leave it to their secretaries. That's about the worst thing you can do." The decision to opt out is based on one of two myths: that intellectual capital doesn't matter (if so, he might ask why the company is paying all that money to manage it) or that it can run by itself (if so, why is the company paying all that money for you?).

CHAPTER 8

Structural Capital II

THE DANGER OF OVERINVESTING IN KNOWLEDGE

THE ONLY IRREPLACEABLE CAPITAL AN ORGANIZATION
POSSESSES IS THE KNOWLEDGE AND ABILITY OF ITS PEOPLE.
THE PRODUCTIVITY OF THAT CAPITAL DEPENDS ON HOW
EFFECTIVELY PEOPLE SHARE THEIR COMPETENCE WITH THOSE
WHO CAN USE IT.
—ANDREW CARNEGIE

Structural capital takes what I know and delivers it to my customers. It marshals the resources of the corporation to augment and support my ideas and my work. But it can also summon the bureaucrats of the corporation to squelch them. It can provide me with the information that will help me do a better job. But it can also overwhelm me with trivial information. With intellectual assets as with any other resource, it's possible to have too much of a good thing. Herein lies the central question of organizational design in the Information Age. What can companies do so that their structural intellectual capital offers the greatest likelihood of supporting people and the least danger of stifling them? In this chapter, we'll explore the theory and practice of information overload and discover ways to prevent knowledge management from becoming just another bureaucracy.

With invention giving birth every day, it seems, to new Web

browsers, new and more powerful chips, and new machines of all kinds, it's important to notice that the retorts and alembics of structural capital are essentially conservative, not innovative. Their role is to gather, test, organize, refine, and distribute existing knowledge more efficiently. In his magisterial *The City in History*, Lewis Mumford wrote about the role the medieval university played in the development of urban life. Universities, Mumford pointed out, did not begin as centers of humanistic scholarship (that was a later upper-class add-on) but as professional schools of law, medicine, and theology, an apotheosis of the craftsman's guild. Substitute "corporation" for "city" and "structural capital" for "university," and you will begin to understand how administrative systems, databases, and other codified forms of organizational knowledge are keepers of the flame, not fuel for it:

> Like other forms of craft association, the aim of the university was to prepare for the practice of a vocation and to regulate the conditions under which its members performed their work . . . In the university, the pursuit of knowledge was elevated into an enduring structure, which did not depend for its continuance upon any single group of priests, scholars, or texts. The system of knowledge was more important than the thing known. In the university, the functions of cultural storage, dissemination and interchange, and creative addition—perhaps the three most essential functions of the city—were adequately performed. The very independence of the university from the standards of the market and the city fostered the special sort of authority it exercised: the sanction of verifiable truth . . .
>
> Too often the major contributions to knowledge, from Newton to Einstein, from Gilbert to Faraday, have been made outside the university's walls. Nevertheless, the enlargement and transmission of the intellectual heritage would have been inconceivable, on the scale actually achieved since the thirteenth century, without the agency of the university.

Structural capital cannot break the mold, because it *is* the mold. The market is the mother of innovation. Yes, new building blocks of structural capital—patents, product and process improvements, databases, networks—can remodel or replace the old architecture. For example, one can make a persuasive case that the mere existence of company-wide electronic mail and data networks inherently threatens and will ultimately destroy a traditional business hierarchy. But these new structures create their own sets of infuriating difficulties—such as replacing the stifling hand of bureaucracy with the choking kudzu of information overload. Says Thomas W. Malone, a professor at the Sloan School of Management at MIT: "In the old world, information was very expensive, so we managed with relatively small amounts of it; we developed organizations that could work in an information desert." Storing, moving, and finding information is so cheap and easy now, Malone goes on, that "we're in something more like an information jungle. Survival techniques that worked in deserts won't be as effective. Those who learn to take advantage of this increasing amount of information economically will be much more successful."

Networks set off a noisy, distracting, and unending information explosion. Wired executives complain—or are they bragging?—of receiving 200 or more e-mail messages a day, on top of the by-now-usual stream of voice messages, an undiminished inflow of memos, faxes, even letters. The infoglut at Sun Microsystems is reminiscent of a hundred-year flood: a million and a half internal messages *every day*, 120 per employee. And, chief information officer Bill Raduchel jokes, "it all comes to my mailbox." There's no way to turn it off. The dangers are obvious. The urgent drives out the important; others impose on your time; everyone's a critic, especially the uninformed. Your mailbox swells with "FYIs" where you don't care and "what do you thinks?" where you don't know. It's enough to make you yearn for the old nuisances, like getting five signatures on a form before you can buy a stapler.

Information overload is an all-too-real phenomenon that points to an important challenge in managing intellectual capital. Though everyone interested in knowledge management can tell stories about underinvesting in knowledge—skills ignored, ideas orphaned—the nonmanagement of intellectual assets is equally likely to lead to the reverse: overinvesting in knowledge. Those of us in the knowledge business—that includes you, dear reader—have been getting away with murder. Because we cannot measure and do not manage what we have, we've been able to escape accountability for what we do.

Look at IBM. Never in history was a company richer in human capital. At one colloquy about intellectual capital I attended, the conversation wandered into a lament for all the brainpower that drained out of IBM as more than 150,000 of the brightest workers in the world left it. True enough: But beauty is as beauty does, and when IBM employed all those smart people, it was performing dreadfully. "Nobody's dumb at IBM," said Tom Whiteside, an ex-IBMer who was the company's chief engineer on the project that developed the PowerPC chip with Apple and Motorola, "but it's like herding cats—they just all have their own agenda."

Passion for the value of intellectual capital should not come at the expense of basic principles of management. A business person must strive unendingly to use assets more efficiently, get more out of them, make do with less. Assets that are unused are a drag on performance. If physical exams followed generally accepted accounting principles, fat would be counted among a body's assets.

Sociologists Sara Keisler and Lee Sproull, in their book about electronic networks called *Connections*, say that studies consistently show that people overinvest in knowledge. Agrees Mats Alvesson, a business professor at the University of Gothenburg in Sweden: "People are often over-concerned with information. For example, they gather more than they can use and often talk about it. This strong emphasis on information is grounded in wishes to be (and perhaps even more, to appear) careful, rational, reliable, even intelligent. Paradoxically, this wish to appear rational accounts for a behavior which is not so rational, *i.e.*, an over-preoccupation with information." I have only to walk into my office to see how much overinvestment in knowledge I do. Annual reports, studies by professors somewhere, reports of surveys and studies by business groups and consulting firms, printed copies of particularly interesting e-mail, torn-out articles from newspapers, stacks of unread books, piles of miscellaneous paper, not to mention tens of thousands of lines of notes, phone numbers, rough drafts, and wire service clips saved in my computer—all stored there *just in case*. We know better than that: Japanese manufacturers taught Detroit and everyone else that just-in-case stockpiles can be wiped out, and parts delivered *just in time*, by substituting information for inventory. Heaps of just-in-case information can be as paralyzing as piles of just-in-case parts.

If people overinvest in knowledge, organizations do the same. IBM did not have too many people; its share of computer-industry employment fell in lockstep with its share of computer-industry sales, which suggests that if Big Blue had been able to hold its market share it could have kept its workers. What IBM had was too much structure, a kludgy and dysfunctional apparatus that prevented the company from moving quickly in a changing market to exploit—and thus retain—the talent it employed.

Step back, then, from the technologies of structural capital, and return to first principles. In Chapter 4, I said that there are two kinds of intellectual capital: First, the semipermanent body of knowledge that grows up around a task, a person, or an organization; second, tools that augment the body of knowledge by bringing relevant data or expertise to people who need them when they need them. To these add this: While plenty of quotidian information processing goes on in all companies, value-added knowledge work is rarely routine; because each sale, each project, each legal brief is unique, it's impossible to predict in advance what specific knowledge it will need to call on.

From this, we can deduce two purposes that structural capital should serve. One, which we discussed in the previous chapter, is to codify bodies of knowledge that can be transferred, to preserve the recipes that might otherwise be lost. These might literally be recipes for a restaurant or a food company; they might be blueprints for a nuclear power plant that will be decommissioned long after anyone who helped build it has gone; they might be plug-and-play business processes, such as those that Skandia AFS uses to open new offices in one-twelfth the time previously required (see Chapter 5); they might be any number of other best practices, so long as they can be adapted, transferred, and reused.

The second purpose of structural capital is to connect people to data, experts, and expertise—including bodies of knowledge—on a just-in-time basis. That's what the rest of this chapter will focus on. Hewlett-Packard does this very well; it's worth spending some time looking at how H-P manages knowledge to see how various ways of managing structural capital can be put together.

The fugleman of Silicon Valley, founded in a Palo Alto, California, garage that has become a state historic landmark, H-P is now a global giant with 110,800 employees and 1995 sales of $31.5 billion. In 1993 it passed Digital Equipment Corp. to become the second-largest computer manufacturer; its line of personal computers, introduced in 1995, immediately jumped to the number-six position in worldwide sales; it controls 70 percent of the computer-printer business; between 1991 and 1995, its return on equity has climbed from 11.1 to 23.3

percent. Yet as recently as October 1990, H-P was wheezing with the same bureaucratic emphysema that afflicted IBM and DEC. Problems, among them a centralized marketing organization and slow, consensus-driven decision-making, were severe enough that autumn—when stock traded at $25 a share, the lowest in years—that David Packard, then seventy-eight, came out of retirement to take an active management role to save the company he co-founded. Within a year the stock had doubled and H-P was on the roll it has sustained ever since. Superior management of structural intellectual capital played a key role in H-P's resurgence.

Two Cheers for Openness

An important first step was to recognize that knowledge-based companies cannot succeed if their most important asset is kept under lock and key. "You can't just take a stodgy organization, hire smart guys, and expect good things to happen," says Julio Rotemberg, an MIT economist who has studied how management style affects innovation. Getting results from investing in knowledge requires corporate systems and culture that allow it to flow freely, which means scrapping rules that stifle new ideas.

Openness had been a touchstone of H-P's young days and company rhetoric still swore by it, but reality had become something else; for example, its 1985 security guidelines read: "Computer systems should be configured in such a way as to reduce the users' capabilities and access rights as severely as possible . . . with capabilities and access being assigned to each user on an as needed basis." In 1991, that policy was turned on its head. H-P issued new information systems principles that said: "Information users should have access to any data which would help them perform their jobs, unless specifically limited by management. The burden of proof must be shifted from the user demonstrating a 'need to know' to the appropriate management documenting a reason to limit access." It's a welcome change, argues Robert Walker, H-P's chief information officer: "With the ability to share information broadly and fully without filtering it through a hierarchy, we can manage the way we always wanted to."

But an information explosion was inevitable in a company where everyone has a computer and they are all connected. By mid-1994 H-P's 97,000 employees every month exchanged 20 million e-mail messages (and 70,000 more outside the company); shared nearly 3 trillion characters of data, such as engineering specs; and executed more than a quarter of a million electronic transactions with customers and suppliers; that's not counting phone calls, voice mail, or paper. Says Chuck Sieloff, who is responsible for providing common information services and technology platforms for H-P's worldwide workforce: "Information used to be scarce within organizations. Now we have more than we can begin to know what to do with."

"Pushing" Information Versus "Pulling" It

H-P's information systems group—the techies—began looking for ways to drain the swamp without stanching the flow. One breakthrough insight, Walker says, was distinguishing between information that is *pushed* at someone and information that he *pulls* for himself. Most of us get information pushed at us. Standard reports—weekly sales numbers, monthly budget figures—land on our desks on a regular schedule; less formal documents like e-mail and memos pour in; other, undocumented stuff is told us at meetings, on the phone, by the coffeepot. Each of these—structured data, media, and people's knowledge—has a "pull" counterpart: Instead of being sent a report, you can have access, the ability to get it if you need it; documents can be placed in repositories like the databases discussed in Chapter 7, instead of in in-boxes; corporate knowledge maps and Yellow Pages can help you pull in experts when you need them.

H-P has helped clear off employees' desktops—both wood and silicon—by pushing less information and putting more where it can be pulled. Policies, phone directories, product descriptions (20,000 of them), and many internal reports go on-line. Rather than have publishers fulfill dozens or hundreds of individual subscriptions to magazines, newsletters, and data sources, H-P negotiates company-wide licenses and puts electronic versions into databases. " 'Pull' dissemination is better than 'push,' " Walker asserts.

Recognizing the danger of overinvesting in knowledge, H-P is actually working to increase areas of deliberate ignorance. The thinking takes off from a topology of knowledge drawn by Babson College's Liam Fahey, which looks like this:

	KNOW	DON'T KNOW
KNOW	KNOWLEDGE THAT YOU KNOW YOU HAVE (EXPLICIT KNOWLEDGE)	KNOWLEDGE THAT YOU KNOW YOU DON'T HAVE (KNOWN GAPS)
DON'T KNOW	KNOWLEDGE THAT YOU DON'T KNOW YOU HAVE (TACIT KNOWLEDGE)	KNOWLEDGE THAT YOU DON'T KNOW THAT YOU DON'T HAVE (UNKNOWN GAPS)

Usually people try to expand the domain of "knowledge that you know you have" by explicating tacit knowledge, closing gaps with training and research, or scanning for areas of ignorance. "But is this really our goal?" Sieloff asks. "You don't have to teach everyone everything. The goal isn't to stuff the same knowledge into as many heads as possible" but "to improve your return on intellectual capital." The easiest ways to do that, he argues, involve recognizing zones of deliberate ignorance—"things you're willing to let go of." Among the ways H-P's information systems group is attacking overinvestment in knowledge:

Leveraging through specialization: You can reduce the efforts of many by leveraging the knowledge of a few. Only 20 deeply expert people—10 engineers and 10 support staff—take care of a common operating environment for 80,000 personal computer users at Hewlett-Packard. They are responsible for distributing and tending the core software (word processing, spreadsheets, electronic mail) that everyone needs, and which before every piece of the organization had to deal with on its own, which not only consumed talent but led to incompatibilities.

Simplification and automation: The five-year cost of supporting a client/server computer network is more than $48,000 per person. By using help desks, decision support software, and artificial intelligence to dumb-down certain data and information management processes, H-P figures it does the job for $10,000 or $15,000 less.

Inventory management: Minimizing the cost of intellectual capital by providing knowledge on demand. "Pulled" knowledge can be much more than reports, phone numbers, or magazine subscriptions. For example, like most companies H-P expects managers to be able to use the skills and technology of project management (see Chapter 12), but decided not to offer formal classroom training. Line managers, says Sieloff, "don't care about project management theory—so we do it." Working with Ernst & Young, H-P developed a series of one- or two-day minicourses around specific project management topics, such as how to define a project's scope. A manager needing to learn that can holler for help and get it right away. Says Sieloff: "They provide the content [that is, managers bring in the problem they are actually facing] and pay my people to lead them through a module when they need it. Suddenly, we have business management who would never have gone to a class, but who are willing to *pay* to get it just-in-time." Similarly, H-P's sales force no longer comes in from the road to attend classes about new product launches—a process that consumed weeks of each sales rep's time. Now the information is available online whenever a rep needs it. On the road, the sales force uses what the company whimsically calls ESP—an Electronic Sales Partner, accessible on-line, which contains more than 13,000 documents (product and pricing information, selling tools like presentations, etc.). Before H-P's sales force got ESP, it got mail: literally tons of stuff pushed into their mailboxes, so much that the company estimated that they threw half of it away.

Market-Driven Knowledge Management

While some at Hewlett-Packard are busily spreading ignorance, others are equally engaged spreading knowledge. H-P builds structural capital economically thanks to the most powerful of all bureaucracy-busters: the market. A fundamental principle of managing intellectual capital is, or should be: *Knowledge is valuable, so make 'em pay.*

That principle was forced on H-P's corporate staff in the early 1990s. Part of the company's plan to battle bloat was to challenge every centralized function to earn its keep. There never were many, but among them was a headquarters advisory group, the Product Processes Organization (PPO), looking out for corporate engineering, procurement, manufacturing, quality, and other functions—in effect, an internal consultancy responsible for promoting organizational expertise. Its leader, Bill Kay, took on the task of showing that these structural assets were worth keeping. Says Judy Lewis, head of one of PPO's teams: "Bill's job was to give sense and meaning to the center. By and large it was viewed in H-P as overhead that provided no added value, and by and large that was true." One of Kay's first moves was the most important one: He converted PPO from a tax-supported organization, whose costs were charged to every business unit's overhead, to a direct-funded one that "sold" its services by negotiating contracts with the businesses. Programs would survive only if customers thought they were valuable enough to pay for. The new arrangement was a success, but there was more to come. In Lewis's words, "We still operated as programs—quality, information systems, procurement. It worked, but we'd missed a really big pony." No other group within H-P knew as much about the workings of all its many businesses. PPO could learn with Peter, then teach Paul. But Paul had to be willing to pay. That meant PPO would have to learn more about the unarticulated needs of its customers and find ways to let them know what it had to sell. It had to get in the business of creating and marketing knowledge.

In 1994, Lewis called some old friends in H-P's test and measurement products business (T&M). With its traditional aerospace market depressed because of falling defense spending, T&M was eager for new ideas. Lewis persuaded them "to bear with us as we did action research" about how to transfer knowledge between H-P businesses. Lewis's team chose a piece of the new-product-development process: business planning and product definition, those early stages when critical decisions are made about the functions and features a product should have. T&M knew lots about product planning, but because of its monochromatic customer base (chiefly military and commercial aerospace companies) it had never learned the art and science of market segmentation—that is, how to recognize when a few added or subtracted or different features might open a whole new market in, for example, universities; how customers in some market segments make purchasing decisions early in the development process, others later; etc. This was knowledge T&M didn't know it didn't know.

But other Hewlett-Packard businesses knew a lot about market segmentation. Says Lewis: "We began gathering stories, case studies, and experiences that we knew T&M wouldn't have heard about." H-P's laser printers had become the industry powerhouse by understanding how to design different products for different market segments. Medical instruments, a business more like T&M, had also used market segmentation to cope with the changes caused by the rise of HMOs and giant hospital chains like Humana. Lewis remembers: "We had a wealth of stories, because people in PPO had worked with all our businesses, and they were fascinating to T&M, because to them it was a new way of doing business."

It was also the beginning of a new way for PPO to do business. What Lewis's team pioneered became KnowledgeLinks, a program in which PPO acts as a go-between, collecting knowledge from one H-P business and translating it so another one can see how to apply it. "We had a proof of concept," Lewis says, "that knowledge-sharing works when you pay attention to organizational needs and processes. You can find the information, and you can create a living mechanism that will continuously update it." Out of the translation process have come packages of business knowledge—structural intellectual assets. PPO itself has become smarter.

The group immediately began thinking about how to increase the return on its new organizational knowledge. One-on-one consulting engagements were great, and PPO had the fee income to prove it, but every internal consulting engagement was a potential source of war stories, best practices, or other knowledge that other H-P businesses could use. PPO wanted to share the wealth as quickly as possible. To do that, PPO began identifying major topics that matter to all H-P's businesses—among them competitor intelligence, product generation, inventory management, decreasing time-to-market, etc. These have become the basis of an on-line version of KnowledgeLinks, using internal Web servers. The KnowledgeLinks web sites are a combination of catalog and anthology, designed to help managers know what PPO has and how it might be valuable; managers can browse through it or type in a subject—managing retail channels, for example—and receive a screenful of documents, case histories, and contacts. Says PPO's Gary Gray, an expert in product development: "We can't possibly maintain all information about all things at all levels of depth, so we try to create stories that capture the essence of a program." A manager thinking about outsourcing manufacturing can learn how others have done it and, more important, who has done it.

The strongest validation of KnowledgeLinks—and its best insurance against becoming an overgrown bureaucracy—is that HP's businesses pay for it. When Gray, Lewis, and others took a prototype of the electronic version of KnowledgeLinks to their clients, they pointed out that it costs time and money to write up stories to put online, manage the system, and respond to users' questions, and popped the question: To fund this, we'll have to charge you 25 percent more for our consulting services. Every business agreed.

H-P businesses don't need to go through PPO to seek and share structural intellectual capita. Complementing PPO's work, for example, is something called the Work Innovation Network. Basically WIN is an opportunity for any H-P business to set itself up as the host for a series of presentations, conferences, and seminars on a topic it is wrestling with—for example, how to cope with ever-shorter product life cycles. Typically, the host business will put together a half-day conference on the subject and broadcast an invitation to the rest of the company. If the topic's hot—i.e., if the "market" responds—it will start taking on a life of its own, with meetings every month or so, speakers from several different divisions, and a continuous diffusion of insight from one part of the company to another; indeed, sometimes meetings that begin as WIN-sponsored conferences evolve into ongoing communities of practice.

Programs like WIN and KnowledgeLinks reflect a healthy balance between the human and technical sides of structural capital. Technology networks are not valuable in and of themselves. "The whole point of a network," says Mel Horwitch, a professor at Polytechnic University in New York, "is that people are important." The role of technology is to support the real knowledge network—the informal one of people talking to people. Says Gray: "As a company grows fast and gets very, very large, the informal network isn't as effective. So there is an opportunity for information systems to create a mechanism that allows access to what the informal network knows." The virtuous cycle begins: People learn to do things that become stories that become documents that go on a network that people use to learn how to do things. Human capital begets structural intellectual capital, which begets human capital.

It's a subtle shift, but it is the key to reconciling the seemingly conflicting demands of human and structural capital: The purpose of knowledge management systems—be they corporate universities, staff experts, or knowledge databases—isn't to heap up knowledge for its own sake, but for the sake of knowledge workers and customers. Knowledge workers, who create value, don't like systems. They take shortcuts, forget to tell the boss, and ignore appeals to teamwork. Customers, who pay for value don't like systems either. Employers are right to want to retain human capital for the group, but the ultimate test of any system for codifying and managing knowledge is not whether it knows a lot, but whether it makes employees' and customers' lives easier. Just as one can express the meaning "customer capital" as "the likelihood that our customers will continue to do business with us," so one can define structural capital as "the reasons smart people will come to work here and want to stay here."

The best organizational structure is one that does not seem to exist: a transparent, superconducting connection between people and customers. In what its author calls a "pilot study" of the relative value of human, structural, and customer capital, Nick Bontis, a Ph.D. candidate at the University of Western Ontario, describes fascinating evidence that the best structural capital is the least noticeable. Bontis asked sixty-four MBA candidates—all of whom had returned to school after several years in business—to answer a series of questions about the companies they had worked for. The questions were designed to elicit ratings—subjective, but there are so far no objective measures— of human, structural, and customer capital; the MBA candidates were asked to agree or disagree, on a scale of one to seven with statements like "employees are bright"; "individuals learn from others"; "the firm is efficient"; "systems allow easy information access"; "customers are loyal"; "the firm is market-oriented"; etc. The ratings were totaled, then checked against measurements of the companies' financial performance, such as return on assets, sales growth, and innovativeness. Intriguingly, Bontis found that it was impossible to infer cause-and-effect relationships between high scores for structural capital, on the one hand, and a wealth of human or customer capital, on the other. Structural capital seemed neither to create the others nor to be created by them: It connected. Moreover, it was human and customer capital, not structural capital, that correlated with financial performance.

The efficiency, the agility, with which a company can augment human capital is the true measure of its effectiveness in the Knowledge Age. Dave Ulrich of the University of Michigan says that the learning capability of a company is G times G—the ability to *Gener-*

ate new ideas multiplied by the ability to Generalize them throughout the company. But the ultimate purpose of this generalizing capability, structural capital, is to connect people to experts and information, and customers to the company, and then to get out of the way. Stan Davis, a consultant who works in the Boston area, puts the challenge even more starkly: He says that in the age of knowledge, companies must configure themselves that they can deliver innovation to their customers so fast that they rarely bother to build fancy structures like departments at all. They just *act*.

CHAPTER 9

Customer Capital

INFORMATION WARS AND ALLIANCES

BEFORE I BUILT A WALL I'D ASK TO KNOW
WHAT I WAS WALLING IN OR WALLING OUT
—ROBERT FROST

Every hour on the hour, a United Airlines flight leaves La Guardia Airport in New York bound for O'Hare Field in Chicago. Just behind or just in front of it is an American Airlines flight, likewise headed for O'Hare. At five o'clock P.M. a week from Friday (as I am writing these words), I will be on one of those planes, en route to my mother's seventy-fifth birthday party. The two aircraft will probably be equally crowded; they will arrive as they depart, within minutes of one another; they will serve meals of identical inedibility; they will have, in their seatback pockets on board, inflight magazines with crossword puzzles of approximately equal difficulty and divertisement. I could have bought a ticket from either airline for the same price. I will be on the American flight. My sister, who is leaving New York the next day, will fly United.

You know why one of us chose American and the other United.

Several years ago we made different ch(
flyer plans to feed. Other things being equ
ask my travel agent to book me on an aii
plan I chose to build up miles. For reasc
made American's plan one of my "core h(
both 1995 and 1996, that preference wa:
Crandall's company. If the creek don't
amounts in 1997, 1998 . . .

My behavior makes me an asset to American Airlines—not as valuable an asset as a neighbor who logs more than 100,000 miles on
American every year, but an asset nevertheless, the kind no company
can have too many of: a steady customer. American makes a few investments to preserve the value of me-as-an-asset. It gives me a small
return on my capital in the form of free trips; it sees to it that Citi-
bank, MCI, and various other companies invite me to buy credit or
telephone service that will add to my account and, perhaps, make me
more loyal to American than I am; it makes partnership arrangements
with hotel and rental-car companies and other airlines; it sometimes
(rarely, alas) gives me an upgrade to first or business class if I remember to ask, if there's room, and if a more valuable asset isn't in the
same departure lounge. It invests enough to maintain my allegiance,
though not enough to deepen it to the point where I'd fly American
even if other things were unequal.*

Every company with customers has customer capital, which Hubert
Saint-Onge defines as the value of its franchise, its ongoing relationships with the people or organizations to which it sells. Of the three
broad categories of intellectual assets—human, structural, and customer capital—customers are the most obviously valuable. They pay
the bills. And because they do, the footprints they leave on financial
statements are easier to follow than those made by people, systems, or
capabilities. Though many companies' financial reporting systems are
not set up to do so, it is relatively easy to track indicators of customer
capital, such as market share, customer retention and defection rates,
and per-customer profitability. Not surprisingly, there is an extensive

---

* And if they keep serving those vile ersatz calzones, I'm switching to United
just as soon as I cash in my miles.

t literature describing how to put a monetary value on, for , customer loyalty (see Appendix) or brand equity (which is xpression of customer capital: a willingness to buy your product n if it costs more).

Despite this, customer capital is probably—and startlingly when you think about it—the worst managed of all intangible assets. Many businesses don't even know who their customers are—newsstands, delicatessens, most supermarkets, bus companies, many retailers. American Express knows if I shop at Bloomingdale's, but Bloomie's doesn't. Procter & Gamble knows a lot about the stores that stock its products, and has detailed demographic information that reveals how many men of my age and income buy its goods, but has no idea whether I brush my teeth with Crest or Colgate. Many companies do know who their customers are but treat them as adversaries rather than assets, with "take it or leave it" arrogance. Clothing and department stores have managed the remarkably self-defeating feat of training customers to wait for markdowns before buying, even in the Christmas season. Only mismanagement of customer capital can explain why U.S. companies on average lose half their customers in five years, or why—despite obvious improvement in the quality of manufactured goods, negligible price increases, and unending rhetoric about treating customers right—customer satisfaction is actually declining in the United States.

That customer capital is valuable may seem obvious, but it's startling just how valuable it is. Ford Motor Company figures that every percentage-point increase in customer loyalty—how many Ford owners buy Fords the next time—is worth $100 million a year in profits. Credit-card issuer MBNA calculates that if it cuts the rate at which customers defect by five percentage points, it will increase the lifetime profitability of the average customer by an astonishing 125 percent. Getting that kind of a return on customer capital requires more than acknowledging that customer relationships are assets, not just events. It demands understanding dynamics of managing this asset: what makes it grow or depreciate, what makes it more valuable or less?

It will surprise no one who has read this far to hear that in the Information Age customer capital cannot be captured by fishing around in the stream of goods and services from buyer to seller, but by casting one's net into the tides of information and knowledge that surge between them. With knowledge the most important component of the value of economic transactions—that is, knowledge being what we buy and what we sell—knowledge is the chief ingredient of customer capital. The story of how Merck & Co.—and its competitors in the prescription drug industry—faced and coped with a rapid and potentially disastrous fall in the value of their customer capital not only shows information's lead role but reveals many of the principles and dynamics of managing this asset.

The Pharmaceutical Industry's Customer-Capital Crisis

With the finest research laboratories in the prescription drug business, superb financial management, and an organization that seemed quick and responsive, Merck was America's Most Admired Company in *Fortune*'s annual survey of corporate reputations for seven straight years, a record that will be hard for any company to match. Merck was blessed in the customer capital department. The company was admired and respected by its customers, who were physicians and hospitals, and it served them with a superb sales force—detail men, in drug industry parlance. These were probably the best sales jobs in the world; if you could imagine sales reps from a dozen businesses unwinding at the same bar at the end of a hard week, the detail man would be the guy sitting at the end, wearing Gucci loafers, drinking Chivas, and paying with a Gold Card while the others covertly and covetously glanced his way.

Intellectual assets are what made Merck successful, but they were not—till recently—chiefly customer capital. They were the human and structural intellectual capital employed in discovering, designing, and patenting new drugs, and getting regulatory approval to sell them. In 1990, Merck generated a return on assets—the ones on the balance sheet—of 22.2 percent. Overall, drug companies on the *Fortune* 500 earned a 13.1 percent ROA while the median for all the companies on the list was 4.7 percent, a disparity that caught the eye and provoked the wrath of politicians concerned about high health care costs. But the financial accounting ignored the price of the knowledge that produced those expensive drugs. Developing a typical new drug costs so much money—about a quarter of a billion dollars—that Merck invests far more in R&D than it does in ordinary capital spending. Internally, Merck correctly counts R&D as capital investment rather than as an expense. If those assets are added to tangible ones, Merck executives said at the time, "we look pretty normal" in terms of ROA. (Let's not entirely believe drug company poor-mouthing: These were fabulously profitable companies.)

Though few saw it then, the drug companies' model for success was about to crack because of changes in customer capital. The story begins, actually, in the early 1980s, with a company called McKesson, a wholesaler/distributor that set up what were then sophisticated computer networks with retail pharmacies. By using McKesson's warehouse and network, and others like it that followed, pharmacists could carry much less inventory, which saved them pots of money, and McKesson also got high discounts because it bought in volume. In addition, the wholesalers' networks offered information about drug interactions that made them especially valuable to small pharmacies. McKesson's system worked so well that the percentage of prescription drug sales that went through wholesalers doubled in just a few years from about 40 percent to about 80 percent—a big change in the industry's value chain. The winners, like McKesson, were distinguished by the fact that they owned information, and were able to substitute it for inventory and still get volume discounts. But the change chiefly affected the retail and wholesale ends of the business; life went on as before for physicians and hospitals, and manufacturers were making more money than ever.

In the late 1980s, beginning almost invisibly, the drug business was reshaped again, this time by changes in the relative value of pieces of intellectual capital. The most valuable knowledge in the industry had been the stuff that was cooked up in the drug companies' labs, but it suddenly became much harder for manufacturers to capture the rewards from those investments. Generic medicines were part of the problem, but far more important was the rise of managed care. Picking up where McKesson left off, companies like Medco Containment set themselves up as "pharmaceutical benefits managers." They struck deals with HMOs and employer-sponsored managed care plans that allowed them to get information about prescriptions and deliver the pills directly to the patient, cutting out the traditional middlemen, drugstores and wholesalers. Medco had information at the *individual* level—knowledge that before was kept bottled up by doctors and druggists. Merck and the other drug companies knew their customers—doctors, hospitals, wholesalers, and drugstores—but Medco knew the ultimate customer—the patient.

Armed with that information, the Medcos of the world could—and did—use it in two ways. First, they bypassed retail distribution entirely for some customers, particularly people who had to take a drug regularly for a chronic condition—and senior citizens account for nearly 50 percent of all prescription drug use; second, they intervened directly with physicians, pressing them to prescribe generic versions of costly brand-name drugs, or suggest less expensive alternate medications for, say, treating ulcers or controlling blood pressure. These guys did terrible damage to retail pharmacies and manufacturers. Their knowledge of customers trumped the drug makers' knowledge of chemistry often enough that the drug makers' profit margins came under attack. Between 1987 and 1992, an analysis by the Boston Consulting Group revealed, managed care companies and pharmaceutical benefit managers—the most knowledge-intensive customers—doubled their market share and more than doubled the discounts they received from the manufacturers. Twenty years ago, out of every dollar spent on prescription drugs, sixty-seven cents found its way back to the manufacturer, according to Mercer Management consulting; now only sixty cents does. As pricing power, based on customer capital, accumulated in the distribution channel, *Fortune* took note of the trend and in 1991 prophesied an end to pharmaceutical companies' palmy days. "We're calling a turn" in the market, the magazine said.

But there was another twist to come. In 1993, Merck bought Medco. At the time, Merck was criticized for overpaying for Medco. Using the highly sophisticated simulation techniques that have made her a celebrity among chief financial officers, Merck's Judy Lewent had calculated not only the cost of buying Medco but the cost of not buying the company. She says: "People asked us why we were buying a distribution arm, since vertical integration had never worked in this business. They missed the point. We were not buying a distribution system but a database and a client service capability. We bought their intangible assets."

Look at that statement: "We were not buying a distribution system"—that is, we were not buying into the *physical* flow—"but a database and a client service capability"—that is, buying access to the *information* flow. In doing so, Merck acknowledged that the intangible assets that controlled the market had changed; specifically, Lewent and Merck's auditors figured that nearly half the $6.6 billion Merck paid for Medco went to acquire "customer relationships." Bargaining power had moved from the drug maker to the customer, the person with a buck in his hands—so Merck moved downstream, too, buying Medco.

All of which might have left the detail sales force feeling like Willie Loman. Indeed, Merck at first thought it might reduce the size of its detail force. Instead, however, the company decided to retrain the detailers. Their skills and knowledge used to be almost exclusively pharmacological; now it has added a business component as they have been given much more expertise in cost, disease management, and other downstream concerns. Instead of just filling prescriptions, Medco is, the company says, "developing health management programs that promote better health outcomes and lower long-term costs associated with certain chronic diseases." The company is pouring money into direct electronic links with doctors' offices and pharmacists that will let doctors see what drugs a patient might have been prescribed by other physicians, for example.

Similar transformations are taking place among other drug makers. At Pfizer, the detail force has been made over into "information brokers," also heavily supported by information-technology links with customers. They make eight to ten calls on customers every day, but don't make any sales—which usually must be placed through a managed care provider or pharmaceutical benefits manager. Instead, they hawk information—and collect it. The rise of managed care provoked Pfizer in 1994 to organize "disease management teams" in each of the areas where the company has important products. The teams include medical, marketing, financial, regulatory, and information specialists. Among other things, they keep track of which doctors are affiliated with which managed care plans and which drugs made by Pfizer and competitors are on the plans' approved lists; they also gather data that shows what categories of drugs and which Pfizer products each physician actually orders.

In less than a decade, the whole structure of the pharmaceutical industry has changed, not because of new laboratory techniques or regulatory regimes but because a new class of customer—pharmaceutical benefits managers and managed care plans—came upon the scene. The drug makers had had valuable relationships—customer capital—with their old customers. The newcomers destroyed it. Their power to negotiate prices and determine what drugs were prescribed vitiated the value of those old relationships. For the drug industry, the collapse in the value of their customer capital was as grave a crisis as plummeting real estate values was for Japanese banks in the 1990s. They had to move fast and aggressively to rebuild it.

The Information Wars

You may remember a wonderful Federal Express television commercial in which a jowly boss comes into a room and harangues an employee about a package that hasn't been delivered to a demanding customer. While he rants at her incompetence, she calmly fiddles with her computer, and after a few seconds announces, No, the package got there, signed for by the angry customer personally. Everyone in the office applauds. They're cheering one effect of information-intensiveness on business—it changes power relationships in a company, something we'll discuss in Part Three. To my mind, however, the most dramatic change is in the relationship between FedEx and its customer. Certainly it's convenient if the customer can track her own packages. But it's more than that. The customer can see inside Federal Express. If FedEx screws up, it has no place to hide. "The check is in the mail" no longer applies.

It is a principle of managing intellectual capital that *when information is power, power flows downstream toward the customer*. Pharmaceuticals are one example, but you can see the principle in action in industry after industry. Says Fred Wiersema, a consultant at CSC Index in Cambridge, Massachusetts, dig a ten-year-old marketing plan out of the file and compare it with a new one: "The distribution channel is a mess. Customers have much more power. There's fragmentation in media and advertising. The activities of the sales force are completely different." In the automobile industry, new electronic marketplaces, which put more information in the hands of customers by allowing them to compare various dealers' prices and inventories on-line, have begun to threaten dealers' profits in used-car sales, which have been the most profitable portion of their business.

Airlines are a third example of bargaining power—and therefore valuable customer capital—moving downstream. The networks of computer reservation systems—Sabre, which is run by American Airlines, Apollo, which is run by United, and others—are just a little over ten years old. Before they existed, consumers and travel agents looking for a flight from New York to Los Angeles had to call airlines one by one. The cumbersome process made comparison shopping difficult. Regulation also limited price competition. The airlines, led by American, set up their reservation networks by installing terminals in travel agents' offices, hoping that they would bias agents toward selling tickets on the network's airline. But antitrust complaints forced them to make it possible to use the network to book seats on every airline, and to design the appearance of the screens so that they didn't favor one airline over another.

The networks transformed the airline industry. First, they made comparison shopping easy for anyone who could use the network—that is, any travel agent. That led to price competition, fare wars, and today's wild, messy pricing system. These, in turn, made it worthwhile for a consumer to use a travel agent, because she could get a better deal—and because the system was complex. Before the networks, two thirds of all airline tickets were sold directly by the airlines. Within five years after the networks were set up, two thirds of all tickets were sold by travel agents—a downstream shift as massive as the one in prescription drugs. (Today, with the rise of on-line services and the World Wide Web, the airlines are trying to leapfrog travel agents. That would be a further downstream devolution of power, but since travel agents are paid by the carriers, it would increase airlines' revenues, unless they give the savings back in fare wars; for travel agents, however, the change is life-threatening.)

Or consider the case of a small manufacturer of housewares, who sells products to Wal-Mart, Kmart, and Target, three of the biggest retail chains in the country. A few years ago, each made him an offer he couldn't refuse. "We were encouraged—or pushed—into electronic data interchange," he says. Using computer-to-computer links rather than phones and faxes, the big stores entered orders straight into his system. Invoices and payment went on-line, too. For both manufacturer and retailer, paperwork vanished, errors disappeared, clerical costs fell. At his customers' request, he bar-coded first every pallet, then every carton, then every piece he shipped, allowing retailers to save more time and money when they received the goods.

Initially, his customers split the expense of the system fifty-fifty with him. A while later, he notes sardonically, "They decided that the savings were so great that I should pay both halves." Still, he says: "The demands keep coming." Some customers make him put on not only a bar code but the store's own price stickers so the merchandise is "floor ready" or demand extra discounts as a condition of stocking his goods in newly opened stores.

What explains the downstream movement of power, away from manufacturers and toward wholesalers, retailers and ultimately consumers? Certainly not simply the old story of the big guy putting the squeeze on the little guy. Medco was smaller than Merck, travel agents smaller than airlines. Indeed, much evidence says that large corporations exercise less economic power than they did a generation ago. For example, the number of employees of *Fortune* 500 companies has fallen 24 percent—3.7 million fewer people—since 1974, while the U.S. labor force has grown 43 percent. If big companies have more power to squeeze their little brethren than they did, it ought to show up in their profits. It doesn't. In 1974, the 500 largest industrials pocketed 27.2 percent of all U.S. corporations' profits; by 1994, the lions' share was down to 20.6 percent. If it's any comfort to the housewares manufacturer, bigness doesn't explain the squeeze. Nor has power migrated toward customers because buyers have become meaner—in fact many are more cooperative with suppliers. The explanation is not that management mantras like "customer delight" have suddenly become all the rage. "The customer is always right" was always right. But he wasn't always heard.

The customer today can call the tune because he knows the score. In a knowledge economy, information is more valuable than ever, and generally speaking customers have more of it than they did. Says Michael Standing, an expert in supply-chain management at Gemini Consulting: "Information used to be much more enclosed. Now it is increasingly available to the customer, which changes the power balance." Electronic data interchange, buyer-supplier partnerships, and other techniques of supply-chain management allow customers to see inside the companies they buy from. Your customer might know how much stock you have on hand and when his shipment left your warehouse; he might have the same dope about your rivals. If you make complex component parts, the buyer might even know details of your manufacturing costs and R&D. Says Robert K. Elliott, vice chairman of KPMG Peat Marwick: "An electronic interface with suppliers is strategic because you can use it to hose them on price. With your customers, it is not strategic, because they can hose you."

Not that they always do it, or that the seller is necessarily hurt. Like people who open their hearts to one another, suppliers curl up with customers because intimacy is worth it, even though the pain is greater if something goes wrong. Shared information is valuable. Elliott points out: "If the entire supply chain is information-transparent, it can create the most value for the least resources." Inexpensive intellectual assets—an electronic link, for example—can replace costly working capital by reducing inventory and order-processing time. Partners can eliminate duplicate information-handling functions like stock management, inspection, billing, and purchasing, putting them on one side or the other of the partnership, or even merging them. Jordan Lewis, author of a study of customer-supplier alliances called *The Connected Corporation*, estimates that 30 to 40 percent of the savings from customer-supplier alliances derive from improving such joint processes.

In the best partnerships, the savings are great enough to give everybody a big slice and a frosting rose, too. The administrative cost of business-to-business transactions—the cost of selling, paperwork, logistics, etc.—is something like $250 billion a year in the United States. In the packaged goods industry alone, excess handling, paperwork, and inventory cost manufacturers, wholesalers, brokers, and retailers about $30 billion annually. Now, reengineering consultants boast of reducing internal administrative costs 40 percent or so. Of course, those are their success stories; they are less forthcoming about failures. But that figure gives an idea of the money available to companies who stop fighting with their customers and start building capital together with them—perhaps $100 billion a year, an amount somewhere between the gross domestic products of Thailand and Denmark.

The Intangible Value Chain

To understand customer capital and the wealth-building opportunities it creates for both buyer and seller, you must look at the intangible value chain, not the tangible one. A value chain, recall, shows how a product or service moves from first seller to end user, from raw material to goods on the shelf. Value is—or ought to be—added at each stage. The idea is to add as much value as possible at as little cost as possible, and to capture that value in your markup.

These days, the most valuable links tend to belong to people who own knowledge—particularly knowledge of what happens at the customer end, where you find the folks who pay for all the upstream hurly-burly. So great is the power of information that whoever controls it in many cases controls the business. The squeeze isn't on suppliers *per se;* it's on anyone who is left out of the information flow, or fails to take advantage of it.

This gets a little subtle, so slow down to read the next bit: First, there's no reason why information has to pool at the customer end of the river. Information is funny stuff: Unlike refrigerators or factories or storefronts, it can move anywhere in nanoseconds. Transporting it costs *bubkes.* If you take your sporty little Nissan 240SX to a dealer to get retrofitted for a car phone, knowledge of what you did can be given to Nissan, others in the dealer network, or the local cellular phone company—provided the dealer agrees to share it. Second, though information about customers is always the most valuable knowledge, that information might be worth most to somebody upstream. The fact that you got fitted for contact lenses is worth several dollars to your optometrist, but potentially worth a lot more upstream at Johnson & Johnson, if that company can make you a regular buyer of its disposable lenses.

An alert manager can look for information everywhere in the value chain, and put it wherever it has the biggest return. Therefore managers have to ask three new questions of the value chain:

What information drives the business?

Who has it?

To whom is it worth most?

Depending on its business, a company might find that it should change the physical activities it performs to take advantage of the flow of intellectual activities—that is, move upstream or downstream to put itself where the fish are biting.

MicroAge is a company that did just that, actually moving a step *upstream*, away from the end-user, to get maximum returns from customer capital. Based in Phoenix, Arizona, fast-growing MicroAge (1995 sales: $2.9 billion, up 32 percent from 1994) began life in 1976.

Says CEO Jeffrey McKeever: "Till five years ago, we were primarily a wholesaler." Through franchised dealers, MicroAge sold computers to corporate clients as an authorized reseller for Apple, Compaq, Hewlett-Packard, and IBM. MicroAge added value the way wholesalers always have: buying in bulk, holding inventory, matching buyers and sellers, and, in its case, using its dealer network to deliver equipment to customer sites nationwide and to provide expert help installing it.

But in these days of open systems and dispersed client-server networks, a new source of value-added has been created. Customers don't want just computers; they want configuration, too. Dozens of manufacturers might contribute to a final system—central processing units from one company, servers from another, keyboards from a third, plus sundry monitors, modems, other peripherals, and preloaded software. If the automobile industry worked the same way, you would be able to buy a Cadillac body with a Ford engine, a BMW transmission, and a Midas muffler, assembled at a Toyota dealership.

In this environment, says McKeever, "A computer is just a part." Possessing the physical goods has become worth relatively less than before; the value of knowing how to configure a system has grown. In 1982, out of every dollar end-users paid for computers, eighty-five cents found its way back to the manufacturers; by 1992, only fifty-five cents did, with the rest going to distributors and service providers. Profits have been redistributed even more dramatically, with the manufacturers' share falling from 71 to 25 percent, according to the Mercer Management consulting firm. Says McKeever: "We saw value shifting from physical attributes to information attributes." The key information: knowing how to fit systems together for customers.

So MicroAge moved to where the value was. The company tore apart one of its warehouses and converted it to a factory. Every day, 125 tons of information technology equipment move through MicroAge's factory-cum-logistics center, which assembles customized systems out of monitors and motherboards and other stuff from more than 500 companies in what amounts to a giant job shop. To exploit an extremely valuable pool of information—knowledge of its customers' needs and of the cost, capabilities, and compatibilities of upstream manufacturers' products—MicroAge redesigned its business. "We changed our place on the value chain," McKeever says.

From Warfare to Alliance: How to Invest in Customer Capital

As information and the economic power it conveys move downstream, it is vital that businesses manage customer relationships in new ways. They must invest in their customers, just as they do in their people and structures. Customer capital is a lot like human capital: You cannot own customers, any more than you can own people. But just as an organization can invest in employees not only to increase their value as individuals but also to create knowledge assets for the company as a whole, so a company and its customers can grow intellectual capital that is their joint and several property. Make no mistake: These are real investments made in the expectation of a return. If you make them wisely, they entitle you to one, just as the right investments in human capital produce value that belongs to shareholders as well as employees. There's a world of investment opportunity:

INNOVATE WITH CUSTOMERS

Successful innovation, even if it's not protected by patents, has always been a superb defense against a margin squeeze. We have discussed innovation as an output of human capital, but it has a customer capital component as well. That point is important, and often forgotten: Whoever you sell to wants to charge a premium to *his* customers, too. Innovation helps you both do that. Aluminum giant Alcoa and its customer Audi worked together for the better part of a decade to create a revolutionary aluminum frame for automobiles. Collaborative innovation was in their mutual best interest. For Alcoa, the advantages were finding new ways to increase aluminum use in the huge car market, developing new alloys and technologies that might be usable in other markets, and supporting its expansion into Europe. But Audi had as much to gain: Engineering cachet has traditionally been a selling point European carmakers use to get a premium price for their products, and an all-aluminum car has both marketing and cost advantages because of German laws that demand that cars be recyclable.

Innovating with customers has another advantage, too: An investment you make in R&D can be more productive if you already have a customer; and the customer benefits by getting first crack at it.

EMPOWER YOUR CUSTOMERS

It's a hot trend, says William Bluestein, director of computing strategy research for Forrester Research, a Massachusetts firm: "Companies that empower their customers." Pursuing cost savings and intimacy at the same time, suppliers and customers rummage around in each other's computers, entering orders directly, checking stock and shipping status. While some information is hidden behind electronic firewalls, much is not. Says Frederick Kovac, vice president for planning at Goodyear: "There will be a day in the not-distant future when customers will get data on the tests of a new tire as soon as our engineers do. They'll see everything—warts and all." That gives your customers a chance to give you feedback before you make costly mistakes. From there it's a short step before customers start comparing notes with each other—maybe on your network. Says Bluestein: "If I were Ralph Nader, I'd set up a consumer chat line so someone who was thinking of buying a Saturn could ask people who have one how they like it. If GM were smart, they'd do it themselves." That's what Lotus does: Hundreds of companies can enter the Lotus Notes technical support database directly. As a result, customers can get help not only from Lotus but also from each other. Results: better service, a wealth of new ideas and information for Lotus, a sense of camaraderie among customers and with Lotus—and substantial savings, for fully half of Lotus's technical support is now handled on-line, and often customers help each other out, at no cost to Lotus.

FOCUS ON CUSTOMERS AS INDIVIDUALS

Empowered customers enormously increase the amount of information a company has about its market (and customers have about it), but turning this knowledge into customer capital—a long-lived asset whose value is greater than the mere sum of transactions—requires the ability to respond flexibly to individual customers' wants. That, in turn, requires that companies break away from the mind-sets of mass marketing and mass production—which are inappropriate for most knowledge work, but which stubbornly endure in practice, however easily they are discarded in theory. The blind pursuit of market share, for example, is much less rewarding than an eyes-open pursuit of an increased share of the business of your best customers. My mailbox is full of envelopes from credit-card issuers eager to increase their market share. But—as card companies learn in every recession, when some customers go broke and become deadbeats—some market share is not worth getting. According to James Moore, a North Carolina consultant, the average bank actually loses money on three out of five retail accounts. (If you rarely use your credit card and never pay interest, you may be one of them.) To build customer capital, share-of-customer is a better strategy than share-of-market: Get your best customers to give you more of their business—not just a credit card, but checking and savings accounts, a mortgage, a retirement plan.

One-to-one dealings with customers depend on human and structural capital to develop the ability to do "mass customization." Motorola, in its Boynton Beach, Florida, factory, can profitably make pagers in up to 29,000 different varieties in lot sizes as small as one; indeed, a Motorola sales rep can design your pager with you on his laptop and dial in the specifications, and the factory can make your pager that day. The technology of mass customization and flexible manufacturing isn't an issue: It's there.

SHARE THE WINNINGS WITH YOUR CUSTOMERS

If the intangibles in customer relationships were not truly valuable, they would go unrewarded, because the market doesn't let a company get away with a price increase it has not earned—at least, not for long. Economists use the phrase "consumer surplus" to describe what happens when consumers get most of the benefit from a company's productivity gains: The computer industry, where rapidly increasing productivity has resulted in plummeting prices *and* reduced profit margins, is an example—though most consumers spend the surplus on souped-up machines rather than pocketing it.

Customer capital is wealth that's accumulated when the producer and the consumer don't wrestle over surplus they have created together (cost savings, for example), but agree tacitly or openly to own it together. The closer the partnership between buyer and seller, the greater that surplus can be. CIBC's Hubert Saint-Onge depicts the stages of buyer-supplier intimacy—and the growth in human, structural, and customer capital (on both sides of the relationship) that accompany moving from stage to stage—in this diagram:

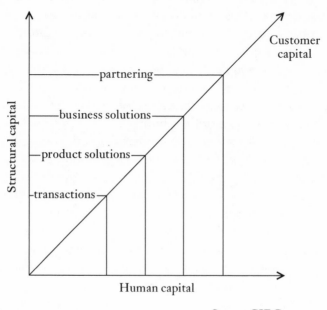

Source: CIBC

At the bottom are transactions, where sellers simply sell, buyers merely buy. If you buy beepers for your sales force off the shelf from an electronics store, you'll buy from whoever sells a decent beeper cheaply; there's little that either of you can do in the way of expertise or structures that will overcome the fact that you'd switch suppliers to get a better price. But say you want beepers made to your specifications, with features your sales force particularly needs. Then you're looking for a product solution. To find it, you'll have to share more information with the supplier, and vice versa. And you will create a tighter bond: Not every manufacturer can meet your specifications or give you the quick service you require. You're still focused on the product, but you will probably pay a premium for the beepers because they have been customized for you.

At the business solution level, the product becomes secondary. You, the buyer, have a business problem: You want your sales force to spend more time on the road but still keep in touch with the office; to do that, you want a communications system that links beepers, voice-mail, and e-mail. Getting that requires that you and the seller share a lot of information about your needs and his capabilities; it's likely that the relationship between you will last a long time, because you value his expertise and he doesn't want to lose your business. In fact, the price you pay will include a substantial fee for the supplier's expertise; he might sell you the beepers for near cost and make his profit from the fee he charges for designing the system. Finally, in a full-fledged partnership, the supplier might actually take over the management of the communications system, an outsourcing deal in which the supplier becomes an extension of your business—and you of his. Rather than negotiate a purchase, you will negotiate a contract, and the supplier will assume financial responsibility for providing the beepers and other equipment needed to run the system.

As you move up from transaction to partnership, the supplier increases his margins, his share of customer, his security—his customer capital. These are intense, demanding relationships. They are also immensely rewarding to both parties.

LEARN YOUR CUSTOMER'S BUSINESS, AND TEACH HER YOURS

The more you know about your customer's business, the better you can serve her. Business people have known that forever, but it's even more important for knowledge work, which is so often customized. The reverse is also true, and also more important in the information economy: Help your customer learn your business. Minnesota Mining and Manufacturing, for example, has always tried to get deep inside its customers—hoary company lore instructs salesmen to head for the smokestacks, where the real customers are, rather than the offices, where the purchasing department sits. Years ago 3M's sales forces became adept at cross-selling—using the fact that a salesman is ped-dling medical supplies to offload some Scotch Tape while he's at it. Now 3M has become much more aggressive about building intellec-tual capital by letting customers learn as much about its business as 3M learns about theirs. Marc Adam, head of marketing, is pushing full-body contact on the 3M side of the relationship by creating ma-jor-customer teams that include representatives from everything from R&D to sales. The idea is to foment a rich conversation that allows 3M to see not only what other stuff it can hawk but also its customers' unarticulated needs, so that 3M can invent products that meet them. Says William Coyne, who is the head of corporate R&D: "The tech-nical community can participate in that, where it couldn't participate in just selling more of what we already have." A recent instance: a fabric that allows water vapor to pass through but blocks liquids, de-veloped after doctors told 3M that they wanted surgical gowns that protected them from patients' blood but didn't leave them soaked in their own sweat.

Most buyer-seller relationships look like a bow tie:

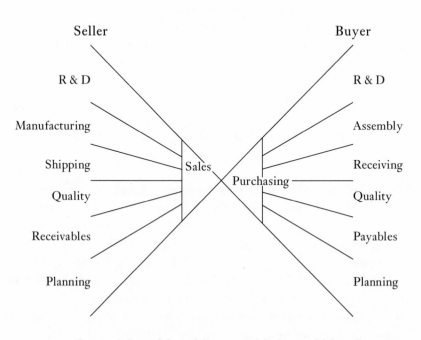

Source: Adapted from Minnesota Mining and Manufacturing

You cannot learn with your customers (or build customer capital) if you leave the relationship entirely in the hands of a salesman or purchaser. Instead, think of a diamond:

Seller   Buyer

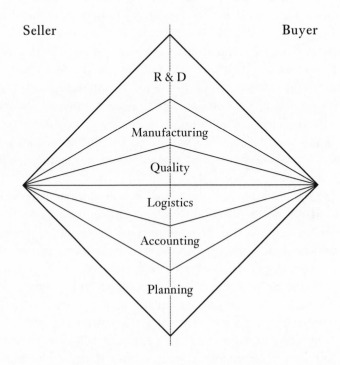

Source: Adapted from Minnesota Mining and Manufacturing

Especially with major customers, field a team that includes logistics, marketing, accounting, engineering, and other people. Their expertise can help your company understand what the other guy needs, how he makes money, and what extras you can provide.

BECOME INDISPENSABLE

Use the information you have to provide a vital service to your customer, making it harder for him to switch to another supplier. For example, a warehouse, by itself, adds no value; but if you manage your

customer's inventory for him, you're very valuable. In close partnerships, you can go further: Companies like Procter & Gamble and
Newell actually manage the stock on Wal-Mart's selling floor, in effect managing a piece of Wal-Mart. When customers depend on a
seller's intangibles—services, technology, etc.—power comes back
into balance.

If there ever was a company that could be vulnerable to a price
squeeze by its customers, it's W. W. Grainger (1995 sales: $3.3 bil-
lion). The Skokie, Illinois, outfit distributes maintenance, repair, and
operating supplies. Light bulbs. Safety glasses. Small motors. Paint
sprayers. Toilet paper. It's one thing to sell valuable components like
antilock brake systems. How do you invest in your customers when
you sell stuff that, however necessary, is often just an expense, not part
of their value-adding activities?*

Grainger's solution: Sell commodities as part of a "value package"
that is decidedly not a commodity. Depending on the customer, it
might include electronic ordering and payment or reengineering consulting services in the supply management field. Because Grainger
already manages large stocks of goods inexpensively—with an average
order worth just $129, it must keep processing and handling costs
low—it can frequently manage a customer's supply closet for less than
the customer would spend to do the job itself, passing on some of the
saving and keeping some for itself. The company will even arrange to
buy and ship supplies from its competitors. By selling an intangible—
management—Grainger has converted itself from a mere seller of
homely products to an indispensable ally. Like brand equity, which is
a form of customer capital, the intangible value of information allows
companies to charge a premium for their services.

Says Jordan Lewis: "Intelligent customers will totally ignore the
low-ball bidder, because he can't afford to keep up the R&D and the

---

* The urge to squeeze the Charmin costs is irresistible. I once worked for a
small book publisher that employed an indomitable wren of a woman named
Rose, who kept the files and bought supplies. Rose one day replaced the toilet-
paper dispensers in the lavatories with new hardware that held huge rolls of
cheaper paper. Based on the prices of the two kinds of paper and the cost of the
dispensers, and estimating how often the staff used the johns and how much toilet
paper was consumed, your correspondent calculated that it would take seven years
before the lower paper cost repaid the investment in new dispensers, not counting
the interest on the money invested. That didn't stop Rose.

cost of bringing in a new supplier is very high." A striking, analogous example of the power of information over price can be found in international trade. One way in which nations try to affect their international trade balances is by adjusting currency exchange rates. If central bankers can make the dollar fall vis-à-vis the yen, then imports to the United States from Japan cost more—in effect, the exchange-rate mechanism imposes a price increase beyond the control of the exporting company. But changes in currency rates have become increasingly less effective. Dennis Encarnation, a professor at Harvard Business School, showed why in his book *Rivals Beyond Trade*. Encarnation found that fully 56 percent of trade among the United States, the European Union, and Japan is intra-company trade—that is, parts or finished goods shipped from one division of a company to a subsidiary or sister division overseas. Intra-company trade is much less price sensitive than arm's-length trade between unrelated companies. A major reason: Intra-company trade includes a much larger knowledge component—design, R&D, management systems, plans and strategies, personal relationships; because these intangibles are not monetized, they are unaffected by exchange rates. In addition, because companies assume a long-term relationship with their subsidiaries (but might not make the same assumption about outside customers or suppliers) they are more willing to sacrifice short-term price advantages to protect the value of the enduring tie.

TEN PRINCIPLES FOR MANAGING INTELLECTUAL CAPITAL

Several key principles of intellectual capital management emerge from a close look at human, structural, and customer capital:

1. Companies don't own human and customer capital; companies share the ownership of these assets with, in the case of human capital, their employees; and in the case of customer capital, with suppliers and customers. Only by recognizing this shared ownership can a company manage and profit from these assets. An adversarial relationship with employees, like one with suppliers and customers, may save or make a few dollars in the short run, but at the expense of destroying wealth.

2. To create human capital it can use, a company needs to foster teamwork, communities of practice, and other social forms of learning. Individual talent is great, but it walks out the door; corporate stars, like movie stars, have to be managed like the high-risk propositions they are. Interdisciplinary teams capture, formalize, and *capitalize* talent, because it becomes shared, less dependent on any individual. Even if group members leave, the knowledge stays behind. If the company provides the locus of learning—if it's the hotbed of new or expert thinking in any area—it will be the chief beneficiary of learning in the field, whether or not some of it "leaks" to other companies.

3. To manage and develop human capital, companies must unsentimentally recognize that some employees, however intelligent or talented they are, aren't assets: Organizational wealth is created around those skills and talents that are (1) proprietary, in the sense that no one does them better and (2) strategic, in that the work they do creates the value customers pay for. People with those talents are assets to invest in. Others are costs to be minimized, as far as your business is concerned; the skills might be assets for someone else.

4. Structural capital is the intangible asset companies own outright; it's therefore what managers can most easily control. Paradoxically, however, it's what customers—who are where the money comes from—care least about. Just as that government is best that governs least, so those structures are best that obtrude least. Manage your company, therefore, to make it as easy as possible for your customers to work with your people.

5. Structural capital serves two purposes: to amass stockpiles of knowledge that support the work customers value, and to speed the flow of that information inside the company. Manufacturers have learned that just-in-time inventories are more efficient than warehouses full of stuff you have just-in-case; so it is with knowledge. What you need should be ready-to-hand; what you *might* need should be easy to get.

6. Information and knowledge can and should substitute for expensive physical and financial assets; every company ought to examine its capital spending and ask: Can inexpensive intangibles do the work of costly physical assets?

7. Knowledge work is custom work. Mass-produced solutions won't yield high profits. Even in businesses long characterized by mass production, there are opportunities to create special relationships—often by providing management services—that will yield value and profits for both you and your customer.

8. Every company should reanalyze the value chain of the industry it participates in—along its whole length, from rawest of raw materials to end user—to see what information is most crucial. Generally, for knowledge work, it will be found downstream, toward customers.

9. Focus on the flow of information, not the flow of materials.

Whether you're looking at human, structural, or customer capital, or their interactions, don't confuse the "real" economy with the "intangible" one. It used to be that information supported the "real" business; now it is the real business.

10. Human, structural, and customer capital work together. It's not enough to invest in people, systems, and customer separately. They can support one another; they can detract from one another. It's worth listing a few of the ways in which this interaction takes place:

Human capital and structural capital reinforce each other when a company has a shared sense of purpose combined with an entrepreneurial spirit; when management places a high value on agility; when management governs more by carrot than by stick. On the other hand, human and structural capital destroy each other when too much of what goes on in an organization isn't valued by customers, or when the corporate center attempts to control behavior rather than strategy.

Human capital and customer capital grow when individuals feel responsible for their part in the enterprise, interact directly with customers, and know what knowledge and skills customers expect and value. An employee who doesn't know or have those skills lowers the value of both human and customer capital. So does an internally preoccupied organization. It's become common to speak of "internal customers" to encourage people to treat their colleagues as if they were as important as those outside. Nonsense. There is no such thing as an internal customer, no substitute for the real thing. Rather than encourage colleagues to treat each other like customers, get them out to mingle with the genuine article.

Customer capital and structural capital grow when the company and its customers learn from each other; when they actively strive to make their interactions informal—to be "easy to do business with." If a cynic in your shop wonders if you're more loyal to the customer than to the company, you're on the right track. On the other hand, if your interactions with customers are limited to writing orders and fielding complaints, your customer and structural capital are working to destroy each other. Every industry has a "most informed vendor"—someone, perhaps not the category leader, who knows the most about the business and is willing to share his expertise with his suppliers and customers. That guy wins.

PART THREE

The Net

▼

CONNECTION

ALL CIVILIZATION BEGINS WITH A THEOCRACY AND
ENDS IN DEMOCRACY. . . . EVERY GREAT POPULAR
MOVEMENT, WHATEVER MAY BE ITS CAUSE AND ITS
FINAL END, ALWAYS SETS FREE, IN ITS LAST
PRECIPITATE, THE SPIRIT OF LIBERTY. . . . AUTHORITY
IS SHATTERED, UNITY BIFURCATED. . . . THE NOBLES
FORCE THEMSELVES A WAY THROUGH THE
PRIESTHOOD. THE PEOPLE FORCES ITS WAY THROUGH
THE NOBILITY.
—VICTOR HUGO

CHAPTER 10

The New Economics of Information

Since 1985, the value of international trade has grown twice as fast as the value of the world's output of goods and services. International financial transactions have grown about twice as fast as trade. Markets for derivative financial instruments (futures, options, and more exotic securities) have grown more rapidly than have markets for the stocks and bonds that ostensibly underlie them. As former Citicorp chairman Walter Wriston has said, "Information about money has become more valuable than money itself." The intangible economy is now arguably of equal or greater size than the tangible economy.

I almost wrote "the tangible economy on which it is based," but that would be wrong. To be sure, the tangible and intangible economic realms coexist, connect, overlap, interweave, interact. They breathe the same economic air. They serve the same human needs for food, shelter, clothing, love, and art—the preservation of the species, the aspirations of the soul. Intangible assets—intellectual capital in its human, structural, and customer manifestations—can powerfully support the work of drilling for oil as well as the work of trading financial instruments nowhere found in nature; conversely, owners and employees of the most disembodied business know that you cannot eat bytes.

But it is no longer accurate to say that the intangible economy is "based" on the tangible one. The ingredients, assets, and outputs of knowledge work, however nearby they lie to the resources of physical work, often differ from them in kind. Many aspects of the production, distribution, and sale of knowledge are amenable to the same analysis and obedient to the same laws as the buying and selling of aubergines or automobiles. Others, however, are as different from the economics of the tangible as quantum physics is from Newtonian. The new rules are the subject of this chapter. If it gets theoretical, bear with it: The economics of information has big and very practical consequences for management and for your career, which the next two chapters will lay out in progressively more concrete fashion. Economics is the terrain on which strategy unfolds. If you do not understand why the new economy is the way it is, you will be less likely to make smart decisions about how to survive in it.

Information: A Weird Resource

Information and knowledge differ from cash, natural resources, labor, and machinery. First, knowledge is what economists call a "public good." That's jargon meaning that knowledge can be used without being consumed. It is nonsubtractive: My obtaining a piece of knowledge in no way diminishes your ability to obtain it, too. This is not so for a chocolate ice cream cone or a seat on the bus. Conversely, the cost of producing knowledge is unaffected by how many people eventually use it; it will have cost me just as much to produce the knowledge in this book if 5,000 people read it as if 500,000 do. To be sure, the particular copy that you are holding cannot be read by a dozen people simultaneously, and the printing cost did depend on the number printed; but those economic facts apply to the *artifact*, not the *knowledge*. As we saw in Chapter 2, knowledge and its wrapper are not the same. Often, furthermore, the means of copying knowledge—tape decks, Xerox machines, television sets, computers—are under the control of consumers, not producers. Production capacity is virtually unconstrained—so that, for example, the annual Oscar telecast is viewed by several billion people at no greater cost to the Academy of Motion Picture Arts and Sciences than if the audience were limited to those who could fit into the Dorothy Chandler Pavilion.

Consequently, knowledge exists independent of space. Like quantum particles, it can be in more than one place at a time. Sell me a cake and you no longer have it. Sell me the recipe and we both have it. Where intellectual assets and intangible outputs are concerned, you can have your cake and eat it too. But you can't take it back. A seller can repossess a car, but not a fact. There's a catch in the economics of information, and it's Catch-22, and both buyer and seller are subject to it: The buyer cannot judge whether it's worth paying for a piece of information until he has it; but once he possesses it, he no longer needs to purchase it.

A further oddity—compared to transactions involving tangible items—is this: The fact that you have sold information to me does not prevent you from selling the same item to someone else, like a college professor who delivers the same lecture year after year. Nor does it prevent me—provided I obey intellectual property laws—from reselling what you taught me; this is what journalists do, after all.

But if knowledge is unconstrained by space, some forms of it are extremely sensitive to time—more so than physical assets. Though these depreciate, sometimes to the point of complete obsolescence (the manual typewriter in my closet isn't worth much nowadays), it's usually a slow slide, whereas a hot tip on a horse, potentially worth thousands before post time, loses all its value the second the betting window shuts. This time sensitivity explains why whole industries have grown up based on anticipating what knowledge will be: weather forecasting; political polling; Wall Street.

Abundance is a second major difference between knowledge and other economic resources. Value in economics, the textbooks say, derives from scarcity. "Buy land," humorist Will Rogers advised; "they ain't makin' any more of it." We make more knowledge every day, however; and, as we will see, frequently knowledge increases in value because it is abundant, not because it is scarce.

Although there is no reliable way to measure the world's stock of knowledge, all manner of indexes point to an ever-growing heap of it.

The number of patent applications filed in the United States, for example, increases inexorably; in 1993, there were 189,000 applications, versus 72,000 in 1953. Though knowledge is frequently superseded, especially scientific knowledge, it rarely vanishes. Says Charles Goldfinger, a French financial-services expert and thinker whose book *L'Utile et le futile: L'Économie de l'immatériel (Useful and Useless: The Intangible Economy)** is the best discussion I have seen about the economic behavior of intangibles: "[Information] is structurally abundant. There is always too much information. Every economic activity produces more information than it consumes." Refining a barrel of oil, for example, depletes petrochemicals but merely *uses* petrochemistry, and produces additional information, such as the characteristics of the oil in the barrel, its cost, whereabouts, and destination. Talent may be scarce, but not knowledge: Humankind knows more than ever before.

In the knowledge economy, the scarce resource is ignorance. Amid information overload, says Eli Noam, head of the Center for Telecommunications and Information Studies at the Columbia Business School: "The value added is the information subtracted." Noam means that selection and screening—deleting knowledge—are critical: extracting the relevant numbers from a mass of data, choosing the best shows for an entertainment network. Because information wants to be free, people pay a premium to bottle it up, for example by having unlisted telephone numbers.

Third, most knowledge-intensive goods and services ("congealed knowledge") have a cost structure that is dramatically different from the cost structure of "congealed material." Costs are heavily frontloaded: That is, the cost of producing the first copy is disproportionately high in relation to the cost of further copies. In book publishing, the up-front cost, which includes the author's time as well as the costs of design and typesetting, is dramatically higher than the paper, printing, and binding costs of subsequent copies. The more intangible a product—the more nearly it is pure knowledge—the greater the discrepancy between sunk and marginal costs; the cost of producing and shipping an electronic copy of a document is a mere spark of electricity, and mostly borne by the recipient rather than the "manufacturer." The same holds true for software, pharmaceuticals, movies, etc. The

* Paris: Editions Odile Jacob, 1994.

tendency of costs to accumulate at the front end of production processes shows up in industrial goods, too, as their information content grows; for airplanes, automobiles, and many other products the cost of design and research and development is rising in relation to direct manufacturing costs. Fuji Electric, Japan's fourth biggest maker of electrical machinery, uses a flexible manufacturing system to turn out magnetic connectors used to control motors. Those Jack-of-all-trades tools are very expensive, but Fuji can now make 8,000 different varieties with virtually no additional cost to tool up for a new variety—almost all the investment in a new product is R&D.

Finally, when it comes to creative work, there is no meaningful economic correlation between knowledge input and knowledge output: The value of intellectual capital isn't necessarily related to the cost of acquiring it, which makes it impossible to use a measure of what you do as a way of revealing how you're doing. A study by the Arthur D. Little firm showed that the productiveness of pharmaceutical companies' R&D couldn't be inferred from their spending; rivals Eli Lilly and Merck & Co., for example, invested about the same amounts from 1980 to 1988, but Lilly had much less to show for it. The benefits of training are similarly unrelated to expenditure. Fixed capital such as machinery is much more predictable, which is why accountants agree that the price paid for equipment, minus accumulated depreciation, reasonably expresses its value and can be entered on a balance sheet, while holding that investment in intangibles, whose ultimate worth is indeterminable, should not be capitalized.

Breaking the Law—and Getting Away with It

Nonsubtractive, structurally abundant, front-loaded, and unpredictable: When the most important economic resource has these characteristics, it's no wonder that information-rich businesses such as finance and computer software are notoriously volatile. Frequently they even venture outside fundamental laws of economics.

The law of supply and demand, for example, holds that there is a point of equilibrium between what sellers produce and what buyers purchase, and that the pricing mechanism prevents them from getting too far out of whack. This law remains on the books of the knowledge economy, but it's less rigorously and often capriciously enforced. Liquid and efficient financial markets, for example, ought to display nearly perfect equilibrium, but instead are increasingly volatile as what's traded moves from the tangible (shares that are a proxy for the value of physical assets) to the intangible—information about the future and about the value of corporations' intellectual assets. One reason supply and demand breaks down: Many intangibles—think of consulting, training, education, entertainment—are created jointly by producers and consumers; who then is the buyer and who the seller? Another reason: Often production capacity (supply) is controlled by consumers rather than the ostensible producers. There are as many "units" of an episode of "Seinfeld" as there are people who want to watch it. Excess capacity, anathema to markets for physical goods, can make intangible markets more efficient.

Knowledge-intensive businesses violate another basic economic law, that of diminishing returns, as often as New Yorkers disregard the prohibition against jaywalking. The law of diminishing returns, which like the U.S. Constitution dates from the eighteenth century when it was described by Thomas Malthus and David Ricardo, says that there comes a point in any business activity where additional investment is less productive than prior investment: Two workers per garbage truck might double its productivity, but four workers won't double it again. Competition for scarce resources, the theory goes, shrinks marginal returns on investment; companies therefore reduce investment to a level consonant with the average profits in their industry and its structure stabilizes. One reason diminishing returns hold sway is the counterintuitive fact that capitalism abhors profits and does its damnedest to destroy them. A highly profitable business attracts competitors who are willing to make a little less or who undercut the first guy's price because they can freeload off his investments in technology or market development. The greater a company's success, the more vulnerable it becomes.

Much economic behavior in the Information Age, however, displays increasing rather than diminishing returns. According to Brian Arthur, the Stanford University and Sante Fe Institute economist:

> The parts of the economy that are resource-based (agriculture, bulk-goods production, mining) are still for the most part subject

to diminishing returns. Here conventional economics rightly holds sway. The parts of the economy that are knowledge-based, on the other hand, are largely subject to increasing returns. Products such as computers, pharmaceuticals, missiles, aircraft, automobiles, software, telecommunications equipment, or fiber optics are complicated to design and to manufacture. They require large initial investments in research, development, and tooling, but once sales begin, incremental production is relatively cheap . . . Not only do the costs of producing high-technology products fall as a company makes more of them, but the benefits of using them increase . . . When one brand gains a significant market share, people have a strong incentive to buy more of the same product so as to be able to exchange information with those using it already.

Where first-copy costs are high and subsequent-copy costs negligible, economies of scale go off the charts. Some quick math: Imagine that two companies each spend $5,000 to develop competing products that sell for $10 and cost $2.50 apiece to manufacture, advertise, and distribute. The first company sells 2,000 copies; its profit is $20,000 – ($5,000 + $5,000) = $10,000. The second company sells 1,000 copies, and makes $10,000 – ($5,000 + $2,500) = $2,500. A two-to-one difference in sales leads to a four-to-one difference in profit, an unsurprising reward for scale.

Now change the picture, by increasing the development cost by half, to $7,500, and cutting the marginal unit cost in half, to $1.25. The first company still makes $10,000: $20,000 – ($7,500 + $2,500). The second company, however, makes just $1,250: $10,000 in sales, minus $7,500 + $1,250. The two-to-one difference in revenues now produces an eight-to-one difference in profit. As the ratio between first-copy and marginal costs increases, so does the return to scale.

Economies of scale matter in every business, but their power is exponentially greater in knowledge-intensive businesses with high upfront costs.* Where the product is dematerialized, merely ones and

---

* There are countervailing cases where technology has lowered up-front costs. Making computers has become a high-stakes business that treats laggards brutally, but *using* computers has lowered up-front costs in, for example, publishing, where inexpensive computers replace expensive typesetting machines. Result: More small companies have come into being. In 1984, the year the Macintosh was introduced, just over a thousand small publishers (some with just one book to peddle) sought International Standard Book Numbers, which allow books to be

zeros, the advantages to scale theoretically approach infinity. The market leader, furthermore, can pour money into research and development, forcing the followers into a nasty Hobson's choice: Match the R&D spending and go broke, or don't match it and go broke. A few years ago I got the chance to play a simple computer game devised by Merck's chief financial officer Judy Lewent to show how high-tech's economics work in the pharmaceutical industry: Players who cannot afford to match the leader's R&D investments die, while the rich get richer. Often high-tech competition is vicious, with no purse money for place and show.

Overwhelming scale economies aren't the only agent of increasing returns in knowledge-based businesses. Another factor: network externalities. This refers to the fact that the value of knowledge increases because it is widely used. A notable instance is Microsoft's Windows operating system: Because so many computers have Windows, software designers flock to write applications for it, and get around to designing versions for Apple's Macintosh or IBM's OS/2 later if at all. The plethora of hot software, in turn, makes Windows more attractive to computer buyers, in a self-reinforcing cycle of positive feedback. The fact that most of your friends and business associates use Windows creates a second virtuous circle encouraging you to join them to be assured of compatibility. The presence of so many customers and so much software strengthens distribution and service networks, a third virtuous circle. VHS videocassette recorders largely drove Sony's Betamax off the market for the same reason of increasing returns: when VHS took the lead in sales, movie companies began issuing more VHS tapes than Beta, which made VHS still more desirable relative to Betamax.

In industries that depend on communication (not many don't), network externalities are especially powerful, because they create the standards required for communication to occur, just as the utility of English as a language—and the value, therefore, of having the language in your capital stock—increases precisely because so many other people have the same asset. Value can also vanish almost overnight, as happened when the fax put the kibosh on the Telex. Maps are littered

---

given bar codes that can be scanned by booksellers' computers; in 1995, 5,514 received the numbers. (See Doreen Carvajal, "Do-It-Yourselfers Carve Out a Piece of the Publishing Pie," *New York Times*, April 28, 1996, pp. 1, 19.)

with old river towns, canal towns, and railroad towns that died after new networks—highways and airline hubs—supplanted them.

Network externalities are a form of customer capital. Their value is jointly created by and mutually benefits both the supplier and the customer. Microsoft is one beneficiary of Windows' network externalities, but far from the only one and not the biggest; the total sales of what one might call the Windows Metropolitan Area—revenues from all makers' Windows-based software and from computers and microprocessors such as Intel's chips—are about $66 billion, of which Microsoft garners only 4 percent.

In games of increasing returns, losers get immured in market niches, like a player struggling in the final stages of the Japanese game Go. Winners can become nearly impossible to dislodge, even by a superior product. The QWERTY keyboard configuration (named for the first letters on the top row of a typewriter) is a classic example of this "lock-in" effect: Designed to prevent keys from jamming on a manual typewriter, it became standard because the Remington Sewing Machine Co., which adopted the QWERTY layout, got a lead in the market that made it more worthwhile for typists to learn it rather than rival keyboards. That, in turn, drove other manufacturers to adopt QWERTY. People have designed keyboards that permit faster typing, but no one wants them. Network externalities resulted in customer capital—typists' investment in learning QWERTY—that is unassailable.

A New Economics Means New Thinking About Strategy

The weird economics of information presents organizations with a corresponding set of new strategic and management challenges. They can't ignore supply and demand or diminishing returns—these laws haven't been repealed, only riddled with loopholes. Nor can they assume that the old rules apply. One new problem: the need to place enormous bets early. We've seen that high-tech businesses often incur huge initial costs, whether in R&D or in network development. Add to this the rich-get-richer effects of lock-in. Once lock-in occurs, where you can go depends on where you are coming from. The sum of these facts is that someone hoping to ride the curve of increasing returns needs the temperament of a gambler but the deep pockets of a big company—not a combination frequently found in corporate cultures.

Information Age companies seeking to exploit information's economics need to understand the strategic armamentarium available to them. There are essentially three kinds—families—of weapons.

USING FRIENDS—SOME OF WHOM MIGHT BE COMPETITORS—TO CREATE AND SUSTAIN EARLY ADVANTAGES IN MARKET SHARE

The economics of information lead to what might seem like strange business bedfellows: For example, it made sense for Matsushita not to be proprietary about its VHS technology for videocassette recorders; by licensing it widely and inexpensively to competitors, Matsushita caused VHS to become the industry standard, walling out Sony's proprietary Betamax. By contrast, Apple for years stuck to the seemingly rational business plan of protecting its profit margins by not letting other companies clone the Macintosh operating system—a decision that in retrospect, *The Wall Street Journal* said, was "one of the seminal blunders of business history."

In the software industry, Netscape and Sun Microsystems have gone Matsushita one better: They *give away* copies of their software. End-users pay nothing to download Netscape's web-browsing Navigator from the Internet—but they create a huge demand for Navigator-based applications, which can be written only by people who have a version of the software they paid for. Sun's Java, a programming language that produces applications that can run on any operating system—Windows, Mac, IBM, Unix, etc.—goes to end-users and application developers for free, unless you want to embed it in your products, in which case you must buy a license. Says Eric Schmidt, chief technology officer at Sun. "We want ubiquity first, then profitability."

Alliances—especially with distributors and suppliers—offer powerful support to any business. General Motors, Ford, and Chrysler wouldn't have gone very far against steam-powered cars and railroads without the support of the oil industry and government road-builders.

Alliances are especially powerful weapons in information-intensive businesses, because the low marginal cost of information—its near-zero manufacturing cost—allows alliances to be assembled quickly, and lock-in makes them strong. (Alliances and virtual corporations will be discussed more in the next chapter.)

COOPERATIVE STRATEGIES FOR DEFENDING LEADERSHIP POSITIONS

Where marginal costs are negligible, market leaders have enormous pricing flexibility. They can spread fixed costs over a large base of customers, seriously squeezing competitors who have to recover equally high research and development costs from a smaller market. The effect potentially surges the full length of the value chain, from suppliers to customers, dropping costs for everyone who takes part—*provided the company uses its leverage to create customer capital, rather than simply squeezing its suppliers and distributors to increase its own profit margins.* A powerful company that uses its leverage to push inventory out of its warehouses and onto the books of its suppliers or customers has simply tilled the soil in which a competitor can emerge; but if the company works with customers and suppliers to drain inventory out of the whole system, lowering costs for all and sharing the savings regardless of who ends up holding the bag, then it locks them into its network. One way to test whether you are riding the market or fighting it: Examine not just your own market share but that of your suppliers and customers. Are your most important and fastest-growing customers also the fastest-growing companies in their industry? Is *your share* of their business growing as fast as (or, better, faster than) their overall business? If so, increasing returns are working for you.

LEARNING AS A COMPETITIVE WEAPON

Like alliances and market power, knowledge of markets, customers, technologies, and processes helps any organization grow; but also like them knowledge gains added power when it is the primary ingredient of a business. Knowledge then becomes, in effect, part of what the two parties trade. Companies that learn with their customers (simultaneously teaching them and learning from them) come to depend on each other. Their people and systems—human and structural capital—mesh better than before.

Oddly, and wonderfully, the very intangibility and volatility of information make it durable; its permanence is a function of its ability to permeate boundaries through which the tangible cannot pass. Until Gutenberg invented movable type, Victor Hugo wrote in *Nôtre-Dame de Paris*, mankind sought to protect knowledge by inscribing it in stone. Architectural monuments like cathedrals were "the great book of humanity," on whose portals and statuary were carved and painted the intellectual and spiritual inheritance of the race, rock-solid and seemingly indestructible. Yet when knowledge is freed of that baggage, it grows stronger, Hugo wrote: "In printed form thought is more imperishable than ever: it is volatile, intangible, indestructible; it is in the air we breathe. In the days of architecture thought became a mountain, and boldly possessed itself of an age or a place. Now it becomes a flock of birds that scatter themselves unto the four winds of heaven, and occupy at once every point of air and space. . . . It is possible to demolish a pile; but how can we destroy omnipresence?"

Now, further dematerialized by the digital revolution, knowledge has become still more available—and indestructible—weaving webs of incalculable and nearly unassailable worth. To thrive in this immaterial economy, organizations and individuals need to find ways of working that are as different from their old ways as birds are from stones.

CHAPTER 11

The Network Organization

What is the management structure of a flock of birds? Geese on the wing form a V, but their leader has no special authority, and cedes his place if he tires or the flight changes direction. No hierarchy determines the direction or order of ducks or pigeons in a flock, or a school of brightly colored sergeant major fish on a Bahamian reef. In response to a stimulus—a breeze, a gunshot, an abrupt move by a watching snorkler, a passing stingray—the flock or school might suddenly veer, reverse, seeming to follow a new leader who actually had nothing to do with the change in direction. By watching films, scientists have found that birds in a flock turn within one-seventieth of a second of one another—faster than their individual reaction time. Simulations by Craig Reynolds, a programmer at Silicon Studio, a developer of multimedia software, show that realistic artificial flocks can be created by giving computer-created birds, bats, and other creatures three "simple steering behaviors": separation (don't crowd your neighbors), alignment ("steer toward the average heading of local flockmates"), and cohesion ("move toward the average position of local flockmates"). Reynolds used these rules, expressed as equations, to create realistic computer-generated flocks of bats and penguins in the film *Batman Returns*. To someone watching a flock of birds, Reynolds says, "most puzzling is the strong impression of intentional centralized control. Yet all evidence indicates that flock motion must be merely the aggregate result of the actions of individual animals, each acting solely on the basis of its local perception of the world." In these man-made flocks, as in nature, there is no leader, no chain of command, no span of control. There is instead a sort of shared brain, a loosely conjoined network of relationships and impulses.

Networking is lots more than a metaphysical idea, a technological phenomenon, or a hot industry. It is the most important development in management since DuPont, General Motors, and others invented the modern corporations—with its headquarters officers and staff, multiple divisions, and functional departments—before World War II. Where once there were pyramids, bosses, departments, troops, now there are webs, nodes, clusters, flocks. In companies whose wealth is intellectual capital, networks, rather than hierarchies, are the right organizational design. In this chapter, we'll show what new forms of organizational design emerge and how they fundamentally alter the nature and agenda of management.

How Technology Destroyed the Hierarchy

There were networks before there were computers: old-boy networks; the skein of contacts that led you to your job; the tangled macramé of connections and back channels in a company's informal organization, which gets things done and fills out the paperwork later. Important as they are, these networks are unofficial. What's new is the deliberately networked organization, made possible because it has become cheap enough to put a computer on every desk. A technology network supercharges social networks. No longer adjuncts of the hierarchy, they supplant it. They become the means by which the organization does work. More and more, the operations companies conduct on-line are critical ones—trading at brokerage houses, stock management at Wal-Mart, design and development of new aircraft at Boeing.

When computers were new, no one imagined they would subvert centralized power—on the contrary. In 1958, thirty-nine years ago, *Harvard Business Review* carried an article called "Management in the 1980s" by Harold Leavitt and Thomas Whisler. Predicting the future, especially in print, is always brave. Leavitt and Whisler did better than most: Just two years after William H. Whyte's *The Organization Man* described the rise of the middle manager, they foresaw his demise, prophesying that the computer would do to middle management what the Black Death did to fourteenth-century Europe. And so it has. Middle managers account for about 5 to 8 percent of the workforce, but nearly 20 percent of recent layoffs. A middle manager should not enter his boss's office alone.

But Leavitt and Whisler got one thing very wrong. In their time, the only computer they knew or could imagine was the mainframe, and so they conceived a workplace in which the surviving middle managers were tightly controlled from on high, just as in George Orwell's *1984* citizens of Oceana mutely obeyed the Telescreen, which was essentially a mainframe hooked to dumb terminals. In 1968, in the prophetic movie *2001*, the same Orwellian vision took the form of the malevolent Hal. Remember "I am a human being. Do not bend, fold, spindle, or mutilate"?

In January 1984—the real 1984, not Orwell's—Apple introduced the Macintosh. The famous commercial shown during the Super Bowl that year paid homage to Orwell's vision by blowing it up. Apple founder Steve Jobs's prophecy—that the personal computer would change the world—has proven more accurate than Orwell's. In business, Frederick Kovac, who is in charge of technology and strategy at the Goodyear Tire and Rubber Company, says: "The PC destroyed the hierarchy." Why was the PC responsible? His gnomic answer: "Because that's not why we bought them."

Actually, Jobs was only half-right. On January 1, 1984, three weeks before Apple brought computing to "the rest of us," a consent degree, signed by AT&T and the U.S. Department of Justice, took effect. It broke up AT&T, ending monopoly telephone service in the United States—Bastille Day in the history of the Information Age. Before, it was illegal to connect any device to a telephone line that was not approved and supplied by Ma Bell. That same year, the U.K. Government privatized British Telecom. Today networks of PCs, linked by telephone lines, are the dominant technology by which companies manage knowledge—which is to say, the dominant means by which they manage, period.

How Networks Change the Work of Managers

The extraordinary economic power of a network—expensive to create, cheap and fast to use, accessible from any point at any time, valuable in geometric relation to the number of its parts—is available to any organization that wants to get the highest returns out of its intellectual capital. The greatest challenge for the Information Age manager is to create an organization that can share knowledge. Networks do that; they connect people to people and people to data. They allow information that once flowed through hierarchies—from me up to my boss and then hers, then down to your boss and to you—to pass directly between us. Information being power, that can greatly hurry the process of cutting slices from the old wedding-cake bureaucracy. Says Bill Raduchel, chief information officer of Sun Microsystems: "E-mail is a major cultural event—it changes the way you run the organization."

For one thing, networks irrevocably subvert managerial authority. They inspire an informal style; bossy behavior—such as bosses are prone to—is not congenial to them. People communicating over electronic networks are less deferential to their superiors and more likely to speak their minds, sometimes intemperately.

Second, in a wired world, basic management jobs such as planning, budgeting, and supervising must be done differently. Tools like e-mail, teleconferencing, and groupware let people work together despite distance and almost regardless of departmental or corporate boundaries, which networks fuzz up or even obliterate. A person might spend most of his day with an interdepartmental team led by someone from another part of the company in another part of the world, doing a project his nominal boss knows little about. Then what, pray, is a chain of command? Says Susan Falzon, a principal at CSC Research & Advisory Services in Cambridge, Massachusetts, who in 1993 made a study of networks in more than seventy-five companies: "When work is carried out through networks, an organization's structure changes whether you want it to or not. I can't find a single case where it doesn't happen." One outfit Falzon studied was a big company's legal department, with offices across the United States. When the lawyers were wired to one another and to the files (as well as to databases such as Lexis), junior attorneys asked for less help from their seniors than before. Instead, they dug through data on the net or asked colleagues in their peer group who worked in other offices. They, and their bosses, spent more time doing legal work, less being managed and managing. Her conclusion: "In a network, supervision changes. There's less supervision of the content of the work, more supervision of a person's overall performance and career." Hellene Runtagh, CEO of General Electric Information Services is blunt: "Communications in a network are absolutely incompatible with a strict, parochial hierarchy."

Indeed, the very nature of knowledge work gives networks an advantage over pyramidal forms of organizational design. Says John Manzo, VP of engineering at Pitney Bowes: "To develop complex products, you need lots of people with specialized knowledge, working together in a little virtual department." Functional organizations do an excellent job of developing experts, but a lousy job of linking them with experts in other fields. In the gabby, "does anybody know?" environs of a network, trolling for brainpower is simple and quick and it's enormously easier to keep your "little virtual department" informed.

The network's edge is that it can deliver information just in time, not just in case. It can add value—particularly information value, the most important kind—more quickly and accurately than a bureaucracy. This happens for two reasons: First, hierarchies filter information—to keep the system orderly, information moves "through channels," up, over, and down. That means information is edited, delayed, politicized, and sometimes destroyed.* News on the Rialto comes secondhand: A salesman's two-page report becomes a paragraph in a district supervisor's weekly roundup, and mere numbers on a chart in

---

* A hilarious example of how information moves in hierarchies appeared in my e-mail. This purportedly is actual correspondence between a London hotel's staff and one of its guests. Readers of Peter Senge's *The Fifth Discipline* will recognize it as a case of the Beer Game run amok.

the regional manager's monthly report. Of course top brass needs summaries. But filtering has dangers. Criticism is toned down; ideas are edited to fit your preconceptions of the boss's viewpoint.

Mind you, hierarchies also add knowledge—for example, senior management's experience. An "adhocracy" needs to find a way to

---

Dear Maid,

Please do not leave any more of those little bars of soap in my bathroom since I have brought my own bath-sized Dial. Please remove the six un-opened little bars from the shelf under the medicine chest and another three in the shower soap dish. They are in my way.

Thank you,
S. Berman

Dear Room 635,

I am not your regular maid. She will be back tomorrow, Thursday, from her day off. I took the 3 hotel soaps out of the shower soap dish as you requested. The 6 bars on your shelf I took out of your way and put on top of your Kleenex dispenser in case you should change your mind. This leaves only the 3 bars I left today which my instructions from the manage-ment is to leave 3 soaps daily. I hope this is satisfactory.

Kathy, Relief Maid

Dear Maid,

I hope you are my regular maid. Apparently Kathy did not tell you about my note to her concerning the little bars of soap. When I got back to my room this evening I found you had added 3 little Camays to the shelf under my medicine cabinet. I am going to be here in the hotel for two weeks and have brought my own bath-size Dial so I won't need those 6 little Camays which are on the shelf. They are in my way when shaving, brushing teeth, etc. Please remove them.

S. Berman

Dear Mr. Berman,

My day off was last Wed. so the relief maid left 3 hotel soaps which we are instructed by the management. I took the 6 soaps which were in your way on the shelf and put them in the soap dish where your Dial was. I put the Dial in the medicine cabinet for your convenience. I didn't remove the 3 complimentary soaps which are always placed inside the medicine cabinet for all new check-ins and which you did not object to when you checked in last Monday. Please let me know if I can be of further assistance.

Your regular maid,
Dotty

restore the perspective delayering might remove. Says James Nesbit, former chief information officer of Monsanto:

> For my first twenty years at the company I relied on corporate staffs over and over—experts in public relations, labor law, antitrust, manufacturing. You went up the hierarchy and lots of 'wise' people looked at what you were doing. When we decentralized, all these capabilities were torn apart and were not replaced in kind. You no longer have George at corporate who is the expert.

Dear Mr. Berman,
The assistant manager, Mr. Kensedder, informed me this A.M. that you called him last evening and said you were unhappy with your maid service. I have assigned a new girl to your room. I hope you will accept my apologies for any past inconvenience. If you have any future complaints please contact me so I can give it my personal attention. Call extension 1108 between 8AM and 5PM. Thank you.

Elaine Carmen, Housekeeper

Dear Miss Carmen,
It is impossible to contact you by phone since I leave the hotel for business at 745 AM and don't get back before 530 or 6PM. That's the reason I called Mr. Kensedder last night. You were already off duty. I only asked Mr. Kensedder if he could do anything about those little bars of soap. The new maid you assigned me must have thought I was a new check-in today, since she left another 3 bars of hotel soap in my medicine cabinet along with her regular delivery of 3 bars on the bath-room shelf. In just 5 days here I have accumulated 24 little bars of soap. Why are you doing this to me?

S. Berman

Dear Mr. Berman,
Your maid, Kathy, has been instructed to stop delivering soap to your room and remove the extra soaps. If I can be of further assistance, please call extension 1108 between 8AM and 5PM. Thank you,

Elaine Carmen, Housekeeper

Dear Mr. Kensedder,
My bath-size Dial is missing. Every bar of soap was taken from my room including my own bath-size Dial. I came in late last night and had to call the bellhop to bring me 4 little Cashmere Bouquets.

S. Berman

George still exists, actually, somewhere on the network. The paradoxical secret of building an efficient network organization is to lay into it enough redundancy to keep everyone in the loop. If you do, says Bill Raduchel of Sun: "People with knowledge almost always get into the discussion, because somebody somewhere draws them in." For example, the consultants at Booz Allen & Hamilton used to be organized in three large functional areas—strategy, operations, and information technology, a setup that produced slow-but-sure knowledge. To gain speed, the firm reorganized by market—financial services, petroleum, telecommunications, manufacturing, etc.—but it protected its expertise by creating "intellectual capital teams" that preserved a functional orientation. The structure is not a matrix. Decision-making authority is not shared—information is. If networks are messy, so what? Says General Electric's CEO Jack Welch; "Neatness

---

Dear Mr. Berman,
I have informed our housekeeper, Elaine Carmen, of your soap problem. I cannot understand why there was no soap in your room since our maids are instructed to leave 3 bars of soap each time they service a room. The situation will be rectified immediately. Please accept my apologies for the inconvenience.

Martin L. Kensedder, Assistant Manager

Dear Mrs. Carmen,
Who the hell left 54 little bars of Camay in my room? I came in last night and found 54 little bars of soap. I don't want 54 little bars of Camay. I want my one damn bar of bath-size Dial. Do you realize I have 54 bars of soap in here. All I want is my bath size Dial. Please give me back my bath-size Dial.

S. Berman

Dear Mr. Berman,
You complained of too much soap in your room so I had them removed. Then you complained to Mr. Kensedder that all your soap was missing so I personally returned them. The 24 Camays which had been taken and the 3 Camays you are supposed to receive daily (sic). I don't know anything about the 4 Cashmere Bouquets. Obviously your maid, Kathy, did not know I had returned your soaps so she also brought 24 Camays plus the 3 daily Camays. I don't know where you got the idea this hotel issues bath-size Dial. I was able to locate some bath-size Ivory which I left in your room.

Elaine Carmen, Housekeeper

and orderliness are not what we are after. We are after getting information to people who can act on it."

A network organization might not look like one on its formal chart; nor should it be entirely unhierarchical, because business organizations need to be pointed in the right direction even if they are not pushed in it. On paper, Minnesota Mining and Manufacturing seems to be a neat, conventional ziggurat of sectors, groups, and divisions, but these are marriages of convenience, their purpose being to school executives in the art of running large organizations and to group 3M businesses that serve the same customers. The work of innovation, 3M's core competence, happens in a dotty, disorderly, and apparently wasteful mangrove swamp of networks. The company wallows in redundancy. Its 8,300 researchers are scattered among so many different labs and types of labs that no one is entirely certain how many there are. There's central R&D; there are labs attached to each of the sectors; more linked to groups or businesses; and eleven centers dedicated to particular "technology platforms"—basic technologies like adhesives and optics, each of which feeds into scores of products and lines of business. A scientist who can't get money for a project from a business unit his lab is linked with is encouraged to see if someone else will pony up or, if no one will, to apply for a "Genesis Grant," money that is not allocated by management but by a panel of fellow scientists.

Dear Mrs. Carmen,

Just a short note to bring you up-to-date on my latest soap inventory. As of today I possess:

On shelf under medicine cabinet—18 Camay in 4 stacks of 4 and 1 stack of 2.

On Kleenex dispenser—11 Camay in 2 stacks of 4 and 1 stack of 3.

On bedroom dresser—1 stack of 3 Cashmere Bouquet, 1 stack of 4 hotel-size Ivory, and 8 Camay in 2 stacks of 4.

Inside medicine cabinet—14 Camay in 3 stacks of 4 and 1 stack of 2.

In shower soap dish—6 Camay, very moist.

On northeast corner of tub—1 Cashmere Bouquet, slightly used.

On northwest corner of tub—6 Camays in 2 stacks of 3.

Please ask Kathy when she services my room to make sure the stacks are neatly piled and dusted. Also, please advise her that stacks of more than 4 have a tendency to tip. May I suggest that my bedroom window sill is not in use and will make an excellent spot for future soap deliveries. One more item, I have purchased another bar of bath-sized Dial which I am keeping in the hotel vault in order to avoid further misunderstandings.

S. Berman

On occasion a stubborn and frustrated researcher has pushed into the CEO's office looking for scratch, and received it.

Similar redundancy exists at the other end of the innovation pipeline, where ideas are evaluated for commercial potential not only by people with hierarchical responsibility for them but also by a "technical audit" panel of scientists, manufacturing folk, and marketers, none of whom work for the sponsoring business. The audit has a dual purpose: to second-guess the hierarchy and, if an idea can't be used by its sponsor, to expose it to other businesses that might want it. Twice annually, in addition, 3M holds technology fairs, one run by scientists hawking inventions that need business sponsors, the other put on by business units promoting a marketing opportunity that needs an invention. Says Morgan Tamsky, head of the adhesives technologies center: "One of the imponderables of 3M is the multiplicity of interaction—it's not explainable, and it's not orderly."

It is, however, efficient—redundancy without waste. Labor productivity bears witness to the achievement. In 1984, when 3M had 88,949 employees, sales per employee totaled $88,814. In 1994, with almost the same head count (85,166), per employee sales had jumped 99 percent to $177,019. In real terms the gain was even higher, 101 percent, since 3M's average prices fell 2 percent in the decade. By comparison, for U.S. manufacturers as a whole, real output per person rose only 39 percent during the same period.

Networks allow 3M to stay lean while seeming not to watch its weight. L. D. DeSimone, 3M's CEO, says, "You never see the productivity issue off the screen," but 3M rarely pursues it in the usual ways—streamlining, chopping, eliminating duplication. Those words have a mechanical feel—fine-tuning the machine, removing superfluous parts. The talk in 3M's offices is more holistic and organic. In a series of interviews with me, top 3M executives said: "We're managing in chaos, and that's the right way to do it"; "We go in helping to shape but not shaping"; "What matters is the climate"; "All you really have to do in management is provide an environment; it's almost alive, always ebbing and flowing"; "I manage an environment"; "An environment to free up your imagination—that's the whole idea."

Consider, says University of Minnesota business professor Andrew Van de Ven, the difference between these mechanical and ecological metaphors. In an environment like the ocean, "every drop of water contains all the elements of the entire ocean. The ocean is full of redundant drops—but the redundancies are supportive, not wasteful."

3M's environment supports hundreds upon hundreds of businesses. Just as every bird in a flock knows the rules that every other bird knows, each 3M business contains the essential elements of the whole; each is an individual, yet none is independent. That is—in this metaphorical version, at least—each business can draw sustenance from the whole and also flourish because a big, varied ecosystem gives it room to grow, compete, and evolve.

Certainly redundancy carries costs; but it also creates opportunities and savings. First, there's knowledge sharing: 3Mers save time and money by adapting one another's ideas rather than reinventing them. Also, because 3M managers swim in the same sea, they seem able to move from one business to another—or to toggle between labs and businesses—smoothly, with no loss of speed and with minimal bureaucratic drag. Marvels Professor Van de Ven, who was the only outsider on a high-level 3M task force assembled a decade ago to study ways to improve the management of innovation: "You see constant self-reorganization and self-redesign, without the need for a whole lot of coordination across the company."

The best structural capital, as we've seen, allows a company to act almost reflexively. The very week Post-it notes was launched in the autumn of 1980, Leon Royer, ostensibly running 3M's labs for commercial office supplies, was given a crash assignment to come up with a new fly-fishing line for the leisure-time products department because a competitor's new product was killing 3M's offering. Royer called in a fluorocarbon expert from a third part of the company, who suggested playing around with a molecule that had been invented for still another piece of 3M. Royer himself spent many a Sunday afternoon testing the line by fly-casting in high school gymnasiums—the only structures around that were big enough, empty enough, and warm enough on those Minnesota winter days. The new line was ready by the time trout season opened, and went gangbusters—the result of an in-house effort that not only ignored the formal organization but also built no permanent structure of its own. Like a flock of birds, 3M simply turned.

The job of management used to be to plan, organize, execute, and measure—POEM. In the networked organization, the manager's job is best described in organic terms—indeed, in terms of the fundamental material of life. The manager's job is DNA: Define, Nurture, Allocate.

Define: Who are we? Why are we in business? What business are we in? What are our mission and vision and what value do we seek to offer to our customers? The networked company often organizes itself; people gather around projects that need to be done. It's not management's job to run those teams and projects; instead, management's role is to decide what needs to be done, to keep those projects from running off every which way by defining the direction in which the organization is headed. Vision-and-values stuff isn't mushy gobbledygook; it's truly important.

Nurture: The human, structural, and customer capital on which organizations depend need to be supported and nourished by managers. What kinds of people and knowledge do we need? What skills are essential to our business? How do we get them, how do we keep them at their best, how should results be rewarded? What kind of environment do they need to do their best? What systems can connect specialist knowledge workers with the least amount of bureaucratic drag? How can we grow relationships with our customers so that they share our fate and we share theirs?

Allocate: Management is about choosing. Among a dozen opportunities, which should we pursue, and with what vigor? What resources do we need? What's the best way to get them—do we grow our own, buy them through an acquisition, or rent them through an alliance? How strictly or loosely do we manage teams' use of those resources? How do we measure results?

Why Webs Win

There's an Information Age moral to the stories of webbed companies like 3M and Sun: The flat, networked organization triumphs because the underlying economics of communication and control have changed in favor of small, flexible organizations, not big ones. We need a bit of theory here, but bear with it. Different organizational structures have different costs—the implications of which are not usually considered by managers. Understanding those differences gives you a powerful tool for analyzing the decisions you have to make as you examine the "DNA" of managing. The argument is derived from an increasingly influential school of economics called transaction cost economics, begun by Nobelist Ronald Coase and further developed by Berkeley's Oliver Williamson and others. Traditionally, micro-economics has focused on factors of production such as labor and raw materials. Williamson argues that those miss a more important element, the cost of transactions: not just labor, but the whole labor transaction, which includes the cost of finding workers, training them, replacing those who quit, etc.; not just the cost of raw materials, but the cost of the transactions required to get the materials to where you want them. Conventional microeconomics never really examined administrative costs—both internal and external—associated with doing business. Department heads mostly ignore them, too; they're overhead, and outside your control. These are huge costs; if the administrative cost of business-to-business transactions is upward of $250 billion a year, the cost of internal transactions is probably even larger.

Oversimplified, Williamson's thinking goes like this: A transaction can be accomplished in one of two basic ways—you can buy something from someone else, or you can produce it yourself. Call the first system a market and the second a hierarchy. (There are hybrid forms, but we're oversimplifying.) Vertically integrated businesses, in which transactions take place between divisions, are hierarchies. Markets, on the other hand, are flat; they are organized only by the value proposition that motivates a buyer and seller to do business.

Each system has its advantages. Markets generally deliver the lowest price, because many sellers compete. Hierarchies usually have lower coordinating costs, because going to market is a messy business that involves searching for customers, setting up systems of purchasing and selling, bill paying and bill collecting, advertising, etc. Depending on how the costs and benefits line up, a given industry will tend to be more or less vertically integrated, feature larger or smaller companies, and display a bureaucratic or entrepreneurial management style.*

---

* Transaction costs are not, of course, the only influence on decisions to integrate vertically or to buy from markets. The cost of capital in relation to corporate profits is another powerful, and usually overlooked, influence, as Margaret M. Blair et al. show in *The Deal Decade: What Takeovers and Leveraged Buyouts Mean for Corporate Governance* (Washington, D.C.: Brookings Institution, 1993). In essence, Blair shows that when the cost of capital is low, mergers and acquisitions do not need to meet as high a hurdle rate as they do when providers of capital

Buy a computer, hook up a network, and the costs change. The cost of transmitting data over networks dropped about 90 percent in the 1985–95 decade—a rate of fall that parallels the steeply declining price of computer-processing power. Other things being equal (they never are, but economists are allowed to pretend otherwise), hierarchies begin to lose their comparative advantage in coordination costs. Sellers and buyers find each other more easily. Paperwork goes paperless, decimating armies of clerks. Electronic ordering and payment cut selling costs and reduce bad debt. Though networks reduce intramural transaction costs too, these were lower to begin with, and the information explosion networks set off favors decentralized decision-making. The net result, if you'll forgive the pun, is to increase the range of transactions for which marketlike structures become more efficient than bureaucratic ones; more companies decide to buy what they once produced in-house.

The effect of information technology on transaction costs explains, for example, why United Airlines' attempt to assemble a vertically integrated travel-service company that offered air transportation, automobile rental, and hotel accommodations was a short-lived failure. In 1985, United bought Hertz, and in 1987 it purchased Hilton and renamed the enlarged company Allegis; within one year, the company undid the deal. The sought-for synergies never materialized. Why? Allegis came into being at the same time as computerized reservations systems took off. The very technology that made it possible and economical to share information among the three travel services made it possible to get those synergies from the market (through travel agents) without incurring the transaction costs—bureaucracy and inefficient pricing—of a hierarchy. Because the costs of creating, manipulating, and transporting information are so much cheaper than before, you can get the coordination benefits of a hierarchy—and the price advantage of the market.

The best thing about this theory is that it checks out. Big companies are breaking up; outsourcing is on the rise (see Chapter 6); entry barriers have fallen in many industries; companies are more tightly focused; networks of "virtual corporations" are springing up; and internal hierarchies, their cost advantage gone, are collapsing like cakes

---

demand a higher return on their investment. Raise the cost of capital, however, and divestitures will become more common.

in the draft from an open oven door. Conference Board figures show that between 1979 and 1991 the number of three-digit standard industrial classifications (SIC codes) in which an average U.S. manufacturer does business dropped from 4.35 to 2.12. Companies are also smaller: Census data show that the number of employees at the average U.S. workplace is 8 percent lower than it was in 1980. The shrinkage is greatest in industries where information technology spending is highest: In an Information Age business, small is beautiful.

It's one thing, and usually a good thing, to go to market to buy paper and pencils rather than make them oneself. It's another thing, and usually an even better one, to use the market to supply important corporate services. Alliances and outsourcing put some of the capital costs of doing business on another guy's balance sheet. The company you outsource to is almost certain to have more than one customer and can spread the cost of the assets among them. A few years ago, for example, GE Capital took over the charge accounts of Montgomery Ward—that is, Monkey Ward outsourced its credit-card business to GE. GE Capital computers are linked directly to the retailer's cash registers; GE approves and issues Ward's credit cards; GE sends and collects the bills. That saved Ward the cost of owning, maintaining, and upgrading its own data processing systems. GE is able to spread that cost, a tremendous one, over several different credit-card lines.

The financial capital is the smallest part of it; both companies get even greater leverage on their intellectual capital. Montgomery Ward's core skills are in merchandising and purchasing, not consumer credit, debt collection, or information systems. By allying with a company whose intellectual capital is complementary to its own, Ward was not only liberated from the need to invest in the machines; it freed itself from the need to invest in the expertise. Clearly, a company that leases its most vital skills is a company that is in danger of losing its very reason for being. But a company that holds on to those vital skills and outsources what it can is, on the contrary, able to *leverage* intellectual capital over a much bigger market than it might otherwise be able to reach.

Three New Organizational Designs

Out of the economics of information and transaction costs emerge three new forms of organizational architecture: the internally networked organization; the virtual corporation, and the economic web. Each is a powerful source of operating efficiency and, perhaps more important, a mechanism for rapid growth by leveraging intellectual capital. We've discussed the internally networked organization above, with the example of 3M, and extensively in chapters 7 and 8. Virtual organizations and economic webs need a bit more explaining, to suggest a few of the principles by which they operate.

Skandia's Assurance and Financial Services (AFS) division defines itself as a virtual corporation. AFS's focus is not on traditional life insurance, but on savings-*cum*-insurance vehicles such as variable annuities (unit-linked insurance, it is sometimes called) where premium payments are invested in mutual funds at the policyholder's direction; the policy's ultimate value is primarily determined by the investment results of those funds. AFS's net premium income grew at a stunning annual rate of 45 percent for the five years from 1991 through 1995, and Skandia is one of the world's top three sellers of variable annuities.

That rapid growth was made possible by Skandia's creation of a virtual organization that produces increasing returns. AFS puts its money and brainpower into developing insurance products, operating its internal and external network, and opening global markets. (Note that these correspond to human, organizational, and customer capital, which must be the most important nodes of any corporate network.) For example, the company's sophisticated internal network exploits common processes worldwide to reap the dramatic economies of scale of intangibles; by leveraging its organizational capital globally, Skandia in 1995 opened a Southeast Asian sales office, headquartered in Malaysia whose back office is in Switzerland.

But AFS neither manages mutual funds nor deals directly with the public. That's done by partners in its virtual network. Downstream there are local sellers—banks, brokerages, and financial advisers—who want to sell insurance and value AFS's product-development expertise. Upstream are well-known fund managers such as J. P. Morgan, Invesco, and Fidelity, who value AFS as a stable source of long-term funds from an inexpensive distribution channel. The network of sellers and fund managers further leverages intellectual capital by providing AFS with an infrastructure it could not have built so quickly on its own. In 1992, AFS had 1,169 employees; today it has 2,086—a modest 917 more. But the number of people who sell and manage Skandia's products through its federation of alliances has more than tripled, from 15,000 to 46,000, and the value of AFS's assets under management has increased even faster, from 25 billion Swedish kroner to 116 billion (about $17.5 billion).

Many companies, like Skandia AFS, have begun to focus on a few core activities and unbundle the rest. In an electronic environment where knowledge is the most important economic good, entire value chains are being dismantled and re-formed. Take distribution. A manufacturer, focusing on his factories, turns over logistics to what used to be a freight forwarder. That company, rather than own and manage a fleet of trucks and ships, rents the vehicles it needs, as it needs them, from a wired leasing company that knows what's where, what's full, what's empty. Each party—manufacturer, logistician, lessor—manages its financial and intellectual assets more efficiently than before.

That—a focus on managing intellectual assets—is the key to making virtual corporations work. Says D. J. Crane, a vice president of GE Information Services, who works with GE Capital (a major lessor of aircraft, freight cars, and trucks) and its customers on just such reconfigurings: "This is changing the business of being a middleman. Forward-thinking companies are taking up positions as middlemen for information, not goods."

McKinsey consultant John Hagel III uses the term "economic web" to describe the ultimate way in which the logic of networks manifests itself in organizational architecture. Economic webs are "clusters of companies that collaborate around a particular technology . . . [and] that use a common architecture to deliver independent elements of an overall value proposition that grows stronger as more companies join the set." We've met one of these creatures before, what I called the Windows Metropolitan Area, but there are others: local, long-distance, and alternate-access telephone companies; automobile manufacturers and their suppliers and dealers; cable-TV companies and companies that provide programming for them, like CNN. When electric utilities are fully deregulated, that industry will probably form webs of power generators, power transmitters, power sellers, and appliance repairers. Webs can also be spun around sets of customers—think of the ancillary services American Express offers cardmembers, or of how on-line services offer access to magazines, travel services, and software companies. The whole financial services industry was invented to serve the set of customers and sellers who gathered at medieval market towns.

Companies in economic webs face a dual challenge of competition and cooperation. Within a web, there may be fierce battles as different participants vie with one another—think of Compaq, Gateway, and Packard Bell, for example. These struggles might even dislodge the prime mover of a web and change its character, which happened in the personal computer business when Microsoft, aided by Intel, pushed IBM to the periphery of a web IBM originally spun; now Netscape and Sun (via its Java software) are trying to make Microsoft a secondary spider in a web based on the Internet. At the same time, however, webs compete with other webs—Greater Microsoft with Apple, the Ford web with Honda's—and every participant stands to gain from increasing returns if its web expands, or to lose if its web is less successful than a rival one.

The key to success in both endeavors—expanding a web, and jockeying for position within it—lies where we have by now come to expect it: information. The richer and faster the flow of information in a web, the better its participants will be able to seize new opportunities for themselves, thereby making the web's value proposition more attractive to customers. As for success in intramural competition, it, too, depends on access to information about what a web's dominant companies are thinking.

The center, the genome, of all these new forms of organizational architecture is intellectual capital. Internally networked companies, virtual organizations, and economic webs partake of the same Information Age economic logic: that ideas, knowledge, information processing, and other intangibles—human, structural, and customer capital—can generate wealth much faster and less expensively than physical and financial assets traditionally deployed. The arithmetic of the goods economy is addition; in the knowledge economy, it's multiplication.

CHAPTER 12

Your Career in the Information Age

THE FUNDAMENTAL PREMISE OF THE NEW MODEL EXECUTIVE . . .
IS, SIMPLY, THAT THE GOALS OF THE INDIVIDUAL AND THE GOALS
OF THE ORGANIZATION WILL WORK OUT TO BE ONE AND THE
SAME. THE YOUNG MEN HAVE NO CYNICISM ABOUT THE
"SYSTEM," AND VERY LITTLE SKEPTICISM—THEY DON'T SEE IT
AS SOMETHING TO BE BUCKED, BUT AS SOMETHING TO BE CO-
OPERATED WITH . . . THEY HAVE AN IMPLICIT FAITH THAT THE
ORGANIZATION WILL BE AS INTERESTED IN MAKING USE OF THEIR
BEST QUALITIES AS THEY ARE THEMSELVES, AND THUS, WITH
EQUANIMITY, THEY CAN ENTRUST THE RESOLUTION OF THEIR
DESTINY TO THE ORGANIZATION . . . [T]HE AVERAGE YOUNG
MAN CHERISHES THE IDEA THAT HIS RELATIONSHIP WITH THE
ORGANIZATION IS TO BE FOR KEEPS.
—WILLIAM H. WHYTE, *THE ORGANIZATION MAN*, 1956

W ell, scratch that. If there's unanimity about any aspect of the Information Age economy, it's that you have a better chance of getting a gold watch from a street vendor than you do from a corporation.

Time was, and not long ago, employees mounted hierarchies as elegant and monumental as Aztec temples. The steps were clear, the path seemed obvious—forget that those who made it to the top were either priests or human sacrifices. Now the worker, the manager, the executive zigzag through organizations that resemble circuit boards more than pyramids, where lines of energy and control run every which way; where chutes are many, ladders few and short; where the organizing principle is ceaseless reorganization; where it's hard to know what a career *is*, let alone how to get one. Asked about the future of middle management, that famously endangered species, David Robinson, president of the CSC Index consulting firm, offers a lonesome-pine of a word: "Extinction."

After more than a decade in which millions of working lives have been disrupted—downsized, outsourced, flattened, reengineered—corporations and people have learned, often at awful cost, new clichés. "We cannot offer job security, but through challenging work you can learn marketable skills." "Act as if you are self-employed, working for 'Me, Inc.'" "Any given job is temporary." "You are responsible for managing your own career." Like mother's milk, these make a nourishing beginning. But then what?

It is one thing to mouth the new truths, another to live them. How can you tell if your career is on track if there is no track? How can you conceive and execute a career strategy when corporate mores and institutions trail behind economic reality? Says Gary Knisley, CEO of Johnson Smith & Knisley Accord, a New York executive recruiter: "Companies haven't accepted the view of temporary employment the way employees have. They're talking about 'this great career opportunity in this great and growing company.' They honestly think they're offering an old-fashioned job, while across the desk the candidate is thinking, 'I know better.'" If you believe otherwise, ask yourself this Hobbesian question: How comfortable would you be if you went to your boss, or if a key subordinate came to you, and candidly said: "Since lifetime employment is no more, I want to discuss how to change what I do here so that I will be more attractive to the next company that hires me?"

Take heart. (Take Prozac, too.) There is a new model for careers in the Information Age. True, confusion and contradiction abound—the CEO who in one breath proclaims that he wants well-rounded managers with broad, generalist skills, next sighs about how vital and how hard it is to keep star technical talent. And true, job security is gone, maybe for keeps. Even if a tight labor market raises employees' bargaining power, says Robert Saldich, chief executive of Raychem Corp., "We'll never slip back to the level of comfort and complacency of the past." Evidence bears Saldich out: In the twelve months that ended in June 1995, according to an American Management Association survey, 50 percent of large and mid-sized companies eliminated jobs. Most of those same companies also created jobs—hiring with one hand, firing with the other. Net-net their labor force shrank just 1.1 percent, and other companies more than picked up the slack: Among the 1,003 surveyed companies, total employment rose 4.5 percent. This churning has become a fixture of life; despite economic growth, the percentage of companies eliminating jobs has risen every year since 1991.

Today's economic seas therefore cannot be navigated by the old stars above, but by internal compasses and gyroscopes. Instead of security, seek resilience. Chart your contribution, not your position. Careers will be defined less by companies ("I work for IBM") and more by professions ("I design RISC chips"); they will be shaped less by hierarchies and more by markets. There are new rules for success and new warning signs of trouble. Because the risks are higher, so as always are the rewards.

NEW SIGNS OF TROUBLE

The old trappings of success—a leather chair, your own secretary—are gone. So are the old signs of trouble. Says Richard Moran, a leader of the change-management practice for Price Waterhouse consulting: "The rule used to be incremental promotions every year or two. If you missed one—hmm—that was a warning. You don't get the little clicks now." Warnings are subtler—many audible only to you, not your boss or colleagues. If several of these click, wake up:

1. *Are you learning?* If you can't say what you have learned in the past six months, nor what you expect to learn in the next, beware. Says Harvard Business School professor John Kotter: "When there's nothing you can learn where you are, you've got to move on, even if they give you promotions." If your job has become easy, someone else will do it for less.

2. *If your job were open, would you get it?* Benchmark your skills regularly. Look at want-ads for jobs in your field. If they ask for skills you don't have—with phrases such as familiarity with Lotus Notes a plus"—get on the stick.

3. *Are you being milked?* When you sacrifice your long-term growth for short-term benefits, especially your employer's, you are living on intellectual capital. A salesman who wants to learn marketing but keeps hearing, "You're so good we need you here" or a finance guy who is

asked to keep the old system running while others learn the new soft-ware—these are people in whom the company has stopped investing.
4. *Do you know what you contribute?* If you can't give anyone a two-minute summary of what you do and why it matters, your boss probably can't either.
5. *What would you do if your job disappeared tomorrow?* If you can't answer that question, you haven't thought about what marketable skills you have. More and more, you have to sell yourself inside the company.
6. *Are you having fun yet?* Sure, they call it "work," but you'll be less eager for new challenges if your heart's not in it.
7. *Are you worried about your job?* Says Moran: "If you are, you probably should be."

The New Career Model

The changed model of a career follows from the changed nature of work, and the importance and dynamics of intellectual capital—not just human capital, but structural and organizational assets too—are central to understanding it. As consultant William Bridges describes it in his book *JobShift*, the "job"—meaning a more-or-less set task you do every day—is disappearing as routine office and factory work are automated.

Instead of jobs, we have projects. A project is simply a task that has a beginning, a defined scope, and an end: designing the wings of a new jetliner, launching a product, preparing a lawsuit, reengineering accounts payable, cleaning up a Superfund site. (Okay, every project supposedly has an end.) These boundaries make managing projects different from, say, overseeing a production line and preparing a weekly tally of costs in and gewgaws out, now and forevermore.

They also redefine managerial careers. Unlike departments or processes, projects are conceived, staffed up, completed, and shut down. According to Warren Bennis of the University of Southern California, this kind of work leads to "adaptive, rapidly changing temporary systems . . . task forces composed of groups of relative strangers with diverse professional backgrounds and skills organized around problems to be solved . . . People will be evaluated not vertically according to rank and status, but flexibly according to competence. Organizational charts will consist of project groups rather than stratified functional groups."

This is not altogether new: Bennis wrote it, albeit in the future tense, in 1968.

Three things are new. First, says Gene Dalton, head of the Novations Group, a Utah consultancy specializing in career management: "You no longer have a choice"; the old career path is gone. Companies used reengineering to jackhammer out the middle-manager staircase and employ computers instead to gather, analyze, and report information. According to American Management Association studies, management and supervisory jobs are being eliminated nearly twice as fast as they are being created. At the same time, professional and technical jobs are being created about 50 percent faster than they are being cut. The man in the gray flannel suit is now a man in a gray sweat suit, running around the lake at ten-thirty in the morning. In late 1995, *The Wall Street Journal* ran an article arguing that these trends weren't quite as overwhelming as some people have said. But the paper's prize exhibit demonstrated exactly the opposite. It was a study of the number of managers per 100 employees among companies with more than 100 employees, which must file reports with the Equal Employment Opportunity Commission. The data showed that there were 12.5 managers per 100 employees in 1983, and 11.2 in 1994. In just over a decade, 1 out of 9 managers disappeared—and nearly half the drop had occurred in the last three years. The equation looks like this: Add professional and technical workers, subtract supervisory work and bosses; more and more, what matters is what you do, not whom you do it for.

Second, businesses have redrawn their boundaries, making them both tight (as they focus on core processes and technologies) and porous (as they outsource noncore work, form internal networks and virtual corporations, and participate in economic webs). Just as the value a business creates derives less from the physical assets it controls than from the knowledge it develops and applies, so the importance and value of a career is marked not by hierarchical position—a badge of the assets one controls—but by one's ability to provide and mobilize knowledge in furtherance of company goals. As the economics of transaction costs dictate, work and labor increasingly follow a contractor-subcontractor market model rather than one of vertical integration.

The third change is of scale. Project-based (versus position-based) work has been the norm for decades in construction and engineering firms, movie studios, many professional services firms, and a few other industries whose book of business is a portfolio of projects. Says David Milligan, director of project technology for Asea Brown Boveri's combustion engineering business: "We had project management before I came here thirty years ago." Now even the bastions of bureaucratic careerism have been breached. Witness Chrysler's bringing out new cars by deploying cross-functional "platform teams" especially chartered and arrayed around a project—the new car—rather than passing work from hierarchical department to department. Those departments still exist, but they function more as "home rooms" for team members than as organizers and managers of work. At the Federal National Mortgage Association, which processes more financial transactions than any other private organization on earth, you'd think operations management would rule the roost. But no, says executive VP William Kelvie, Fanny Mae's chief information officer: "Automation and empowerment take away the need to have managers oversee the steady-state structures. Everything has become projects. This is the way Fanny Mae does business today."

How the New Career Model Affects You

Life in the projects has profound implications for careers. "There are basically four levels, and four types of career," says Frank Walker, president of GTW Corp. This Seattle outfit sells project management consulting services and software (in an alliance with Microsoft) and construction management services. Among other projects, GTW helped Boeing and contractors from Baugh Industrial choreograph and manage an enormously complex schedule to design and build a 500,000-square-foot testing lab for airliners. In Walker's schematic, the top level sets strategy: It is the land of presidents and CEOs and executive VPs. Few people live there. Next come resource-providers: These folks develop and supply talent, money, and other resources; they are CFOs and CIOs, human resources managers, temporary services firms, or heads of traditional functional departments like engineering and marketing. Next come the project managers: They buy or lease resources from the resource-providers—negotiating a budget and getting people assigned to the project—and put them to work. Finally there is talent: chemists, finance guys, salespeople, bakers, candlestick makers.

Look at the work you do; chances are good this four-piece template—strategist, resource-provider, project manager, talent—fits better than the old system of every-other-year steps up the rung. Take Andersen Consulting, where about 80 percent of employees are busy with one or more consulting engagements—that is, projects—that may last a few weeks or several years. (Most of the others have long-term assignments—for example, to Andersen units that run information systems for companies that choose to outsource that function.) Newcomers to the firm (talent) are assigned to a regional office. There an HR group (a resource-provider) is responsible for helping the fledgling consultant grow. It works with lead consultants (project managers) to find assignments for her, coordinates feedback, and helps her develop the analytical, technical, and communication skills against which her progress is measured. Soon, this orientation and apprenticeship over, she joins an industry group, such as financial services or telecommunications; it, too, has an HR team that acts as a resource-provider and career developer; in addition to the generic skills she learned while attached to the regional office, she begins to pick up industry-specific knowledge. As her ability grows, she tries her wings as a project manager, leading teams of talent in engagements of increasing importance and complexity. Not everyone aspires to or attains that level; some remain journeymen (programmers or analysts, say), valued more as experts than as project managers.

Though Andersen has levels—"consultant," "manager," "experienced manager," and eventually partner—which determine pay, the real career action isn't defined by the hierarchy but by increasing levels of skill and by a market of buyers (lead consultants staffing up projects) and sellers (HR, representing the talent). Says Carol Meyers, the firm's worldwide head of human resources: "Demand comes into the pipeline when someone makes a deal with a client and says 'I need twenty-five people to do X on such-and-such a date.' Supply comes in as people free up. Your career happens as we match supply and demand."

To be sure, at Andersen as anywhere, there are traditional careerists whose ambition is to climb the ladder (even if it's a stepladder) toward that great executive suite in the sky. Says Gene Dalton of the Novations Group: "People at Exxon used to say that the company did two things: It looked for oil, and it looked for the next president of Exxon—not necessarily in that order. Every manager who came in was considered a candidate." That career track will persist in some places. Mostly these will be industries where skills and markets are not quickly eroded by the pace of change (not many of those left), or where high capital requirements raise entry barriers (though many of those—telephone companies, for example—have flattened hierarchies to leverage their capital investment).

For the rest of us: How much more ambiguous, now, are the paths ahead, and more various the strategies we might pursue. This way of working affects career choices in six important ways:

A career is a series of gigs, not a series of steps. Familiar signs of career progress—promotions from junior engineer to engineer to senior engineer to manager et cetera—have gone the way of the Taylorist division of labor. Says Daniel Burnham, president of Allied-Signal's $4.6 billion-in-sales aerospace business: "The signs of career progress are the richness of your work's content and the size of its impact on the organization." You might toggle back and forth between roles—now a project manager, next month talent. Says television writer Terry Curtis Fox, a member of the board of the Writers Guild of America West: "Someone who works for you on one TV series might be your boss on the next one."

What distinguishes a star in the corporate firmament from a dim bulb in the basement is not his level in the organization but the complexity and value of the projects he works on. "The goal is growth in your profession, not turning into a supervisor," says Michael Hammer, the consultant and author whose proselytizing for reengineering has probably made him the world's number-one cause of white-collar career disruption. For models, Hammer looks to the professions and to sales: "A great lawyer like Joe Flom [of Skadden Arps Slate Meagher & Flom] couldn't waste his time being managing partner. Great sales people don't want to be managers—they want big accounts. Sales managers are burnouts."

Hammer predicts that a summary of a successful career—that is, a résumé—will look different. Rather than describe a man or woman who has had few changes of company but many changes of title, a résumé will show fewer titles but many more employers. Titles will matter little. Says Linda DiMello, executive director of Alumnae Resources, a nonprofit career management service in San Francisco: "People who identify themselves with their title are the first to go, because they don't have the flexibility to move with the organization. Résumés will tell the story of what I did for the customer. Whom I did it for is just a by-product."

Project management is the furnace in which successful careers are forged. In the mid-1980s I had a boss who, whenever he heard that someone had been assigned to "special projects," jokingly made the sign of the Cross, as if warding off a vampire, against the chance of its happening to him. Says Chris Holt, an organizational improvement expert at Chevron Products Co.: "Special projects used to be the kiss of death. Now it means you've been pulled out for something important."

Projects package and sell knowledge. It doesn't matter what the formal blueprint of an organization is—functional hierarchy, matrix, or the emerging process-centered organization, whose lines of communication and power are drawn along end-to-end business processes such as order generation and fulfillment, new product development, and customer management.* Routine work doesn't need managers; if it cannot be automated, it can be self-managed by workers. It's the

---

* "Horizontal" organizational design is a powerful way in which companies can configure themselves to manage information and knowledge better; such process-centered organizations are inherently more capable than functional ones of producing the customized work that is characteristic of knowledge-intensive businesses; as my periodontist said while trying to sell me a $130 ultrasound mechanical toothbrush, "I recommend it." The biggest source of the horizontal organization's greater flexibility, however, comes from the fact that its customer focus makes it more amenable to cross-functional projects to improve processes, products, and services.

Horizontal organizations are spawning a fifth kind of Knowledge Age career: The "process owner" joins the strategist, resource-provider, project manager, and talent. Process owners are senior executives who, as the name implies, are responsible for the smooth functioning of a process or subprocess. There won't be many of them; a benefit of the horizontal organization is that it needs much less administration than a functional hierarchy. Reengineering guru Michael Hammer estimates that even the largest companies will have no more than 100 slots for process and subprocess owners. (Michael Hammer, *Beyond Reengineering* (New York: Harper Business, 1996.)

never-ending book of projects—for internal improvement or to serve customers—that creates new value. It draws information together and does something with it—that is, formalizes, captures, and leverages it to produce a higher-valued asset.

Consequently, if the old middle managers are dinosaurs, a new class of managerial mammals—project managers—is evolving to fill the niche they once ruled. Like his biological counterpart, the project manager is more agile and adaptable than the beast he's displacing, more likely to live by his wits than by throwing his weight around. Says William Dauphinais, a consultant at Price Waterhouse: "Project management is going to be huge in the next decade. The project manager is the linchpin in the horizontal-slash-vertical organizations we're creating."

As I said above, project management has its roots in the construction and engineering industries. (Actually, its technique and art are literally as old as time, the first practitioner having been God, who gave himself six days in which to turn the void into the world, then turned operations management over to Adam, who promptly made a hash of it. Unlike corporate project managers, however, God got to define what He meant by "six days" and had unlimited resources.) Project management is spreading rapidly from these redoubts into aerospace and defense, banking and insurance, computer hardware and software, and almost every other industry as managing projects evolves from a specialty into the central task of middle managers. Put it the way Roger Glaser of San Diego Gas & Electric does: "Project management is the management of change. We're here. We want to get there."

People who lead or work on winning projects will get first crack at the next hot gig. The best project managers will seek out the best talent, and the best talent—offered a choice as it often will be—will sign on with the best managers. Seniority matters less than what-you-have-done-for-me-lately. Says Anthony Miles of the Boston Consulting Group: "This is a system that favors the strong. It's a negotiated relationship between employer and employee"—a market transaction, not a hierarchical *fait accompli*. Bargaining power belongs to people who know stuff or show that they get stuff done. Says Scott McNeely, CEO of Sun Microsystems: "You have to somehow get into a position where you can come into me and say, 'I did the deal with AT&T' or 'I was the chief architect of such-and-such new product' or 'I ran manufacturing operations and brought inventory turns up from 3 a year to 30.' That's what I'm looking for."

Not everyone can or should be a project manager, but those who can will be winners. When an organization ceases to be defined by its functional departments and becomes a portfolio of projects and processes, it's much easier to claim credit for success—the results are obvious. Conversely, it's harder to blame "them" for failure because "they" are on your cross-functional project team.

In the new organization, power flows from expertise, not from position. The dirty secret of flat organizations is that they still need authority—defined as the ability to say, "Do it, dammit"—and no one has it. Project managers talk about being "caught in the matrix" of cross-functional work. They might as well speak of being stretched on the rack. Janine Coleman has been on that rack for a decade as a project manager for Lucent Technologies' strategic opportunities division, which installs multimillion-dollar switching systems, mostly for big corporations. Says Coleman—cheerfully, mind you: "The company tells the client, 'We assign you a project manager and she's in charge.' If it fails, it's my fault." But does she have power as well as responsibility? "No. If a VP doesn't go along, it's up to the project manager to get him to go along." A project manager is like a car's differential gear: He transforms the power coming from the driveshaft—the functions or processes—into forward motion. That isn't easy. Most of the time, Coleman says, "I don't have a budget per se." Like the people who work for her, the money comes from departments whose leaders might want it back. In most companies where project management is well established, there are ways to appeal for help. Coleman's boss, national project director Daniel Ono, leads a swat team of twenty-five project managers and reports to national headquarters. In theory (and probably more often in practice than people will tell a journalist) that structure allows a beleaguered project manager to call for reinforcements.

"Why, so can I, or so can any man," said Shakespeare's Hotspur: "But will they come when you do call for them?" For the Information Age manager, power doesn't flow from position or budget but from subtler springs, as intangible as the assets that create value. The first is expertise—in project management more than in a technical field. That capability must include knowing how the business makes money. Unlike a functional supervisor, a project manager needn't be an expert in cash flow or procurement or engineering change orders, but she must know how each of these can make the difference between a trot around the bases and a slow walk to the dugout. This management discipline has a boxful of great tools, ranging from planning software to business school courses to a "body of knowledge" published by the Project Management Institute. Says Coleman, who has managed projects as diverse as software development, building construction, and switch installation, and is helping her church start a credit union: "I don't need to be a technical person. But I need to know enough to tell if a project is on track, if people are telling me the truth." Knowing the tools gives the power to plan and to manage "scope creep," the plan-aglaying contingencies that occur when someone wants lilies gilded or runs into unforeseen problems.

Second is reputation. Nail enough coonskins to your wall and you'll find that the company's best designers and engineers and other experts—the talent—want to join your next hunting party. That means fewer problems—and strong voices to support you back in the functions.

Call the third source of power honest salesmanship. Based on informal surveys, William Dauphinais estimates project managers spend 75 percent of their time jawboning. In each consulting project, he assigns team members to make regular visits to everyone who has a stake in it—the ultimate beneficiaries of the work and the resource-providers who supply people, money, or equipment—to keep them informed and on board. The key to doing it well: Focus on the work, and the personalities will take care of themselves. Says AT&T's Ono: "Executives need specifics, and the management layer that used to provide them is gone. We do it now."

Fourth, project managers need the entrepreneurship and negotiating ability to put themselves up for project management roles, land them, and profit from their team's performance. Ultimate authority in a well-run company comes from the customer, of course. Whether the customer is external or internal, smart project managers hitch their wagons to his star with a formal contract: I'll give you X work for Y price; bells and whistles cost extra. Project managers don't do favors; they do deals. The one-shot nature of the work gives them the cordite perfume of hired gunmen, which many are, in fact or in *Weltanschauung*. In this way, the new middle manager is the market-driven antithesis of a sinecurist hierarch. The project manager's world, like all markets, is an uncertain, intense, even scary place, noisy with bargaining and bidding, highly competitive, and going full speed all the time. Says Coleman, a twenty-six-year veteran at AT&T: "In the old organization, I had job security. Now each job has a beginning and an end—and then what? If I did well, my next assignment will be harder and better, and it's 'Here we go again' till you get back up to that high in the middle. Whatever it takes, that's what we do."

Most roles in an organization can be performed by either insiders or outsiders. Whether you're a strategy-setter, resource-provider, project manager, or talent, you don't have to work in a company to work for it. Yes, even strategists—who in fact were the first out the door. As Harvard Business School professor John Kotter points out, only the top cadre of corporate strategists remains on the payroll: "The internal strategy guys all said bye-bye and became investment bankers and consultants, where they had a lot more upside opportunity." The rise of the contingent worker began long before the 1990–91 recession accelerated the process. Between 1983 and 1994, the number of temporary jobs in the United States increased from 619,000 to 2.25 million, and the Bureau of Labor Statistics expects it to increase 60 percent by 2005. By 1992, 13.6 percent of federal income tax returns reported Schedule C income—nonfarm sole proprietorships—up from 7.8 percent in 1970.

Increasingly these people are freelance professionals, not typists or security guards. Large numbers of others are *de jure* employees, but of companies that are independent resource-providers—"talent guilds" is the apt name given them by Mel Warriner, head of human resources for Walt Disney Imagineering. Manpower, Inc., whose payroll of 750,000 temporaries makes it the nation's largest employer, gets 15 percent of its revenues from placing high-technology workers. The total payroll for professionals and managers employed by temporary services companies has jumped from $335 million in 1991 to over $1.6 billion in 1995. Plug-and-play knowledge workers, you might call them.

Talent guilds are becoming a significant part of business life. In a 1994 survey, 37 percent of designers, engineers, and other contract employees working for companies in the National Technical Services Association, a trade group for employers of contingent workers, said contract employment is "my career choice," versus 23 percent who said, "I am between 'permanent' jobs." Bill Wickham is an executive who has chosen to work from outside as a project leader. When I met Wickham, forty-six, he was at Coca-Cola for a nine-to-eighteen-month stint helping to reorganize Coke's New York metropolitan area sales and distribution system. "I get bored in everyday situations," says Wickham. "I like the jazz, the excitement." When this gig is done, a regular Coke employee will take Wickham's job and he will find his next. Wickham got a reputation as a change expert and turn-around manager while employed by Occidental Petroleum, Xerox, and Amax. In 1992, he went on his own. Says Wickham: "Given the temporary nature of most change projects, it doesn't matter whether you're internal or external." He has a little company—Wickham and Associates, what else?—hires occasional help on a project basis, and contracts with small resource-providing companies to handle benefit plans and other administrative work. Wickham finds that his freelance life has an unexpected fringe benefit—its own form of stability. Though he has seen the inside of more hotel rooms than most people would like, he says: "I don't have to relocate my family every five minutes."

Careers are made in markets, not hierarchies. Whether you're "permanent" or an outsider, it helps to conceive of yourself as a self-employed participant in a market for work. Partly, a self-employment mind-set is smart defense—a prudent mental preparation for the likelihood of becoming unemployed and job seeking. But it's more than that: Insiders more and more often must compete among each other and with outsiders for spots on projects. AlliedSignal, Andersen Consulting, Chevron, and Lotus Development, among others, already build databases showing which employees have what skills, using them to create a virtual marketplace where resource-providers and project managers shop for talent. It behooves you, therefore, to hang your shingle in the internal agora.

These markets won't be efficient until sellers—that's you—have as much access to them as buyers. A handful of progressive companies have taken first steps in that direction. New hires at Sun Microsystems receive in their orientation packets information about Sun's Career Resilience Center. It began in 1991 as an outplacement service, but now offers a full range of assessment and counseling services to help people in the internal labor market—and for those who want out, even an introduction to the Career Action Center down the road in Palo Alto. The Career Action Center is a knowledge-workers' hiring hall, where people can network with fellow seekers, meet with counselors, research a library of fat clip files about local companies, check job listings, or attend seminars on subjects like résumé writing, entrepreneurship, and careers in biotechnology or multimedia. Like its sibling Alumnae Resources in San Francisco, the Career Action Center began in the 1970s as a job-hunting resource for women and, unisex now, is jam-packed with people who want to change careers or learn about the markets for their skills: 95 percent of Alumnae Resources' members have college degrees, for example, and seven out of ten are currently employed.

Where project-based work is long established, these markets are in full swing. Jeff Leon, managing director of the Russell Reynolds headhunting firm, points out: "In Hollywood there's a whole world of casting people and agents who are dealing people." As virtual corporations become widespread in other sectors of the economy, predicts Mel Warriner of Walt Disney Imagineering: "If you're not in a company's core group, you'll end up a free agent, connected with human-resources brokers. Talent brokers are the analogue for the new millennium of the financial dealmakers of the 1980s."

The fundamental career choice is not between one company and another, but between specializing and generalizing. Psychologists say adults pass through three phases in the development of a sense of identity. The stages (not everyone goes the distance) as summarized by Carl Sloane, the founder of Temple Barker & Sloane, who with Shoshanah Zuboff now runs midlife career seminars for Harvard Business School alumni:

Interpersonal: You learn to be a grown-up by copying parents and peers. The young MBA whose dream is to raise honeybees joins a bank because it's the done thing.

Institutional: You pledge your troth to a group and take on its coloration. The college cutup turns into a pinstriped poop because bankers don't laugh.

Interindividual: You define yourself. Our banker not only keeps bees, he tells his colleagues that he does: "Banker, beekeeper, father, lover—they're all me."

In the days of the Organization Man, we looked to our employers for the crucial institutional phase. They not only paid us, they defined us: We were IBMers in white shirts, Alcoans in black wing tips, Citibankers, Ford men. Nowadays, that way lies a career crisis and an identity crisis too.

Far better to peg your soul to your talent. As Dan Hatch, Pepsico's highly regarded human resources chief, puts it: "Loyalty to the profession is greater than loyalty to the company."

"I'm a salesman," says William Paine, twenty-seven, when someone asks about work. Where do you work? "Six hundred California Street." What do you sell? "Bonds." It takes four questions—Do you work for a company?—before he says, "Gruntal & Co.," where Paine is one of ten bond salesmen in the San Francisco office. Not that Paine doesn't feel loyal to Gruntal: "I'm *very* loyal. I'll remain loyal if they supply me the things I need. They owe me phones, a computer, execution, and inventory. I owe them production and integrity." Paine's self-description—you are what you do for your customers—is as clear a description of the new career contract as there is.

It leads directly to a crucial, career-defining choice: specialist or generalist? Do you follow your talent to a lofty acme of expertise, or make it the central massif of a range of skills? Consider the management structure of a football team, Michael Hammer suggests: One group of coaches are generalists—the offensive and defensive coordinators (in effect, they are "owners" of the "offensive process" and the "defensive process") and train the team to execute plays. Another group are specialists—position coaches for the quarterbacks, linebackers, receivers—whose job is to develop players' particular functional talent. The basic unit of work—the play—is a project, the management of which is also a generalist's responsibility, unlike in a traditional organization, where tasks, supervised by specialists, are the basic building blocks.

The conventional wisdom is that generalists are better off. "Major in people," Scott McNeely advises. (Then, about his days at Stanford University, he jokes: "I majored in golf.") Says Daniel Burnham of AlliedSignal: "A designer can't be just a designer. He has to have a broader dimension of skill—got to start reading *The Wall Street Journal*, got to understand Peter Drucker's thinking" in order to understand the whole business, not just a specialty. When you come to a fork in the road—say, a choice between two projects, one of which will broaden your knowledge, one deepen it—choose the path that will increase your flexibility, headhunter Gary Knisley says. He explains: "Never narrow your options. To the extent that technical expertise narrows your market, you've made a bad career decision. Companies may love it at the moment, but if you've got that good a crystal ball, get out of a job and into investing." Someone who bets his career on a specialty is like an investor who puts all his money in one stock.

On the other hand, that stock might be Microsoft. Says Dan Hatch of Pepsico: "It's a little dangerous to be esoteric, but companies treat specialists very well—as the scarce resource they are—compared to people who are more interchangeable." A growing number of businesses follow the path DuPont blazed long ago when it set up a separate career ladder so scientists could be richly rewarded without having to become managers. For example, the consulting arm of Price Waterhouse redesigned career paths for its 3,300 staffers, eliminating its traditional "up-or-out," twelve-years-to-partner timetable. The new structure creates three levels—consultant, principal consultant/ director, and managing director/partner—with no clock, which makes it easier for specialists to stay. The old model worked fine in a stable business environment. Now customers demand deep expertise in, for instance, computer networking. Says Fran Engoron, a partner who was chief architect of the new system and has since been named the firm's director of intellectual capital: "You can't go to the table with people who are just smart people; they have to have deep, hard skills. We were shoving people out the door just as they began delivering the most value to our client."

Often, Engoron says, specialists left to join or start niche consulting firms—talent guilds. That's not surprising. Independent resource-providers will be found most in technically specific fields like law, computer science, architecture, and so on. It makes sense for people with one skill to make themselves available to more than one customer. They might forgo a secure wage, but are likely to compensate for it with an equity position in a smaller shop or a business of their own. In occupations where an individual's human capital is the single most valuable asset—writing, acting, lawyering, deal-making, design—the gap between the highest-paid and the worst-paid practitioners tends to be enormous, and at both extremes are the freelancers; those on-staff fill the somewhat attenuated middle. As a rule of thumb, therefore, your choice between generalizing and specializing should be powerfully influenced by frank self-assessment: A specialist should be willing to bet on the long-term value of his specialty, do whatever it takes to be among the very best, and take the risks and seek the rewards of a more entrepreneurial career.

Intellectual capital is the source of wealth for individuals as well as for organizations—and it is held in common between them. Not only the content but also the structure of knowledge work reinforce the by-now-obvious fact that value comes from, and therefore rewards accrue to, skills and knowledge. People who move from project to project in what Warren Bennis calls "floating crap games of temporary teams and groups" cannot be paid according to the number of direct reports they have any more than a road warrior can flaunt her status by the number of windows her office has. Instead, "competencies" and "skill sets"—indeed, the full panoply of intellectual assets, including intra-organizational and customer relationships as well as human capital—determine career success.

Intellectual capital is like a joint checking account on which both you and your employer can draw. Much writing and thinking about the economy of the Information Age—including some of my own—has skirted, perhaps obliviously, around what seems to be a fundamental tension: On the one hand is "Me, Inc.," an every-man-for-himself universe of individual initiative and reward, in which the "contract" between employee and employer is a fling, not a marriage; on the other is the team, which may hire its own members, manage its own work, receive rewards as a group and parcel them out to members according to its collective view of their contribution to the group's enterprise. Team members' ostensible managers might not know enough to evaluate their work in projects they do not directly supervise. The economics of intellectual capital explains this contradiction, though it cannot resolve it. Knowledge work, like knowledge itself, is a collaborative product, the joint and several property of the people who do it. What I give to the team I still have, and I also have what the team makes that I did not give it. It is appropriate, then, that the team mediate between me and our customer, the organization-at-large, as the agent dispersing the organization's rewards.

But we are, all of us, our own agents, too, with a portfolio of intellectual assets to manage. We're free to go where we can get the best return on those assets—and in an economy whose chief resources are not factories or land but are instead ourselves and our fellow-passengers on the elevator, we're more able to seek our fortune than ever before. A century and a half ago, in "Self-Reliance," his great, prescient excoriation of Organization Man, Ralph Waldo Emerson wrote: "If our young men miscarry in their first enterprises they lose all heart. If the young merchant fails, men say he is *ruined*. If the finest genius studies at one of our colleges and is not installed in an office within one year afterwards . . . it seems to his friends and to himself that he is right in being disheartened and in complaining the rest of his life." There is a better path, Emerson cried: "A sturdy lad . . . who in turn tries all the professions, who teams it, farms it, peddles, keeps a school, preaches, edits a newspaper, goes to Congress, buys a township, and so forth, in successive years, and always like a cat falls on his feet, is worth a hundred of these city dolls. . . . He has not one chance, but a hundred chances."

Afterword

When I first started looking into the management of corporate brainpower in 1990, the quest for ways to measure and manage knowledge was just beginning. Today it is becoming a business reality, something that can be and is being put to use by managers, investors, and people planning their working lives. It is, I hope, the principal contribution of this book that it offers a framework upon which business people can build useful and valuable strategies for increasing both their intellectual capital and their return on it. The subject is too young for fads, let alone for tried-and-true disciplines; but it is old enough to need a vocabulary. Human capital, structural capital, and customer capital are all intangible—all reflect the knowledge assets of a company—and yet all describe things that business people can get their arms around.

Back then, I knew most of the people who were interested in intellectual capital; now every day's mail brings news of a person or a company I've never heard about that is making significant contributions to the field. The day I am writing these words, in July 1996, I received a fax of the annual report of Celemi, a Swedish multinational that develops training programs for corporate clients, which includes a supplementary balance sheet of its intangible assets. Waiting in my office at *Fortune* is a thick transcript of a two-day symposium held in April 1996 by the U.S. Securities and Exchange Commission, titled "Financial Accounting and Intangible Assets." There are a dozen Web pages I have to check out, a couple of conferences I will attend, and a couple of others I will have to miss. Far from being confident that I know the field, I'm certain, now, that it is growing faster than I can keep up.

The torrent of news shouldn't overwhelm something far more important. As I wrote in Chapter 5, there are only two kinds of intellectual capital. The first is the semipermanent body of knowledge, the expertise, that grows up around a task, a person, or an organization. The second kind of knowledge assets are tools that augment the body of knowledge. In the course of writing this book, I reread most of what I have published in *Fortune* about the subject. My reading brought me at least one gratification: the realization that much of what I wrote even a half decade ago still holds true—indeed, is more obviously true than it might have seemed then, even to me. In 1991, for example, in my first short piece about intellectual capital, I wrote (briefly) about the peculiar economics of increasing returns, a subject that received a new, louder burst of attention from my colleagues and from others (in the *McKinsey Quarterly*, for example) five years later. I also wrote about networks and network externalities, again briefly; but I never mentioned the word "Internet." I'd never heard the word, which isn't surprising: There were about 3,000 networks attached to the Internet then, mostly in defense-related industries and academe; today there are some nine million host computers on the net, mostly commercial, and it's clear to anyone who had not spent the last half-decade in a cabin without electricity that this network of networks will change business life. My point isn't to brag about my foresight, about which, as my stockbroker knows, I have little to boast; instead it is to say that the persistence and increasing relevance of principles and trends I wrote about then argues that a "semipermanent body of knowledge" about intellectual capital exists, ready to be augmented by new tools and more real-world experience: *Your* real world experience, I hope.

I also noticed, as I read through my stuff and that of others, that some of the stories we hopefully told have so far had less than happy endings. Some companies that eagerly and thoughtfully identified and invested in corporate knowledge have not done well. Polaroid, for example, is struggling with weak profits and a stubbornly low stock price. Hewlett-Packard, about which I write enthusiastically in Chapter 8, took a beating on Wall Street in the summer of 1996. Perhaps by the time you read this, that will appear in retrospect simply to be the traditional summer tech-stock slump or a general computer-industry cyclical downturn; perhaps it will turn out to be something else.

A few hard swallows don't make for summary judgment, however. Some companies profiled in Tom Peters's *In Search of Excellence* didn't find it and some of reengineering's glister turned out to be pyrite; that doesn't make their insights and techniques wrong. Business is complicated. Nothing works always. The management of human, structural, and customer capital is part—a major part, an increasingly important part, but only part—of an uncertain and complex endeavor that must deal with technology and competitors that won't stand still, must formulate strategy and place multimillion-dollar bets on the basis of highly imperfect information, and that adds to the mix the most intangible and least describable asset of all, plain old good business judgment. No book can lead an organization. Maybe, though, it can help leaders see a little more clearly.

Tools for Measuring and Managing Intellectual Capital

I LOVE FOOLS' EXPERIMENTS. I AM ALWAYS MAKING THEM.
—CHARLES DARWIN

Measuring the acquisition and use of knowledge assets excites great interest and great skepticism. Even people who decry the inadequacy of today's accounting worry about putting untried, possibly subjective, nonfinancial measures into annual reports. Corporate financial statements are cluttered enough with good will, restructuring charges, and other items, that many complain that they no longer describe financial performance clearly. Stick in measures of nonfinancial assets, Microsoft's chief financial officer Michael Brown says, and you'll simply be adding to the confusion: "The more stuff the accountants put in, the more the analysts take out."

Yet if it would be a mistake to mingle measures of intellectual capital with financial data, it would be a greater one not to use them at all. Ultimately managing intellectual capital depends on finding rigorous ways to track it, which correlate with financial results. The data we want should, first, allow management to evaluate year-to-year performance—to measure progress toward goals—and, second but more difficult, permit company-to-company comparisons. Undoubtedly measuring knowledge assets must be imprecise, but there is a lot of informed guesswork in "hard" numbers, too. If the process of valuing tangibles were foolproof, companies would never have to take write-offs for those assets or argue with tax authorities about whether their useful life (and hence the rate at which they should be depreciated) is five, ten, twenty, or more years. More to the point, enthusiastic experimentation with measurements is the best way to improve them.

There are many tried-and-true ways to measure parts of intellectual capital. Dollar values can be ascribed to brand equity and sets of customers, for example. A generation ago, "human capital accounting" attempted to put numbers on that component of intellectual capital. Other measures don't attempt to put a dollar figure on the *value* of intangibles, but do measure processes or results that depend on it; 3M and Hewlett-Packard, for instance, are among many companies that track the percentage of sales generated by new products, a revealing measure of innovativeness, part of human capital.

In what follows, I offer a smorgasbord of approaches to measuring intellectual assets and the processes that use them. I've made no effort to be comprehensive: My purpose is to share ideas I've found interesting and to provoke companies to experiment with their own.* As I said

---

* Several recent publications discuss nonfinancial performance measurements, some of which apply to intellectual capital. Four deserve mention here, both for their own merits and because their notes and bibliographies offer pointers to other sources. Robert S. Kaplan and David P. Norton's *The Balanced Scorecard* (Boston: Harvard Business School Press, 1996) is an excellent description of the management accounting technique Kaplan and Norton have developed and described in several influential articles in *Harvard Business Review*. A 1995 research report from The Conference Board in New York, *New Corporate Performance Measures* (report number 1118-95-RR) is an excellent discussion of the need for new measurement systems and contains several very good examples. A 1995 report prepared for the Ontario (Canada) Premier's Council with the support of the Canadian Institute of Chartered Accountants, *Performance Measures in the New Economy*, also cogently describes the need for new measures and has the advantage of surveying some pioneering work of Scottish, British, and other non-U.S. thinkers too often overlooked in the United States. Finally, "The Valuation of Intangible Assets," prepared by Arthur Andersen with the Economist Intelligence Unit in London (Special Report No. P254, 1992) contains an excellent discussion of the need for measurements of intangibles together with a survey of methods used to

in the Foreword, the field of intellectual capital is too new for cookbooks. It would be a mistake for any company slavishly and simply to adopt the ideas that follow; each company needs to think through its own sources and uses of intellectual capital. I hope the ideas here will get you started. I've grouped them in four areas—ways to measure the overall value of intangible assets; human capital measurements; structural capital measurements; customer capital measurements. I then conclude with an approach that I've never seen tried, but that I think would result in a powerful way to visualize several dimensions of intellectual capital simultaneously and could act as a "navigator" to guide companies managing knowledge assets.

Measures of the Whole

MARKET-TO-BOOK RATIOS

Value is defined by the buyer, not the seller: Something is worth what someone is willing to pay for it. A company, therefore, is worth what the stock market says: price per share × total number of shares outstanding = market value, what the company as a whole is worth. The simplest, and by no means the worst, measure of intellectual capital is the difference between its market value and its book equity. "Book value," which can be found in every annual report and in *Value Line*, is the equity portion of a company's balance sheet, what's left after all debt is stripped from it. The assumption here is that everything left in the market value after accounting for the fixed assets must be intangible assets. If Microsoft is worth $85.5 billion and its book value is $6.9 billion, then its intellectual capital is $78.6 billion.

It's quick, easy, and reasonable. If the value of a company is greater than the value of what shareholders own, it makes sense to attribute the difference to intellectual capital—for as we discussed in Part Two, human and customer capital are assets companies own jointly with employees and customers. But market-to-book ratios have three prob-

---

evaluate intellectual properties and brands, some of which can be adapted to put values on softer intellectual assets.

lems. First, the stock market is volatile and responds, often strongly, to factors entirely outside the control of management. If the Federal Reserve Board raises interest rates and Microsoft's stock drops 5 percent, does that mean the value of its intellectual capital has dropped, too? If a company trades for less than its book value—as happens sometimes—does that mean it has no intellectual assets whatsoever? Second, there's evidence that both book value and market value are usually understated. To encourage companies to invest in new equipment, IRS rules deliberately permit companies to depreciate assets faster than the rate at which they really wear out; and companies can (within limits) fiddle with depreciation methods to make profits look better or worse than they are. Because the right side of a balance sheet (liabilities plus shareholders' equity) must equal the assets on the left, any understatement of assets results in a corresponding undervaluation of book value. The understatement of market values shows up when companies are acquired. Friendly or unfriendly, takeovers almost always cost a premium over market capitalization. For example, Duracell International's stock was trading at $49 on September 11, 1996; the following day, Gillette offered $60 a share to buy the company. Third, while it's nice to say that Microsoft has $78.6 billion in intangible assets, so what? What can I, as a manager or investor, do with this information?

A way to improve the reliability and usefulness of the difference between market and book value is to look not at the raw number but at the *ratio* between the two. You can then compare one company with similar competitors or its industry average and also make year-to-year comparisons of the ratios. Since exogenous factors like interest rates or general stock market bullishness or bearishness presumably affect every company in an industry more or less equally, that noise is filtered out; and managers and investors can gauge, albeit roughly, how one company is doing vis-à-vis its rivals. A declining market-to-book ratio (over time, or compared to competitors) would then act as a warning.

TOBIN'S Q

A little more work produces a better number than the market-to-book ratio. "Tobin's *q*" is a ratio developed by Nobel prizewinning economist James Tobin. It compares the market value of an asset with its replacement cost. Tobin developed it as a way to predict corporate investment decisions independent of macroeconomic factors such as interest rates. If q is less than 1—that is, if an asset is worth less than the cost of replacing it—then it's unlikely that a company will buy more assets of that kind; on the other hand, companies are likely to invest if similar assets are worth more than their replacement cost.

Tobin's q wasn't developed as a measure of intellectual capital, but it's a good one. Federal Reserve chairman Alan Greenspan has noted that high q and market-to-book ratios reflect the value of investments in technology and human capital. Among other things, q says something about the effect of diminishing returns: When q is very high (say 2: an asset is worth twice its replacement cost) the company is getting extraordinary returns on that class of asset and not feeling the bite from diminishing returns. In this sense, Tobin told me, q is a measure of what economists call "monopoly rents"—i.e., a company's ability to get unusually high profits because it's got something no one else has. That's not a bad definition of the manifest power of intellectual capital: You and your competitors presumably have similar fixed assets, but one of you has something uniquely its own—people, systems, customers—that allows it to make more money.

It's possible to figure Tobin's q for individual assets—a truck, a building—or for a company as a whole: Market value divided by the replacement cost of fixed assets. The down-and-dirty way to figure replacement costs for a company's entire basket of fixed assets is to take the reported value of a company's fixed assets—land, buildings, machinery, equipment, etc.—add back accumulated depreciation, and account for inflation. (If you spend a million dollars on computers, they would be booked as worth $1 million the first year, $800,000 the second year, $600,000 the third year, etc., assuming five-year, straight-line depreciation.) Using Tobin's q instead of market-to-book ratios neutralizes the effects of different depreciation policies. As with market-to-book ratios, Tobin's q is most revealing when like companies are compared over a period of several years.

CALCULATED INTANGIBLE VALUE

An elegant way to put a dollar value on intangible assets has been developed by an Evanston, Illinois, outfit called NCI Research, which is affiliated with the Kellogg School of Business at Northwestern University. NCI got into the question of measuring intangibles out of an interest in helping cities nurture new, knowledge-intensive businesses. Investors like banks are leery of putting money into businesses that have few tangible assets as collateral. If a way could be found to put a monetary value on intangibles, NCI president James Peterson hoped, banks would open their checkbooks.

Leading the NCI project was Thomas Parkinson, who runs the Evanston Business Investment Corp., a seed-money fund that has invested in a score of high-tech companies, mostly startups. Parkinson's group assumed—as we did with market-to-book ratios and Tobin's *q*—that "the market value of a company reflects not only its tangible physical assets but a component attributable to the company's intangible assets." To find the assets that create that extra value, the group then adapted a method used to evaluate brand equity: Brands confer economic benefits (pricing power, distribution reach, improved ability to launch new products such as line extensions) that give their owners a higher return on assets than unbranded competitors. Calculate the premium, and you can infer the value of the brand.

Parkinson, Peterson, and crew applied that thinking to whole corporations: The value of intangible assets equals a company's ability to outperform an average competitor that has similar tangible assets.* Here is how the method works, using Merck & Co. as an illustration. (Even I can do this math, dear reader, so fear not.)

1. Calculate average pretax earnings for three years. For Merck: $3.694 billion.
2. Go to the balance sheet and get the average year-end tangible assets for three years: $12.953 billion.

---

* After I wrote about NCI's work in *Fortune* in 1995, I received letters from a couple of accountants who pointed out that the Internal Revenue Service permits the use of a similar method for calculating intangible assets. The NCI team hadn't known about the IRS method. The IRS's original ruling—"Appeal and Review Memorandum 34" (ARM 34)—was developed in 1920 because breweries and distilleries needed to be able to calculate, for tax purposes, how much Prohibition cost them in terms of lost goodwill and other intangibles. ARM 34 was updated in 1968; the ruling now in force is called Revenue Ruling 68-609. According to the IRS, it "may be used to determine the fair market value of the intangible assets of a business."

3. Divide earnings by assets to get the return on assets: 29 percent. (A nice business, pills.)

4. For the same three years, find the industry's average ROA. NCI used figures from Robert Morris Associates' Annual Statement Studies for companies with the same Standard Industrial Classification code. For pharmaceuticals, the number is 10 percent. (If a company's ROA is below average, stop: NCI's method won't work.)

5. Calculate the "excess return." Multiply the industry-average ROA (10 percent) by the company's average tangible assets ($12.953 billion). That tells you what the average drug company would earn from that amount of tangible assets. Now subtract that from *this* company's pretax earnings, which we got in step one ($3.694 billion). For Merck, the excess is $2.39 billion. That's how much more Merck earns from its assets than the average drugmaker would.

6. Pay Uncle Sam. Calculate the three-year-average income tax rate, and multiply this by the excess return. Subtract the result from the excess return, to get an after-tax number. This is the premium attributable to intangible assets. For Merck (average tax rate: 31 percent), that's $1.65 billion.

7. Calculate the net present value of the premium. You do this by dividing the premium by an appropriate percentage, such as the company's cost of capital. Using an arbitrarily chosen 15 percent rate, that yields, for Merck, $11 billion.

And there you have it: The "calculated intangible value" (CIV) of Merck's intangible assets, the ones that don't appear on the balance sheet. This is not their market value. The market value is higher (Merck's market capitalization minus tangible assets is $45.6 billion), in part because it reflects what it would cost a buyer to create those assets from scratch. What it is, NCI says, is a measure of a company's "ability to use its intangible assets to outperform other companies in its industry." That makes it a number managers should be interested in.

Like the Oracle at Delphi, CIV is as good as the questions you ask it. Certainly the number is a useful addition to a manager's kit, as a tool for benchmarking, for example: A nice feature of CIV is that it permits company-to-company comparisons using audited financial data. Private companies can also use it, comparing themselves to their publicly held brethren; and by using internal figures a business unit such as GE Appliances could compare its intangibles with competitors like Whirlpool. It can also be used to compare divisions or business units within a company, provided they're in the same industry.

In addition, a weak or falling CIV might be a tip-off that you're spending too much on bricks and mortar and not enough on research or brand-building. A rising CIV can help show that a business or division is generating the capacity to produce future cash flows, perhaps before the market—or the budget committee—has recognized it. Over time, the market's valuation of intangibles (market-to-book ratio or Tobin's q) ought to parallel the CIV. It's possible to plot the two numbers on the same graph. NCI did this for twenty-three small companies that had recently gone public, and also, at my request, for Merck, Intel, and International Flavors & Fragrances. A pattern—not unvarying, but noticeable—appears. First, whenever the CIV declined, the market-to-book ratio—and the stock price—did too, often dramatically. But if the market value of intangibles fell while the CIV was rising, that in most cases signaled a buying opportunity. This is another way of saying that when a stock trades close to book value, it's worth a look, but with this twist: Knowing a company's CIV could help you judge whether a low price-to-book ratio reflects a fading business, or one that's rich with hidden value that isn't yet reflected in the stock.

Human Capital Measures

INNOVATION

As we saw in Part Two, human capital's "output" is innovation, structural capital's efficiency. There are a number of ways to track innovation. The simplest is to tally the percentage of sales attributable to new products or services—a measurement that 3M has used for years and to good effect, setting a goal that at least 25 percent of its annual sales should be from products that are less than four years old. Other companies tally numbers of new products or of patents.

A sophisticated variation: Add a measure of *gross margin* from new products. It's possible to cheat on a simple measure of percentage-of-sales-from-innovation by making trivial changes in an existing product: Paint it blue, call it new, and bingo, you've met your goal. But customers, who are rarely stupid, won't pay for cosmetic or minor incremental improvements. They expect these, and expect you to pay for them. Real innovation, however, should command a premium. In some industries, moreover—information technology is the obvious and important example—the pace of change is so great that the measure of innovativeness is not whether you're doing a lot of it but whether you're doing so much so well that you can stay ahead of the industry's fast-falling price curve. Measure, then, gross margins from new products, and compare them to gross margins from old ones. The former should be substantially higher.

EMPLOYEE ATTITUDES

No, this isn't merely feel-good stuff. Studies consistently show a correlation between high morale and superior financial performance. The mere fact that financial excellence cohabits with shiny, happy people doesn't establish causality, of course: It could be that a fat bottom line makes for smiling faces rather than vice versa. But you don't need regression analysis to believe that people who feel as if they are learning, needed, and useful will be more productive than people who are idle and uncertain of their role in the company's success; they're also likely to treat suppliers, customers, and each other better. Studies show a strong relationship between employee attitudes and customer attitudes—evidence of the interplay between human and customer capital.

A word of caution: Employee attitude surveys often turn up discursive, anecdotal information about what's on people's minds, which can be valuable; but to be useful as an index of human capital they need to gather more structured data—On a scale of one to ten, how happy are you at work? Compared to a year ago, are you happier, about the same, less happy? Do you understand how your work benefits customers (not at all, a little, somewhat, pretty much, completely)? Etc.

TENURE, TURNOVER, EXPERIENCE, LEARNING

Another approach to measuring human capital is to maintain indexes of your "inventory" of knowledgeable employees. This is tricky:

Youth and experience both have their virtues and age discrimination is immoral as well as illegal. In Chapter 6 we saw that the human capital that belongs on a company's intangible balance sheet resides in expert employees who are doing work that adds value for customers. In that chapter I discussed how Canadian Imperial Bank of Commerce's "competency maps" allow individuals and department heads to match their skills or the skills of their staffs against the skills customers expect them to have. Keeping records of the gap between accomplishment and expectation results in one measure of human capital, especially useful at the general manager level. It is not enough to identify these gaps, of course: You need plans—real plans, with funding—to close them.

A Swedish company named Celemi International, which provides human resources consulting, training, and change management services, published several interesting measurements of tenure and expertise in its 1995 annual report. They include:

▼ The average number of years of experience employees have in their professions
▼ Turnover among experts (defined as "employees working directly with customers in projects"; top managers count only if they work actively with customers)
▼ Seniority among experts (average years with the company)
▼ Value-added per expert and per employee
▼ The percentage of customers who are "competence-enhancing." I like this a lot, though it's fuzzy: "Competence-enhancing customers," the report says, are those "who bring projects challenging the competence of Celemi's employees. These customers are valuable because Celemi's employees learn from them."*
▼ Rookie ratio (the percentage of employees with less than two years experience)

* Competence-enhancing customers are a human capital asset because they improve Celemi's people. Celemi also measures the percentage of customers who are image-enhancing (prestigious customers whose testimonials are valuable), a number that could be used to measure customer capital. The firm also tracks customers who are organization-enhancing (whose demanding projects force Celemi to use its resources more efficiently or to acquire new structural intangible assets), a possible measure of structural capital. A customer may be counted in more than one of the three categories.

MORE HUMAN CAPITAL MEASURES

Answering the following questions won't result in quantitative data about human capital, but will yield a rich harvest of qualitative information:

▼ Among the many skills possessed by your employees, which do customers value most? Why?
▼ Which skills and talents are most admired by your employees? What accounts for any difference between what customers value and what employees value?
▼ What emerging technologies or skills could undermine the value of your proprietary knowledge?
▼ Where in your organization do high-potential managers most want to be assigned? Where do they least want to work? How do they explain their preference?
▼ What percentage of managers have completed plans for training and developing their successors?
▼ What percentage of *all* employees' time is spent in activity of low value to customers? What percentage of *expert* employees' time is spent in activity of low value to customers?
▼ When competitors are hiring, do they hire from you?
▼ Why do people leave you to accept jobs elsewhere?
▼ Among experts in your labor market—including headhunters— what is your company's reputation vis-à-vis its competitors?

THE KNOWLEDGE BANK

Every company builds a bank of knowledge—research, skills, customer lists, tradecraft, and more. Says Alan Benjamin, former director of SEMA Group, one of Europe's leading computer-services companies, with 1994 sales of $853 million: "The knowledge bank, not the buildings, is the reason people invest in your company or come to work for it." What's it worth?

Now retired, Benjamin, sixty-three, developed a measure of the value of the knowledge bank for the "Tomorrow's Company" inquiry, a study of the sources of competitive advantage sponsored by a veritable *Debrett's Peerage* of British industry and conducted by the Royal Society for the Encouragement of Arts, Manufactures, and Commerce. Benjamin recast the income statement of a division of an actual company to show how it would look if the main measurements were the creation of knowledge and cash—not bad criteria for the Information Age. The pseudonymous outfit is "Brilliant PLC." Here is a snapshot of Brilliant PLC's cash account:

Sales (12 mo.)	£2,788,011
Minus overhead (rent, raw material, supplies)	−£506,386
capital spending	−£98,000
labor	−£1,594,602
Cash surplus at year-end	£589,023

In ordinary accounting, the capital expenses would be moved to the balance sheet and put on the asset side. The income statement would be charged only for depreciation from it and prior years' capital spending. Benjamin upended the rules to calculate the knowledge bank—the "real" profit of Brilliant PLC. First, treat capital spending as an expense, not an investment. Benjamin's argument: "In a people world, capital spending just houses people and equips them and gives them something to work with." The long-term investments are intellectual.

On the other hand, he deferred a portion of salaries, treating it as investment—what he calls "real value." To do this, calculate how much of an employee's work is devoted to current-year tasks and how much to seeding the future (training, planning, research, business development, etc.). Thus, all the salary of a clerk is expensed, but half the pay of the marketing staff might be treated as capital spending and booked as an asset, because half the value of their work will be realized in future years. Most of the pay of a new hire, who accomplishes more learning than doing, would also be banked. In the lab, researchers' entire salaries are capitalized, as are all training costs. You can come up with these figures by guess and by gosh, but don't. If knowledge is your most important asset, these books matter more than the ones auditors check; before you defer employee cost by capitalizing it, you should seriously analyze what employees do and learn. That will take work, but not much more than, say, rethinking job descriptions.

One group of employees gets special treatment. Brilliant PLC's ninety-one technical employees, whose combined pay is £1.1 million, are highly skilled, key people. Though their time is spent generating this year's revenue, they are in such demand that recently 30 percent a year have been wooed away; hiring and training replacements costs £10,000 a head. Their value, therefore, is based on these figures: Sixty-four of the ninety-one will probably stay; their replacement cost is £10,000; so £640,000 goes in the bank and the balance is expensed. Taking all this into account for Brilliant PLC, Benjamin apportioned the payroll as follows:

Deferred labor cost (added to knowledge bank):	£871,979
Expensed labor cost (no residual value):	£722,623

Next, Benjamin conservatively estimates the value added by R&D: the net present value of estimated sales from forthcoming products, minus contingency deductions for failure and unforeseen competition or costs. That, too, goes in the knowledge bank.

Now it's possible to draw a new bottom line:

Sales (12 mo.)	£2,788,011
Minus overhead (£506,386), capital spending (£98,000), and expensed labor (£722,623)	−£1,327,009
	£1,461,002
Plus R&D value added	£40,097
Surplus at year-end	£1,501,099

That surplus consists of £589,023 in cash (the same as in the first, conventional figures above) and £912,076 in banked knowledge—capitalized pay plus the R&D value added—which the company can call on in the future and which, like any asset, will depreciate. Resist your lawyers' argument to keep these calculations to yourself. There's some guesswork in these figures—how fast to depreciate the knowledge bank, for example—and the best way to reduce the subjectivity is to expose them to sunlight.

As with tangible assets, so with the knowledge bank: Knowing the size of your stash is the first step, but you really want to measure your return on assets. The return-on-human-capital (knowledge bank divided by profit) will probably be lower than ROA conventionally measured. It ought to be: The entire argument of this book is that the intellectual capital of Information Age companies is greater than their financial capital. If your CFO has time to kill, she might try to construct a q ratio for the knowledge bank.

Structural Capital Measures

To picture structural intellectual assets, you need two kinds of data: measures of the value of accumulated stocks of corporate knowledge, and measures of organizational efficiency, i.e., of the degree to which the company's systems augment and enhance the work of its people rather than obstruct them.

VALUING STOCKS OF KNOWLEDGE

Structural capital takes innumerable forms and each company's will be different. Accountants and lawyers have developed many methods to put price tags on patents, processes, trademarks, and copyrights from work they have done in licensing or selling such structural intangibles; we won't go into them here. It's harder to put a value on intellectual assets that take less defined form. Weston Anson, an MBA and lawyer who runs a La Jolla, California, company called Trademark & Licensing Associates, Inc., and has worked with Procter & Gamble, Du Pont, and other companies and helped the Roman Catholic Church evaluate the Vatican library, has a method of identifying and evaluating structural intangibles that can be applied to some of the more oddball assets as well as familiar ones.

To find them, Anson thinks of intangible assets as falling into one of three groups. These are (1) a technical bundle (trade secrets, formulas, proprietary test results, etc.; (2) a marketing bundle (copyrights, corporate name and logo, warranties, advertising, package design and copyrights, trademark registrations, etc.*); and (3) a skills and knowledge bundle (databases, manuals, quality control standards, asset management processes, security systems, business licenses, noncompete clauses; proprietary management information systems, etc.). He then applies three basic tests to see if an asset has marketplace value: Does it differentiate your product or service from another's? Does it have value to someone else? Would someone else pay a fee for it? To answer those questions, you should look at an intangible asset's uniqueness, breadth of use, incremental profit margins, legal status, life expectancy, and so on.

How should one price these assets? Cost is one way, but as we have seen it's a lousy one; the cost of creating intellectual capital is not necessarily related to the value of what's created. But business is so rich with stories and data that there's usually something out there that's somehow comparable even to the most amorphous intangibles. From industry scuttlebutt, published information, and so on, you can find it. For a glass-making technology, what have comparable technologies sold for, or what royalty rates have been paid to license them? For a noncompete clause in an executive's contract, have there been any court fights or negotiations involving similar deals in your business or ones like it?

The next step is to rate the relative strength of your asset versus the comparables. Anson uses a scorecard he calls Valmatrix. It lists twenty factors such as pretax margins, breadth of product line, potential for line extensions, barriers to entry, and licensing potential; for more curious intangibles, you might need to design a special list. For each factor, score the asset from 0 to 5 based on your assessment—buttressed by numbers about market share, attributable cash flow, etc., wherever you can get them—of its relative value compared to the five best comparable assets. The best possible score is 100, which would be earned by that rare intangible asset that was top-of-the-line for all twenty factors; the highest score Anson has ever given was a 91, and that was under unique circumstances, in one Latin American market.

You can use the Valmatrix score in several ways. First, its twenty factors with ratings of relative strength are a managing agenda: You now have a factor-by-factor comparison of how you stand compared

---

* Anson puts brand names in this bundle; I think they go better in customer capital than structural.

to your best competitors. Second, the score can be plugged into an established method of evaluating intangibles (such as royalty rates, asset sales, or even costs). If you know the particulars of licensing or sales agreements for an asset that earned a 50 on your scorecard, and your comparable asset merits a 60, then the higher Valmatrix score tells you to value yours relatively more.

WORKING CAPITAL TURNS

One way structural capital improves performance is by allowing companies to substitute information for inventory. To track that, measure working capital turnover—the number of times each year that working capital cycles through a company. The measure, devised by George Stalk of the Boston Consulting Group and used by Allied-Signal, GE, Hillenbrand Industries, and others, is a powerful index of operating efficiency, and you can calculate it on the back of a cocktail napkin. First write down your working capital: receivables plus inventory, minus payables. To eliminate seasonal variations, do this at the start of each year and the end of each quarter, then average the five numbers. Divide the average into the year's sales. The higher the number, the less money you have tied up to get your sales.

You can compare working capital turns across divisions or with competitors (receivables, payables, and inventories are published in annual reports), but be careful: For example, LIFO and FIFO inventory numbers aren't comparable. Because working capital measures everything from purchasing through billing, it is almost impossible for managers to claim improvement in one area by hiding the mess elsewhere. Receivables won't fall unless billing and shipping errors vanish. You can't cut inventories without reducing idle machine time, picking top-notch suppliers who deliver small lots just in time, and shortening distribution pipelines—all indicators of strong structural capital. (Some service companies might need to develop a proxy for inventories, such as hours of work spent but not yet billed.)

MEASURING BUREAUCRATIC DRAG

There are any number of ways to see whether your company's systems are standing between your people and your customers. A trio:

▼ *Suggestions made versus suggestions implemented.* If employees come up with 1,000 new ideas and the company puts only 279 of them into effect, you're hog-tying your people.
▼ *Time-to-market.* How long does it take to develop and introduce new products or services?
▼ *The too-many-chiefs test:* What is the ratio between revenues and SG&A (sales, general, and administrative) costs?
▼ *Set-up times, minimum profitable lot sizes, etc.* Measures of flexibility can be good proxies for measures of structural capital.

MEASURING THE BACK OFFCE

Markets, we agree, establish value; but some work is never sold, though it costs money to produce—for example, back-office information services, such as creating purchase orders and invoices or collecting and crunching numbers for internal reports. The lack of an objective measure of *value* for such processes bedeviled Thomas Housel, who was responsible for reengineering at Pacific Bell and is now teaching at the University of Southern California. Says Housel: "Reengineering ought to increase value, not cut costs—and especially not cut costs at the expense of value. But when a process doesn't have a salable output, we had no way of knowing if we increased value or of figuring a return on investment."

Working with Valery Kanevsky, an expert in the mathematics of complexity who is a three-time winner of Moscow University's top math prize, Housel found a recherché but ingenious solution for his dilemma. Be warned: This is wild. But Hewlett-Packard, which like many information technology companies sells reengineering services on the side, has adopted the Housel/Kanevsky technique, which it calls business process auditing. The technique is a lens through which companies can measure how efficiently they create value from information; as such, it can be used to evaluate and improve the management of intellectual assets that never see the clarifying light of a market.

The premise of Housel's and Kanevsky's work is that value-added equals change; that is, raw material enters a process, work is performed that alters it, and something new and more valuable comes out. No change, no added value. When knowledge work has a reasonably well-defined output (such as a purchase order; the technique can't be used for creative processes like designing dashboards or writing punch lines for jokes), it's possible to measure the change in terms of information—the more information has been added or changed, the more value has been created. In its most precise form, this would be done by counting up how many bits and bytes are changed during the work, but a plain-language description will often serve as well. Because digital code is a universal, it permits comparisons between different processes or between companies. For example, one could compare telephone order-taking at L.L. Bean versus Lands' End in terms of information-value-added as well as cost. From there it's easy to calculate return on investment in an intangible process or how efficiently an operation uses information.

To make sure it's value that is being added, not just verbiage, Kanevsky adapted work done by Andrey Kolmogorov (1903–87), a renowned Russian mathematician who in the 1960s developed ways to describe complex systems in the shortest possible mathematical form. This means compressing all repeats and all patterns in the equations. Don't write $2 \times 2 \times 2$; write 2^3. If you don't compress repeats and patterns, says Kanevsky: "You will confuse redundancy with change and reward lousy work."*

Pac Bell used the technique to evaluate new software to support

---

* Murray Gell-Mann, the Nobel prizewinning physicist who is the head of the Santa Fe Institute, illustrates the process of removing redundancies by telling the story of a schoolboy whose homework assignment is to write a 300-word theme about something that happened to him on the weekend. He forgets the assignment until he is finishing breakfast Monday morning, whereupon he grabs a piece of paper and writes: "Saturday morning, I looked out my window and saw smoke and flames pouring from the building next door. I shouted: 'Fire! Fire! Fire! Fire! Fire! Fire! Fire! Fire! Fire! Fire! Fire! . . .' "

Kolmogorov, Gell-Mann says, would strip the theme of redundancies by making it read: "Saturday morning, I looked out my window and saw smoke and flames pouring from the building next door. I shouted: 'Fire!' 280 times."

the process of placing orders for phone service; it got the go-ahead when Housel and Kanevsky reported that it produced 80 percent more information per dollar of cost than the old system. A Hewlett-Packard client learned that its testing process cost a lot but added little new information, and decided to put the job up for bids by outside suppliers.

Customer Capital Measures

CUSTOMER SATISFACTION

Of course you measure it. But do you measure it well? Big "how did we do?" surveys are of trivial value. Says David Larcker, professor of accounting at the Wharton School: "Measurements of this sort are well known to be unreliable. Customer satisfaction is too complicated to measure by means of an unscientific sample's knee-jerk rating on a scale of one to five." (And have you noticed that those surveys seem designed to monitor employees rather than gauge customer satisfaction? Yes, the front desk clerk was courteous, but my room wasn't ready.)

If you can't demonstrate the link between increased customer satisfaction and improved financial results, you're not measuring customer satisfaction correctly. Happy customers should exhibit at least one of three measurable characteristics: loyalty (retention rates), increased business (share-of-wallet), and insusceptibility to your rivals' blandishments (price tolerance).

MEASURING ALLIANCES

Customer capital is jointly owned by you and your customers. There are a number of financial and nonfinancial ways to see if you're creating it.

—Quality data, information on savings (for both parties) from shared processes such as inspection or electronic data interchange, figures on inventories (again, for both buyer and seller) and availability all help establish the value of intimate relationships between you and your customers or your suppliers.

—It is also worth keeping track of your customers' financial strength and growth and your share of their business: If you are a key supplier to a strong customer, you have a valuable asset. Someone with better math skills than I might be able to construct a measurement of customer capital based on key customers' financial strength and growth versus their competitors'. Some sophisticated buyers, such as Marks & Spencer and Motorola, have begun trying to measure, in qualitative terms, their suppliers' creative contributions, responsiveness, flexibility, and the like.

WHAT'S A LOYAL CUSTOMER WORTH?

Customers are the most important asset a company has. You know this in your heart. Surely, then, you have at your fingertips answers to some simple questions: What is the net present value of your customer base? How much is a new customer worth? How much is it worth to keep an old one?

Though customer loyalty is an intangible asset, the math needed to evaluate it is straightforward. Finding out what numbers to plug into the formula requires legwork, however, making it a perfect project for the first-year MBA students you hire next summer. The effort will be repaid many times if it helps you keep customers. Says consultant Frederick Reichheld, a principal at Bain & Co.: "Raising customer retention rates by five percentage points increases the value of an average customer by 25% to 100%." Here, based on Reichheld's work and that of Claes Fornell, an economist at the University of Michigan Business School, is how to calculate how much a customer is worth.

1. Decide on a meaningful period of time over which to do the calculations. This will vary depending on your planning cycles and your business: A life insurer should track customers for decades, a disposable-diaper maker for just a few years, for example.

2. Calculate the profit your customers typically generate each year you keep them. Track several samples—some relative newcomers, some with long histories—to find out how much business they gave you each year, and how much it cost you to serve them. (If possible,

segment them by age, income, sales channel, etc.) Make sure you look at the whole panoply of costs and benefits for your customers. On the cost side: For the first year, remember to subtract the cost of acquiring new customers, such as advertising, commissions, the portion of sales overhead devoted to serving new customers, back-office costs of setting up a new account; for subsequent years, figure in maintenance costs, such as customer service; these will be lower than the cost of acquiring the customer in the first place, but still are important to track. (If you find you spend almost no money retaining customers, that alone speaks volumes.) On the revenue side, make sure you get specific numbers that reveal the buying behavior of long-term customers—profit per customer in year one, year two, etc.—not averages for all customers or all years. Long-term customers tend to make bigger purchases, pay higher prices than newcomers (who are often lured by discounts), and create less bad debt; they also buy additional items (Post-its as well as Scotch Tape, savings accounts as well as checking accounts), and bring in additional business through referrals.

If you've done the work thoroughly, you will end up with a chart like this:

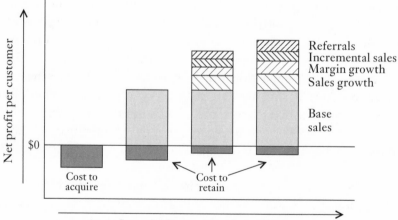

3. Then chart customer "life expectancy," using the samples to find out how much your customer base erodes each year. Again, specific figures are better than an average like "10 percent a year"; cus-

tomers who have been with you a long time are much less likely to leave than freshmen are.

4. Once you know the profit per customer per year and the customer-retention figures, calculate the net present value of a customer. Pick a discount rate—if you want a 15 percent annual return on assets, use that, since customer capital is an asset. Apply the discount rate to each year's profit, adjusted for the likelihood that the customer will leave. In year one, the NPV will be profit $\div$ 1.15. Next year, NPV = (year-two profit $\times$ retention rate) $\div$ 1.15^2. In year n, the last year in the period you chose, the NPV is the nth-year's profit $\div$ 1.15n. The sum of years 1 through n is how much your customer is worth—the net present value of all the profits you can expect from his tenure: In effect, it's what someone else would pay to get the customer.

This is invaluable information. You can use it to find out how much to spend to attract customers, and, if you analyze customers by segment, which customers to pursue and which to let slide. Better still, you can exploit the economic leverage customer satisfaction offers. You probably spend more money attracting new customers than you do retaining old ones. Repeat business—the ultimate manifestation of customer capital—almost certainly merits bigger investments than you make. To see how much, go back to your figures, and calculate how much more your customers would be worth if you increased your retention rate by 5 percent. Reichheld and his colleagues at Bain did this for several industries. For advertising agencies, a 5 percent increase in retention rates translated into a 95 percent increase in customer value. For credit-card companies: 75 percent. Even software makers, hotfooting after new business in a fast-growing industry, would see a 35 percent increase in customer value if they lost fewer old accounts. And customer retention is the best possible growth strategy; as Reichheld says, "You can fill a bucket a lot faster if it's not leaking."

An Intellectual Capital Navigator

No single measurement will ever describe a company's stocks and flows of intellectual capital. Just as financial accounting looks at a number of indexes—debt-to-equity ratio; cash flow; returns on sales, assets, and equity, to name but a few—to paint a picture of financial performance, intellectual capital accounting needs to look at corporate performance from several points of view. What might be a key indicator for one company could be trivial for another, depending on the industry it's in and the strategy it has chosen to follow. For example, in my business—magazine publishing—measures of customer capital might include subscription renewal rates, average discounts for advertisers, number of letters to the editor, or number of requests to reprint articles; for Campbell's Soup, key measures might include brand equity, market share, supermarket shelf space, or the ability to introduce line extensions.

Yet the existence of so many possible nonfinancial measurements creates the risk that companies will use too many of them, cluttering their corporate dashboard with instrumentation and, in the end, learning nothing important because they know so much about what's not important. Three principles should guide a company in choosing what to measure:

Keep it simple. Shoot for no more than three measurements each of human, structural, and customer capital, plus one number that gives you a picture of the whole.

Measure what's strategically important. If your company is selling old-fashioned reliability, why track the number of new patent applications?

Measure activities that produce intellectual wealth. Lots of important stuff that companies should measure is only sketchily related, if it's related at all, to intellectual capital—not just financial data like quarterly earnings but also nonfinancial information like occupational health and safety records. For God's sake measure safety, but not as part of an effort to identify and manage knowledge formation. Focus—here—on items that tell you something about intellectual capital.

My editors at *Fortune* don't like radar charts, but I do, so here's my chance. Radar charts allow you to create a coherent picture from several, heterogeneous kinds of data. They start with a circle, like a radar screen, from the center of which radiate as many lines as you have items to measure. I've put ten on the examples that follow, but you can use any number. Then mark each axis with a relevant scale. They can vary: One might be ratios, another percentages, another raw numbers, and the hash marks don't have to be equally spaced. For most measures, you'll put zero at the center of the chart, but you can do the opposite. For a measure like "knowledge-worker turnover rate," low numbers are better than high, so you should put zero at the outside end of the axis, where it crosses the arc of the circle.

The chart that follows is an intellectual capital navigator for an imaginary company. It uses one overall measurement (market-to-book ratio) and three indicators each for human, structural, and customer capital. I put scales (but no numbers) on the axes. If this were a real company, I'd set up the scales so that in each case the company's goal was on the rim, where the axis crosses the circle: For something like market-to-book ratio, I might put −0.5 at the center and whatever's best-in-class for the industry (+2.0, +6.0 . . .) on the circle; for working capital turns, if the company currently got three turns a year and we wanted to double the number, I'd put 3 halfway along that axis and 6 at the rim.

Then plot where you are on each scale. Connect the dots and you'll get an irregular polygon that might look like this:

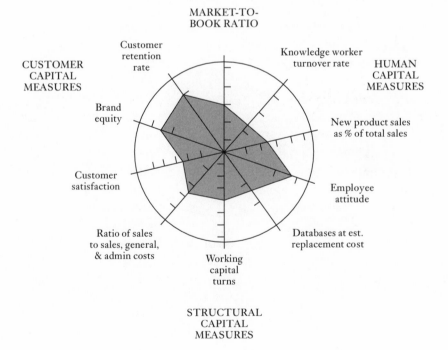

What's inside the polygon is what you've got; what's outside it is what you want.

There's a lot of information in a chart like this, but its greatest value is the overall picture it creates. A navigation tool should not only tell you where you are but also show you where you should be going: Gee, we're doing great with customers, but we're losing good people and if we don't get our systems up to snuff, we'll be in trouble. If you can get comparable data for competitive companies (or benchmark data for your industry), you can set your chart against others and get a picture of your relative strengths and weaknesses; you can also compare one year's chart with another's and see where you are progressing toward your goals and where you are struggling. The chart might also point out anomalies that bear investigating: A chart like the second one here, which shows relatively high customer satisfaction and brand equity but mediocre customer retention, suggests that something strange is happening in your market.

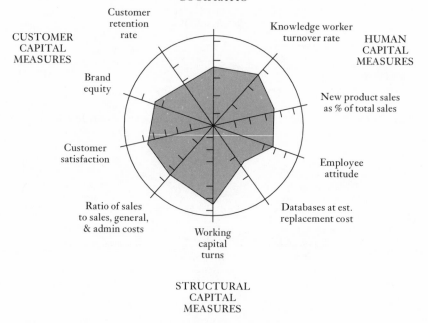

Notes

FOREWORD

p. XI   Nokia: Haswerner Voss, "Virtual Organizations: The Future Is Now," *Strategy and Leadership*, July–August 1996, p. 14.

p. XIII   In 1768, a Swede: Gunnar Eliasson, an economist at the Royal Institute of Technology in Stockholm, told me about Westerman.

pp. XIII–XIV   In 1940, Buckminster Fuller: "Industrialization," *Fortune*, February 1940, pp. 50 ff.

p. XIV   "When I was a kid . . .": Interview with Walter Wriston, quoted in Thomas A. Stewart, "Brainpower," *Fortune*, June 3, 1991, p. 44.

p. XIV   Drucker says: Peter F. Drucker, "Planning for Uncertainty," *The Wall Street Journal*, June 22, 1992, p. A12.

p. XVIII   "The vast bulk . . .": A. Lawrence Lowell, *What a University President Has Learned* (New York: Macmillan, 1938), p. 41.

CHAPTER ONE: THE KNOWLEDGE ECONOMY

p. 4   In 1958, the Adolph Coors Company: William F. Hosford and John L. Duncan, "The Aluminum Beverage Can," *Scientific American*, September 1994, Volume 271, Number 3, pp. 48–53.

pp. 4–5   One of the world's largest: Interviews with Alcoa officials, 1992 and 1996.

p. 7   Growth of railroad freight service: U.S. Department of Commerce, Bureau of the Census, *Historical Statistics of the United States Colonial Times to 1957*, Washington, D.C., 1960, p. 428.

p. 7   The eight o'clock whistle: For a discussion of how difficult it was to create the labor discipline needed by industry, see Shoshana Zuboff, *In the Age of the Smart Machine* (New York: Basic Books, 1988), pp. 31–36.

p. 8   Eventually the Industrial Revolution: Patrick O'Brien and Gaglar Keyder, *Economic Growth in Britain and France 1780–1914: Two Paths to the Twentieth Century* (London: George Allen & Unwin, 1978), pp. 163, 168. Peter F. Drucker, "The Age of Social Transformation," *The Atlantic Monthly*, November 1994, p. 54.

p. 8   One can make a persuasive case: See, for example, John Ellis, *Brute Force: Allied Strategy and Tactics in the Second World War* (New York: Viking, 1990), and Daniel Yergin, *The Prize: The Epic Quest for Oil, Money and Power* (New York: Simon & Schuster, 1991).

pp. 8–9   Shortly after the Civil War: U.S. Department of Commerce, Bureau of the Census, *Historical Statistics of the United States Colonial Times to 1957*, Washington, D.C., 1960, p. 141.

p. 9   Today only 3.4 million Americans: U.S. Department of Commerce, Bureau of the Census, *Statistical Abstract of the United States 1995*, Washington, D.C., 1995, pp. 416–17.

pp. 9–10   "The downsizing of America": The *Times* series ran for a week beginning March 3, 1996. For an examination of misleading statistics and emphasis in the series, see John Cassidy, *The New Yorker*, April 22, 1996, pp. 51 ff.

p. 10   In 1994, *Business Week:* "The Spawning of a Third Sector: Information," *Business Week*, November 7, 1994, p. 116.

p. 11   In 1977, the U.S. Department of Commerce: Marc Uri Porat, *The Information Economy: Definition and Measurement* (Washington, D.C.: U.S. Department of Commerce, Office of Telecommunications, 1977 [OT special publication 77-12]).

p. 12   Even Pope John Paul II recognized: Pope John Paul II, *Centesimus Annus,* quoted in the *New York Times,* May 3, 1991, p. A10.

pp. 12–13   The original IBM personal computer: Interview by Ani Hadjian with Sarafina Estie of IBM, October 1993.

p. 13   "The electro-mechanical boxes": Jodie Glore, quoted in Thomas A. Stewart, "Welcome to the Revolution," *Fortune*, December 13, 1993, p. 66 ff.

p. 13   Steel, of course, was the quintessential: Thanks to my *Fortune* colleague Geoffrey Colvin for the thinking, and some of the language, in this comparison of steel and microchips.

p. 14   Three out of ten large U.S. industrial companies: Thomas A. Stewart, "Welcome to the Revolution," *Fortune*, December 13, 1993, pp. 66 ff.

p. 14   According to *Purchasing* magazine: V. Mirchandani, "Procurement: The Under-Exploited Line in the Supply Chain," Gartner Group Research Note, January 19, 1996.

p. 14   Chrysler outsources 70 percent: Shawn Tully, "You'll Never Guess Who Really Makes . . ." *Fortune*, October 3, 1994, p. 124.

p. 14   "the convergence of goods and services": Steven Goldman, Roger Nagel, and Kenneth Preiss, *Agile Competitors and Virtual Organizations* (New York: Van Nostrand Rheinhold, 1995).

p. 14   International voice telephone . . . data traffic: Charles Goldfinger, "Intangible Economy and Its Implications for Statistics and Statisticians," unpublished paper delivered at Eurostat-ISTAT Seminar, Bologna, Italy, February 7, 1996; interview with Danielle Danese, October 8, 1993.

p. 15   in 1995, after the airlines: "American to Make Reservations System a Separate Unit," *New York Times,* April 17, 1996, p. D4.

p. 15   "Money has been changing": Joel Kurtzman, *The Death of Money* (New York: Little, Brown, 1994), pp. 15–16.

p. 15   Americans need so much less muscle power: U.S. Department of Commerce, Bureau of the Census, *Statistical Abstract of the United States 1995,* Washington, D.C., 1995, p. 146; U.S. Department of Commerce, Bureau of the Census, *Historical Statistics of the United States Colonial Times to 1957,* Washington, D.C., 1960, p. 774.

p. 16   "a Pearl Harbor attack on our information infrastructure": Stewart Baker, e-mail to "Interesting People" mailing list (interesting-people@eff.org), April 24, 1996.

p. 16   "congealed resources": Interview with Brian Arthur, November 12, 1990.

p. 17   The new era is already here: For a rich discussion of the social and economic changes of the Information Age, see Peter F. Drucker, "The Age of Social Transformation," *The Atlantic Monthly,* November 1994.

CHAPTER TWO: THE KNOWLEDGE COMPANY

p. 20   Take capital spending: Thomas A. Stewart, "Welcome to the Revolution," *Fortune*, December 13, 1993, pp. 66 ff. Using slightly different statistics, Charles Jonscher compared production-technology capital spending to information-technology spending from 1965–83. Some of his data (in billions of 1985 dollars):

YEAR	PRODUCTION TECHNOLOGY SPENDING	INFORMATION TECHNOLOGY SPENDING	RATIO OF INFORMATION TO PRODUCTION TECHNOLOGY SPENDING
1965	60.3	18.8	0.31
1970	63.4	28.6	0.45
1975	68.6	27.4	0.40
1980	96.7	52.0	0.54
1983	77.2	61.5	0.80

Charles Jonscher, "An Economic Study of the Information Technology Revolution," in Thomas J. Allen and Michael S. Scott Morton, eds., *Information Technology and the Corporation of the 1990s: Research Studies* (New York and Oxford: Oxford University Press, 1994), p. 27.

p. 21   In the first half of the 1990s: Thomas A. Stewart, "What Information Costs," *Fortune*, July 10, 1995, p. 120, based on data from Stephen Roach, chief economist of Morgan Stanley, Inc.

p. 21   "If R&D investment begins to surpass": Fumio Kodama, *Analyzing Japanese High Technologies: The Techno-Paradigm Shift* (London and New York: Pinter Publishers, 1991), p. 2.

p. 21   "the anticipated technical ones": Lee Sproull and Sara Kiesler, *Connections: New Ways of Working in the Networked Organization* (Cambridge, Mass.: MIT Press, 1991), p. 4.

p. 22   "Information technology is characterized": Shoshana Zuboff, *In the Age of the Smart Machine*, pp. 9–10.

p. 23   Many of those studies: For a discussion of research on IT and productivity, see Erik Brynjolfsson and Lorin Hitt, "New Evidence on the Returns of Information Systems," MIT Sloan School, Cambridge, Mass., March 15, 1993 (Revised June 1993 and October 1993).

p. 23   Recent company-level figures: Brynjolfsson and Hitt, *op. cit.*, 1993; Erik Brynjolfsson and Lorin M. Hitt, "Three Measures of Information Technology's Contributions: Creating Value and Destroying Profits?" MIT Sloan School, Cambridge, Mass., December 1994. The numbers are for improvement "at the margin"—that is, they show the return on each additional dollar of spending.

p. 25   For most of business history: For example, inventory was the secret behind the world dominance of the Dutch economy, and Amsterdam in particular, in the seventeenth century: Amsterdam's huge warehouses allowed the Dutch to control European and, to a considerable extent, all of world trade in an environment where information was slow, imperfect, and uncertain. See Fernand Braudel, *The Perspective of the World* (New York: Harper & Row, 1984).

p. 25   "new computerized control systems": David D. Hale, "The Weekly Money Report" (Chicago: Kemper Financial Services, Inc.) October 6, 1993.

p. 26   "A nineteenth-century farmer": Seth Lloyd, "Learning How to Control Complex Systems," *Bulletin of the Santa Fe Institute* (vol. 10, no. 1: Spring 1995), p. 17.

p. 26   Pioneer Hi-Bred: See Thomas A. Stewart, "Brainpower," *Fortune*, June 3, 1991, pp. 44 ff.

p. 27   "We've got to substitute information": Interview with Richard Karcher, June 2, 1996.

p. 28   CUC International: Stratford Sherman, "Will the Information Superhighway Be the Death of Retailing?" *Fortune*, April 18, 1994, p. 98.

p. 28   "If you had to do the banking industry over": *The Wall Street Journal*, November 3, 1995, p. C2.

p. 28   Wells Fargo: *New York Times*, November 22, 1995, p. D1.

p. 32   This is how reengineering began: The reengineering gurus rarely phrased their insights this way, but it's evident that that is, in fact, what reengineering's great contribution was. See, for example, Michael Hammer and James Champy, *Reengineering the Corporation* (New York: Harper Business, 1993), pp. 36–44.

p. 33   A dollar invested in a corporation: Margaret M. Blair, *Ownership and Control: Rethinking Corporate Governance for the Twenty-First Century* (Washington, D.C.: Brookings Institution, 1995), chapter 6.

p. 34   "an inside-out holding company": Dee W. Hock, "Institutions in the Age of Mindcrafting," speech to the Bionomics Annual Conference, San Francisco, Calif., October 22, 1994.

p. 35   A third of large banks' revenues: American Bankers Association, *Report of the Market Share Task Force*, Washington, D.C., June 27, 1994, pp. A18–25.

p. 35   "The game of financial intermediation": Interview, March 10, 1995.

p. 35   The Equitable Companies administers: Equitable 1993 annual report.

p. 35   Only five of the twenty-eight Major League baseball teams: Interviews by Joe McGowan with Major League baseball and the National Football League, January 12, 1996.

p. 36   "For a lot of asset-intensive businesses": Interview with Adrian Slywotzky, January 4, 1996.

p. 36   Even an asset-heavy utility: Moody's International Company Data Report, 1995.

p. 36   "Today, we are thinking in terms": Quoted in Thomas A. Stewart, "Welcome to the Revolution," *Fortune*, December 13, 1993, pp. 66 ff.

CHAPTER THREE: THE KNOWLEDGE WORKER

p. 37   A dozen or so men and women: Information about GE's Bayamón plant comes from my visit there in February 1992, and is partly recounted in "The Search for the Organization of Tomorrow," *Fortune*, May 18, 1992, pp. 92 ff.

p. 40   Overall, according to calculations: Stephen R. Barley, "The Turn to a Horizontal Division of Labor: On the Occupationalization of Firms and the Technization of Work," paper prepared for the Office of Educational Research and Improvement, U.S. Department of Education, January 1994.

p. 40   A four-piece division: Dennis A. Swyt, "The Workforce of U.S. Manufacturing in the Post-Industrial Era," paper accepted for publication in the *Technological Forecasting and Social Change Journal*.

p. 40   Secretary of Labor Robert B. Reich: Robert B. Reich, *The Work of Nations: Preparing Ourselves for 21st-Century Capitalism* (New York: Alfred A. Knopf, 1991), pp. 173–80.

p. 41   The growth in service sector employment: Council of Economic Advisers with the U.S. Department of Labor, "Job Creation and Employment Opportunities: The United States Labor Market 1993–1996," cited in *New York Times*, April 24, 1996, p. D4.

p. 41   The major exception: James Aley, "Where the Jobs Are," *Fortune*, September 18, 1995, pp. 53 ff. Aley's article cites detailed studies of 290 industries by econometrician Nuala Beck, author of *Shifting Gears: Thriving in the New Economy* (New York: HarperCollins, 1995).

p. 43   "These days, with computerized factories": Quoted in Myron Magnet, "The Truth About the American Worker," *Fortune*, May 4, 1992, pp. 48 ff.

p. 43   two thirds of the employees of Corning: James R. Houghton, "Global Competition: Unleashing the Power of People," remarks to the Cornell Corporate Forum, Cornell University, Ithaca, N.Y., November 3, 1994, p. 8.

p. 43   Not surprisingly, manufacturers: Neal Templin, "Auto Plants, Hiring Again, Are Demanding Higher-Skilled Labor," *The Wall Street Journal*, March 11, 1994, p. 1; John Holusha, "First to College, Then the Mill," *New York Times*, August 22, 1995, p. D1; Robyn Meredith, "New Blood for the Big Three's Plants," *New York Times*, April 21, 1996, Sec. 3, p. 1; David Wessel, "Scanning the Future, Economic Historian Plumbs Distant Past," *The Wall Street Journal*, February 13, 1996, p. 1.

p. 44   Now secretaries say: Steven Greenhouse, "For Secretaries, E-Mail Beats Typing Pool," *New York Times*, April 24, 1996, p. B1.

pp. 44–45   In 1995, writer Susan Sheehan: Susan Sheehan, "Ain't No Middle Class," *The New Yorker*, December 11, 1996, pp. 82–93.

p. 45   Much has been said and written: David Hale, "How Do We Reconcile America's Economic Success with Its New Sense of Insecurity?" (Chicago: Zurich Kemper Investments, Inc., March 4, 1996), pp. 1–2.

pp. 45–46   The one set of numbers: see, inter alia, Gary Burtless, "Worsening American Income Inequality: Is World Trade to Blame?" *Brookings Review*, vol. 14, no. 2, Spring 1996, p. 30; Don L. Boroughs, "The Economics of Income Inequality," *U.S. News and World Report*, January 22, 1996, p. 47; David Hale, "How Do We Reconcile America's Economic Success with Its New Sense of Insecurity?" (Chicago: Zurich Kemper Investments, Inc., March 4, 1996), p. 2.

p. 46   An economist at the University: James E. Rauch, *Productivity Gains from Geographic Concentration of Human Capital: Evidence from the Cities* (Cambridge, Mass.: National Bureau of Economic Research, working paper no. 3905, November 11, 1991).

p. 46   The more computers are used: Peter Cappelli and Kermit Daniel, *Technology, Work Organization, and the Structure of Wages* (Philadelphia: Wharton School, 1996).

p. 46   "Among economists, the leading": Gary Burtless, op. cit., p. 31.

p. 46   Otherwise, why go to school?: Information about Sweden from interview with Magnus Henekson, August 1993; U.S. educational attainment from U.S. Department of Commerce, *Statistical Abstract of the United States, 1995* (Washington, D.C.: Government Printing Office, 1995), p. 157; German enrollment from *The Economist*, April 6, 1996, p. 21.

p. 48   One company in the top: Thanks to my colleague Geoffrey Colvin for this anecdote.

p. 48   Hundreds of years ago: Christopher Locke, "Duelling Axioms for Concurrent Engineering: Automating Autocracy vs Empowering Local Knowledge," unpublished paper, 1993.

p. 48   It has a professional flavor: See Michael Hammer, *Beyond Reengineering* (New York: Harper Business, 1996), p. 44 et seq.

p. 49   "As firms hire increasing numbers": Stephen R. Barley, "The Turn to a Horizontal Division of Labor: On the Occupationalization of Firms and the Technization of Work," paper prepared for the Office of Educational Research and Improvement, U.S. Department of Education, January 1994, pp. 21, 32.

p. 50   Karl Marx noted: See, for example, Karl Marx, "Economic and Philosophical Manuscripts (1844)," *Early Writings*, Lucio Colletti, ed. (Harmondsworth, England: Penguin, 1975), pp. 279–400.

p. 50   Management could replace: Christopher Locke and John West, "Concurrent Engineering in Context," *Concurrent Engineering*, November–December 1991.

CHAPTER FOUR: THE HIDDEN GOLD

p. 56   "A low-value product": quoted in Thomas A. Stewart, "Brainpower," *Fortune*, June 3, 1991, p. 44.

p. 56   it almost always comes wrapped in some tangible form: Charles Goldfinger,

"Intangible Economy and Its Implications for Statistics and Statisticians," unpublished paper delivered at Eurostat–ISTAT Seminar, Bologna, Italy, February 7, 1996.

p. 57 "In most organizations": Tom Davenport, "Can We Manage Information Behavior?" Ernst & Young Research Note, 1992, p. 3.

p. 58 "It has been 500 years since Pacioli": David Wilson, presentation to "Exploring New Values and Measurements for the Knowledge Era," conference sponsored by Ernst & Young, December 8, 1993.

p. 58 "It focuses on tangible assets": Robert K. Elliott, "The Third Wave Breaks on the Shores of Accounting," *Accounting Horizons*, vol. 6, no. 2 (June 1992), p. 68.

p. 58 "the accounting system": Lewent and Jenkins quoted in Thomas A. Stewart, "Intellectual Capital," *Fortune*, October 3, 1994, p. 68.

p. 59 "Ideas have power by themselves": Interview with Michael Brown, May 16, 1996.

p. 59 But time is simply a proxy: Karl Erik Sveiby and Tom Lloyd, *Managing Knowhow: Add Value . . . By Valuing Creativity* (London: Bloomsbury, 1987), p. 69.

p. 60 The case of Cordiant: *The Wall Street Journal*, May 3, 1995.

p. 60 In 1976, Andrew Lloyd Webber: For the history of The Really Useful Company's adventures in finance, see Steven Albert and Keith Bradley, *The Management of Intellectual Capital*, unpublished monograph (London: Business Performance Group Limited), February 1995, pp. 31–40.

p. 61 In a well-documented study: Michael E. Porter, *Capital Choices: Changing the Way America Invests in Industry* (Washington, D.C.: Council on Competitiveness, 1992), pp. 11, 62.

p. 63 A recent poll of executives: Arthur Andersen, *Highlights of the Knowledge Imperative Symposium Fall 1995* (Chicago: Arthur Andersen & Co., 1995), pp. 10–11.

p. 64 "Imagine the implications": Quoted in Thomas A. Stewart, "Intellectual Capital," *Fortune*, October 3, 1994, p. 68.

CHAPTER FIVE: THE TREASURE MAP

p. 67 "an individual's accumulated knowledge": Steven Albert and Keith Bradley, *The Management of Intellectual Capital*, unpublished monograph (London: the Business Performance Group Limited, 1995), p. 1.

p. 67 "ability, skill, and expertise": Karl Erik Sveiby and Tom Lloyd, *Managing Knowhow: Add Value . . . By Valuing Creativity* (London: Bloomsbury, 1987), pp. 35–36.

p. 67 "knowledge that exists": Thomas A. Stewart, "Brainpower," *Fortune*, June 3, 1991, pp. 44 ff.

p. 67 "to account for intellectual capital": David A. Klein and Laurence Prusak, "Characterizing Intellectual Capital," multiclient program working paper (Boston: Ernst & Young Center for Business Innovation, March 1994), p. 1.

p. 67 "Ideas are the instructions": Paul M. Romer, "Two Strategies for Economic Development: Using Ideas and Producing Ideas," Canadian Institute for Advanced Research Program in Economic Growth and Policy (Working Paper No. 4), 1992, pp. 1–2.

p. 68 "We get 6% and 7% productivity": Interview with John F. Welch, September 15, 1991.

p. 70 "People in companies know intuitively": Rob van der Spek, Knowledge Management Network & Kenniscentrum CIBIT, posting to Knowledge Management Internet discussion group, April 23, 1996.

p. 72 "Out of these beliefs and assumptions": Hubert Saint-Onge, "Building the Intellectual Capital of the Organization," presentation to the 1996 Strategic Management Conference of the Conference Board, New York, January 18, 1996.

p. 73 Only then did they realize: David Kearns and David Nadler, former CEO of

Xerox and head of the Delta Consulting Group, in their book *Prophets in the Dark*, vividly describe how difficult it was to change their own and the corporate thinking to instill the ideas of Total Quality Management.

pp. 73–74 "E-mail and telecommuting are fine": Hubert Saint-Onge, "Building the Intellectual Capital of the Organization," presentation to the 1996 Strategic Management Conference of the Conference Board, New York, January 18, 1996.

p. 74 technicians in one division of AMP: Thomas A. Stewart, "Brainpower," *Fortune*, June 3, 1991, pp. 44 ff.

p. 74 Second, much intellectual capital is tacit: Asking whether knowledge can be sold is one way to distinguish between tacit and explicit intellectual capital. In "Extracting Value from Innovation," a draft paper from March 1994, lawyer Patrick H. Sullivan and David J. Teece, a professor at the University of California at Berkeley, both intellectual property experts, write: "Intellectual capital (IC) has two major components: *intellectual resources* and *intellectual assets*. The intellectual resources of the firm reside within the minds of the employees . . . This resource includes the collective experience, skills, and general know-how of all of the firm's employees. We call it a resource because it is available to the company to use for profit generation, yet it would be difficult for the company to sell these assets in disembodied form . . . Intellectual assets, the second component of IC, are the codified, tangible or physical descriptions of specific knowledge to which the company can assert ownership rights, and they can readily trade these assets in disembodied form."

p. 75 They divide intellectual capital: Edvinsson's taxonomy differs slightly from Saint-Onge's. For Edvinsson, the most important distinction is between the intellectual capital that goes home at night, and that which is left behind; accordingly, he considers customer capital to be part of structural capital. His classification scheme looks like this:

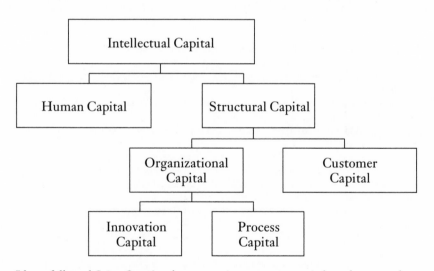

I have followed Saint-Onge's scheme, putting customer capital on the same plane as human and structural capital, on the grounds that customers, like employees, are not the property of the organization.

p. 76 "Leif gave us the idea . . .": In 1990, a Swedish group completed a book in which they drew the distinction between human and structural capital: E. Annel, S. Axlesson, P. M. Emilsson, H. Karlsson, K. E. Sweiby, and C. J. Vikström, *Den Osynliga Balansräkningen* (Stockholm: Affärsvärlden Forlag AB, 1990). The definitions of human, structural, and customer capital are from Hubert Saint-Onge, "Intellectual Capital as a Business Reality," presentation, October 3, 1995.

p. 76 "Universities are a collection": Interview with Betty Zucker, November 13, 1995.

p. 78 The Coca-Cola brand name: Kurt Badenhausen, "Brands: The Management Factor," *Financial World*, August 1, 1995, p. 50.

p. 78 "intellectual capital is useless": Quoted in Thomas A. Stewart, "Brainpower," *Fortune*, June 3, 1991, p. 44.

CHAPTER SIX: HUMAN CAPITAL

p. 83 There is a huge economic and management literature: For an excellent discussion of attempts to understand human capital in economic and accounting terms, see Riel Miller, *Measuring What People Know: Human Capital Accounting for the Knowledge Economy* (Paris: Organization for Economic Cooperation and Development, 1996).

p. 85 In the aftermath of AT&T's notorious: Tom DeMarco, "Human Capital, Unmasked," *New York Times*, April 14, 1996, Sec. 3, p. 13.

p. 85 Meet Robert Zemsky: See National Center on the Educational Quality of the Workforce, "The Other Shoe: Education's Contribution to the Productivity of Establishments (Philadelphia: University of Pennsylvania, 1995).

p. 87 "The only ideas": Thomas A. Stewart, "GE Keeps Those Ideas Coming," *Fortune*, August 12, 1991, p. 40.

p. 88 Kodak, for example, a great company: Information about Kodak's digital imaging from Mark Maremont, "Kodak's New Focus," *Business Week*, January 30, 1995; 1996 sales estimate by Jack L. Kelly of Goldman Sachs, interviewed by Joe McGowan, November 8, 1996.

p. 89 Any task, process, or business: Interview with Michelle Darling, Canadian Imperial Bank of Commerce, March 1996.

p. 90 the four quadrants of this grid: This diagram is based on conversations with Leif Edvinsson.

p. 91 One group at Hewlett-Packard: Tom DeMarco, "Human Capital, Unmasked," *New York Times*, April 14, 1996, Sec. 3, p. 13.

p. 92 "The first thing I did": Quoted in Thomas A. Stewart, "GE Keeps Those Ideas Coming," *Fortune*, August 12, 1991, p. 40.

p. 93 Canadian Imperial Bank of Commerce has devised: Thomas A. Stewart, "Intellectual Capital," *Fortune*, October 3, 1994, p. 68; Hubert Saint-Onge, "The Learning Organization at CIBC," presentation to the British Columbia Human Resources Management Association, May 6, 1994, pp. 23–30.

p. 94 "The false correlation": Quoted in Lewis J. Perelman, "Kanban to Kanbrain," *Forbes ASAP*, June 6, 1994, p. 84.

p. 96 "A group of professionals": P. Brook Manville, "Harvest Your Workers' Knowledge," *Datamation*, July 1996, p. 80.

p. 96 "you can define them in terms": Interview with Etienne Wenger, March 1996.

p. 96 copier repairers who exchange tips: John Seely Brown, "Research That Reinvents the Corporation," *Harvard Business Review*, January–February 1991, pp. 102–111; John Seely Brown and Paul Deguid, "Organizational Learning and Communities-of-Practice," *Organizational Science* 2:1 (February 1991), pp. 40–57; John Seely Brown and Estee Solomon Gray, "The People Are the Company," *Fast Company*, Premier Issue (Autumn 1995), pp. 78–82.

p. 97 A study by three academics: Ronald E. Purser, William A. Pasmore, and Ramkrishnan V. Tenkasi, "The Influence of Deliberations on Learning in New Product Development Teams," *Journal of Engineering and Technology Management*, 9 (1992) pp. 1–28.

 p. 98 In Silicon Valley, National: John Seely Brown and Estee Solomon Gray, "The People Are the Company," *Fast Company*, Premier Issue (Autumn 1995), pp. 78–82; interview with Estee Solomon Gray and Skip Hovsmith, 1996.

 p. 99 Brevetting people to work: Kathryn Rudie Harrigan and Gaurav Dalmia, "Knowledge Workers: The Last Bastion of Competitive Advantage," *Planning Review*, November–December 1991, p. 48.

 p. 100 "As communities of practice proliferate": Stephen R. Barley, "The Turn to a Horizontal Division of Labor: On the Occupationalization of Firms and the Technization of Work," unpublished paper, January 1994, p. 21.

 p. 100 In the late 1980s, Eric von Hippel: Eric von Hippel, "Cooperation Between Rivals: Informal Know-How Trading," *Research Policy*, 16:6 (December 1987), pp. 291–302; interview with Eric von Hippel.

 p. 101 "I believe that corporations": Quoted in Joel Kurtzman, "An Interview with Charles Handy," *Strategy and Business*, Fall 1995, pp. 5–6.

 p. 101 "Knowledge workers . . . are likely": Kathryn Rudie Harrigan and Gaurav Dalmia, "Knowledge Workers: The Last Bastion of Competitive Advantage," *Planning Review*, November–December 1991, p. 8.

 p. 103 "I would never invest one nickel": Interview with Robert A. B. Monks, January 23, 1995.

 p. 103 "According to the American Productivity and Quality Center": Erik Brynjolfsson, "Information Technology and the Re-Organization of Work: Theory and Evidence," CCS TR #144 (Cambridge, Mass.: Massachusetts Institute of Technology, 1993), pp. 165–66.

 p. 103 "Fifteen or twenty": Interview with Michael Brown, May 16, 1996.

 p. 105 "For pure information age companies": Interview with Michael Brown, May 16, 1996.

 p. 106 "the true investment": Peter F. Drucker, "The Age of Social Transformation," *The Atlantic Monthly*, November 1994, p. 71.

CHAPTER SEVEN: STRUCTURAL CAPITAL I: KNOWLEDGE MANAGEMENT

 p. 108 "Only the organization can provide": Peter F. Drucker, "The Age of Social Transformation," *The Atlantic Monthly*, November 1994, p. 68.

 p. 109 Few products that Clorox makes: David S. Marshak, *Understanding and Leveraging Lotus Notes* (Boston, Mass.: Patricia Seybold Group, Inc., 1993), pp. 50–51.

 p. 109 But also among the elements: Patrick H. Sullivan and David J. Teece, "Extracting Value from Innovation," draft research report, 1995, p. 4; Hubert Saint-Onge, "Intellectual Capital as a Business Reality," presentation in Calgary, Ontario, October 3, 1995, p. 29.

 p. 110 "Systematic management of": Skandia Corporation, *Intellectual Capital: Value-Creating Processes*, supplement to 1995 annual report, p. 20.

 p. 111 "At any moment of time": Fritz Machlup, *Knowledge and Knowledge Production* (Volume 1 of *Knowledge: Its Creation, Distribution, and Economic Significance*), (Princeton, N.J.: Princeton University Press, 1980), p. 161.

 p. 113 A 1994 study of sixty-four companies: Scott C. McCready and Ann M. Palermo, "Lotus Notes: Agent of Change" (Framingham, Mass.: International Data Corporation, 1994), pp. 4, 9.

 p. 114 better than average: Frederick H. Reichheld, *The Loyalty Effect: The Hidden*

Force Behind Growth, Profits, and Lasting Value (Boston: Harvard Business School Press, 1966), p. 1.

p. 116 Ward also measures: Arian Ward, panel discussion at The Knowledge Advantage II, conference sponsored by The Strategic Leadership Forum and Ernst & Young, Chicago, December 8, 1995.

p. 118 "I read somewhere that everybody": John Guare, *Six Degrees of Separation* (New York: Random House, 1990), p. 81.

pp. 118–19 "we learn to manage the 'mechanics' ": David J. Skyrme, "History & Future of KM," posting to Knowledge Management Forum (http://www.bonewman@cbvcp.com), May 21, 1996.

p. 121 At Young & Rubicam: See David S. Marshak, *Understanding and Leveraging Lotus Notes* (Boston, Mass.: Patricia Seybold Group, Inc., 1993), pp. 167–85.

p. 123 "The vertical processing of information": Quoted in Thomas A. Stewart, "Managing in a Wired Company," *Fortune*, July 11, 1994, p. 44.

p. 124 "Does he need an answer": Quoted in Thomas A. Stewart, "The Search for the Organization of Tomorrow," *Fortune*, May 18, 1992, p. 92.

pp. 124–25 For example, McKinsey & Co.: Jon R. Katzenbach and Douglas K. Smith, *The Wisdom of Teams: Creating the High-Performance Organization* (Boston: Harvard Business School Press, 1993), pp. 98–104; Philip Brook Manville, "McKinsey & Co: Thoughts on the Past and Future of Our Knowledge Strategies," presentation to The Knowledge Advantage, forum sponsored by the Planning Forum and Ernst & Young, Boston, September 27, 1994.

CHAPTER EIGHT: STRUCTURAL CAPITAL II: THE DANGER OF OVERINVESTING IN KNOWLEDGE

p. 129 "Like other forms of craft": Lewis Mumford, *The City in History: Its Origins, Its Transformations, and Its Prospects* (New York: Harcourt Brace Jovanovich, 1961), pp. 275–76.

pp. 129–130 the mere existence of company-wide electronic mail: See, for example, Sara Keisler and Lee Sproull, *Connections: New Ways of Working in the Networked Organization* (Cambridge, Mass.: MIT Press, 1991); Thomas A. Stewart, "Managing in a Wired Company," *Fortune*, July 11, 1994, p. 44; and Thomas A. Stewart, "Welcome to the Revolution," *Fortune*, December 13, 1993, p. 66.

p. 130 "it all comes to my mailbox": Interview with Bill Raduchel, April 22, 1994.

p. 131 "Nobody's dumb at IBM": Quoted in Steve Lohr, "For Big Blue, the Ones Who Got Away," *New York Times*, January 1, 1994, Sec. 3, p. 1.

p. 131 "People are often over-concerned": Mats Alvesson, "Organizations as Rhetoric: Knowledge-Intensive Firms and the Struggle with Ambiguity," *Journal of Management Studies:* 30:6, November 1993, p. 1010.

p. 133 Yet as recently as October 1990: Andrew Pollack, "Hewlett's Sprightly New Mood," *New York Times*, March 21, 1991, p. D1.

p. 133 "You can't just take a stodgy": quoted in Thomas A. Stewart, "Brainpower," *Fortune*, June 3, 1991, p. 44.

p. 133 Openness had been a touchstone: Information about Hewlett-Packard's corporate information systems comes from Robert R. Walker, "HP's Holistic Approach to Information Management," presentation to The Knowledge Advantage, conference sponsored by the Planning Forum and Ernst & Young, Boston, September 26, 1994; author's interview with Robert R. Walker, April 24, 1994; Thomas A. Stewart, "Managing in a Wired Company," *Fortune*, July 11, 1994; and Chuck Sieloff, "Practical Strategies for Leveraging Intellectual Capital," presentation to Managing Intellectual Capital Strategically, conference sponsored by International Business Communications in cooperation with Knowledge Advantages, New York, December 7, 1995.

p. 136   On the road, the sales force: Kathleen Murphy, "HP's Internal Web Aids Worldwide Sales Force," *Web Week*, March 1996, p. 25.

p. 136   That principle was forced on H-P's: Information about Hewlett-Packard's KnowledgeLinks and Innovation Network comes from interviews with Judith Lewis and Gary Gray, October 12 and 16, 1995.

p. 140   They take shortcuts: Kathryn Rudie Harrigan and Gaurav Dalmia, "Knowledge Workers: The Last Bastion of Competitive Advantage," *Planning Review*, November–December 1991.

p. 140   In what its author calls: Nick Bontis, "Intellectual Capital: An Exploratory Study that Develops Measures and Models," paper prepared for the seventeenth McMaster Business Conference, London, Ontario, Canada: Richard Ivey School of Business, University of Western Ontario, January 24–26, 1996.

CHAPTER NINE: CUSTOMER CAPITAL: INFORMATION WARS AND ALLIANCES

pp. 143–44   Not surprisingly, there is an extensive: See, for example: Robert E. Wayland, "Customer Valuation: The Foundation of Customer Franchise Management," *Mercer Management Journal* 2 (1994), p. 45; Frederick F. Reichheld, *The Loyalty Effect: The Hidden Force Behind Growth, Profits, and Lasting Value* (Boston: Harvard Business School Press, 1996), pp. 33–90, 219–57; Don Peppers and Martha Rogers, *The One-to-One Future* (New York: Doubleday/Currency, 1996); Jean-Noël Kapferer, *Strategic Brand Management* (New York: Free Press, 1993); David A. Aaker, *Managing Brand Equity* (New York: Free Press, 1991).

p. 144   Only mismanagement of customer: Frederick F. Reichheld, *The Loyalty Effect: The Hidden Force Behind Growth, Profits, and Lasting Value* (Boston: Harvard Business School Press, 1996), p. 1.

p. 144   customer satisfaction is actually declining: See Thomas A. Stewart, "After All You've Done for Your Customers, Why Are They Still Not Happy?" *Fortune*, December 11, 1995, pp. 178 ff.

p. 144   Ford Motor Company figures: Special advertising section, *Fortune*, September 19, 1994; MBNA calculations: Frederick F. Reichheld, *The Loyalty Effect: The Hidden Force Behind Growth, Profits, and Lasting Value* (Boston: Harvard Business School Press, 1996), p. 61.

p. 144   Credit-card issuer MBNA: Frederick F. Reichheld, *The Loyalty Effect: The Hidden Force Behind Growth, Profits, and Lasting Value* (Boston: Harvard Business School Press, 1996), p. 61.

p. 145   The story of how Merck: Information about Merck comes from interviews with several Merck officials, including Roy Vagelos, Frank Spiegel, and Judy Lewent, mostly in 1991 and 1995; from Thomas A. Stewart, "Brainpower," *Fortune*, June 3, 1991; Peter Petre, "How to Keep Customers Happy Captives," *Fortune*, September 2, 1985; Brian O'Reilly, "Drugmakers Under Attack," *Fortune*, July 29, 1991; Shawn Tully, "Super CFOs," *Fortune*, November 13, 1995; and Thomas A. Stewart, "The Information Wars: What You Don't Know Can Hurt You," *Fortune*, June 12, 1995, p. 119.

p. 147   senior citizens account for: Merck & Co., *1995 Annual Report*, p. 22.

p. 147   "We're calling a turn": Editor's Note, *Fortune*, July 29, 1991; Brian O'Reilly, "Drugmakers Under Attack," *Fortune*, July 29, 1991, p. 48.

p. 148   Lewent and Merck's auditors figured: Merck & Co., *1995 Annual Report*, p. 41.

p. 148   "developing health management": Merck & Co., *1995 Annual Report*, p. 3.

p. 148   At Pfizer, the detail force: Alice Dragoon, "Rx for Success," *CIO*, July 1995, p. 54.

p. 149 "The distribution channel": Quoted in Thomas A. Stewart, "Welcome to the Revolution," *Fortune*, December 13, 1993, pp. 66 ff.

p. 149 In the automobile industry: Keith Bradsher, "Moving Motors Through Modems," *New York Times*, February 12, 1996, p. D8.

p. 150 The networks transformed: See Peter Petre, "How to Keep Customers Happy Captives." *Fortune*, September 2, 1985, and Bridget O'Brian, "Ticketless Plane Trips, New Technology Force Travel Agencies to Change Course," *The Wall Street Journal*, September 13, 1994, p. B1.

p. 151 "Information used to be much more enclosed": Quoted in Thomas A. Stewart, "The Information Wars: What You Don't Know Can Hurt You," *Fortune*, June 12, 1995, p. 119.

p. 152 The administrative cost of business-to-business transactions: Interview with D. J. Crane of General Electric Information Systems, July 1, 1993.

p. 152 In the packaged goods industry: Bill Saporito, "Behind the Tumult at P&G," *Fortune*, March 7, 1994, p. 74.

p. 153 MicroAge is a company: See Thomas A. Stewart, "The Information Wars: What You Don't Know Can Hurt You," *Fortune*, June 12, 1995, p. 119.

p. 157 According to James Moore: Marc Levinson, "Get Out of Here!" *Newsweek*, June 3, 1996.

p. 157 Motorola, in its Boynton Beach: B. Joseph Pine II, Bart Victor, and Andrew C. Boynton, "Making Mass Customization Work," *Harvard Business Review*, September–October 1993, p. 116.

p. 157 The technology of mass customization: To learn about mass customization, see, among others, B. Joseph Pine II, *Mass Customization: The New Frontier in Business Competition* (Boston: Harvard Business School Press, 1993); Ramchandran Jaikuma, "Minimalist Manufacturing: Doing More, Better, with Less," *Prism* (Cambridge, Mass.: Arthur D. Little), first quarter, 1995, pp. 5–24.

p. 165 It's worth listing: Hubert Saint-Onge deserves credit for several of the items on this list.

CHAPTER TEN: THE NEW ECONOMICS OF INFORMATION

p. 169 International financial transactions: Charles Goldfinger, "Intangible Economy and Its Implications for Statistics and Statisticians," unpublished paper delivered at Eurostat-ISTAT Seminar, Bologna, Italy, February 7, 1966, p. 2; World Bank, *Global Economic Prospects and the Developing Countries*, Washington, D.C., 1995; Charles Goldfinger, "Financial Markets as Information Markets: Preliminary Exploration," paper prepared for the ENSSIB Conference "Économie de l'information," Lyon, France, May 20, 1995, p. 6.

p. 169 "Information about money": Walter Wriston, *Twilight of Sovereignty: How the Information Revolution is Transforming the World* (New York: Scribners, 1992).

p. 170 what economists call a "public good": Roger G. Noll, "The Economics of Information: A User's Guide," in Institute for Information Studies, *The Knowledge Economy: The Nature of Information in the 21st Century* (Queenstown, Md.: Aspen Institute, 1993), pp. 29–30.

p. 171 Although there is no reliable way: For a discussion of the imponderables of measuring stocks of knowledge, see Fritz Machlup, *Knowledge and Knowledge Production* (Volume 1 of *Knowledge: Its Creation, Distribution, and Economic Significance*) (Princeton, N.J.: Princeton University Press, 1980), pp. 161–73.

p. 172 "[Information] is structurally abundant": Charles Goldfinger, "Financial Markets as Information Markets: Preliminary Exploration," paper prepared for the ENSSIB Conference "Économie de l'information," Lyon, France, May 20, 1995, p. 7.

p. 172   "The value added": quoted in Thomas A. Stewart, "Everything that Communicates Must Converge," *Fortune*, January 14, 1991, p. 35.

p. 173   Fuji Electric: Thomas A. Stewart, "Brace for Japan's Hot New Strategy," *Fortune*, September 21, 1992, p. 62.

p. 173   no meaningful economic correlation: See Thomas A. Stewart, "Brainpower," *Fortune*, June 3, 1991, p. 44; Arthur D. Little study cited in Brian O'Reilly, "Drugmakers Under Attack," *Fortune*, July 29, 1991, p. 48.

p. 174   Competition for scarce resources: Zafer Achi, Andrew Doman, Olivier Sibony, Jayant Sinha, and Stephan Witt, "The Paradox of Fast Growth Tigers," *McKinsey Quarterly*, 1995, No. 3, pp. 6–7.

pp. 174–75   "The parts of the economy": W. Brian Arthur, *Increasing Returns and Path Dependence in the Economy* (Ann Arbor, Mich.: University of Michigan Press, 1994), pp. 3–4. For those with a taste or tolerance for economists' complicated equations, Arthur's book, which collects various articles he has published in academic journals over several years and includes a foreword by Kenneth J. Arrow, is an excellent guide to the economics of increasing returns. Those who would prefer a layman's version should see two articles by James Aley—"The Theory that Made Microsoft," *Fortune*, April 29, 1996, and "Give It Away and Get Rich!" *Fortune*, June 10, 1996—and, quite briefly, two by me: "Brainpower," *Fortune*, June 3, 1991, and "Now Capital Means Brains, Not Bucks," *Fortune*, January 11, 1991.

p. 175   Where first-copy costs are high: Roger G. Noll, "The Economics of Information: A User's Guide," in Institute for Information Studies, *The Knowledge Economy: The Nature of Information in the 21st Century* (Queenstown, Md.: Aspen Institute, 1993), pp. 30–31.

p. 177   Microsoft is one beneficiary: John Hagel III, "Spider vs. Spider," *McKinsey Quarterly*, 1966, No. 1, p. 15.

p. 178   There are essentially three: See Zafer Achi, Andrew Doman, Olivier Sibony, Jayant Sinha, and Stephan Witt, "The Paradox of Fast Growth Tigers," *McKinsey Quarterly*, 1995, No. 3, pp. 11–13.

p. 178   "one of the seminal blunders": *The Wall Street Journal*, February 6, 1996.

p. 178   "We want ubiquity first": Quoted in James Aley, "Give It Away and Get Rich! Plus Other Secrets of the Software Economy," *Fortune*, June 10, 1996, p. 90.

p. 180   Architectural monuments like cathedrals: Victor Hugo, *Nôtre-Dame de Paris* (Boston: Little, Brown, and Company, 1888), Book V, pp. 259–76.

CHAPTER ELEVEN: THE NETWORK ORGANIZATION

p. 181   By watching films: Kevin Kelly, *Out of Control: The Rise of Neo-Biological Civilization* (New York: Addison Wesley, 1994), p. 10; Craig Reynolds, "Boids," (http://www.reality.sgi.com/craig/boids.html).

p. 183   "The PC destroyed": Interview with Frederick Kovac.

p. 184   People communicating over electronic networks: Sara Keisler and Lee Sproull, *Connections: New Ways of Working in Networked Organizations* (Cambridge, Mass.: MIT Press, 1992).

p. 185   "In a network, supervision changes": Interviews with Susan Falzon, and Hellene Runtagh, April, 1994.

p. 185   "To develop complex products": Interview with John Manzo.

p. 186   filtering has dangers: See Thomas A. Stewart, "Managing in a Wired Company," *Fortune*, July 11, 1994, p. 44.

p. 187   "For my first twenty years": Interview with James Nesbit, October 17, 1995.

pp. 188–89   "Neatness and orderliness": Interview with John F. Welch, September 15, 1991.

p. 189 On paper, Minnesota Mining: See Thomas A. Stewart, "3M Fights Back," *Fortune*, February 5, 1996, p. 94.

p. 192 The argument is derived: The discussion of transaction cost economics is based on interviews with Oliver Williamson and Thomas W. Malone. For more, see Oliver E. Williamson, ed., *Organization Theory: From Chester Barnard to the Present and Beyond* (New York: Oxford University Press, 1990); Oliver E. Williamson and Sidney G. Winter, eds., *The Nature of the Firm: Origins, Evolution, and Development* (New York: Oxford University Press, 1991); and Oliver E. Williamson, *The Mechanisms of Governance* (New York, Oxford University Press, 1996).

p. 193 Markets, on the other hand: Willard Jule, posting to Learning-organization newsgroup, January 5, 1996.

p. 194 The cost of transmitting data: Letter from Randall S. Hancock, director of strategic research, C⁴ Lab of Gemini Consulting, June 6, 1995.

p. 194 Other things being equal: Erik Brynjolfsson, *Information Technology and the Re-Organization of Work: Theory and Evidence*, CCS TR 3144, Sloan School WP #3574-94 (Cambridge, Mass.: Massachusetts Institute of Technology, Sloan School of Management, May 1993), pp. 82–100.

p. 195 Census data show: Erik Brynjolfsson, Thomas W. Malone, Vijay Gurbaxani, and Ajit Kambil, "Does Information Technology Lead to Smaller Firms?" *Management Science*, 1994, p. 1628.

p. 196 Skandia's Assurance and Financial Services: Information about Skandia comes from company reports, including its 1994 and 1995 intellectual capital supplements to its annual report; a February 1995 report on Skandia by stock market analysts Alfred Berg UK Ltd.; and interviews with Leif Edvinsson, Björn Wolrath, and Jan Carendi.

p. 197 "This is changing the business": quoted in Thomas A. Stewart, "Boom Time on the New Frontier," *Fortune*, September 27, 1993, p. 153.

p. 197 "clusters of companies": John Hagel III, "Spider *versus* Spider," *McKinsey Quarterly*, 1996, No. 1, pp. 5–6.

p. 198 As for success in intramural: For a fascinating look at how Microsoft and Intel keep abreast of one another's thinking, see Brent Schlender, "A Conversation with the Lords of Wintel," *Fortune*, July 8, 1996.

CHAPTER TWELVE: YOUR CAREER IN THE INFORMATION AGE

p. 200 "Extinction": Quoted (as are others in this chapter, except where noted) in Thomas A. Stewart, "Your Career in a World Without Managers," *Fortune*, March 20, 1995, p. 72; and "Corporate Jungle Spawns a New Species: The Project Manager," *Fortune*, July 10, 1995, p. 179.

p. 202 As consultant William Bridges: William Bridges, *JobShift* (Reading, Mass.: Addison Wesley, 1994).

pp. 202–203 "adaptive, rapidly changing": Warren G. Bennis and Philip E. Slater, *The Temporary Society* (New York: Harper & Row, 1968), p. 98.

p. 203 In late 1995, *The Wall Street Journal*: Alex Markels, "Restructuring Alters Middle-Manager Role but Leaves It Robust," *The Wall Street Journal*, November 25, 1995, p. A1.

p. 207 the emerging process-centered organization: For more about process-centered organizations, see Thomas A. Stewart, "The Search for the Organization of Tomorrow," *Fortune*, May 18, 1992; Rahul Jacob, "The Struggle to Create an Organization for the 21st Century," *Fortune*, April 3, 1995, p. 90; Michael Hammer, *Beyond Reengineering*, (New York: HarperCollins, 1996).

p. 210   This management discipline: The Project Management Institute is at 130 S. State Rd., Upper Darby, Pennsylvania 19082.

p. 211   Between 1983 and 1994: Timothy Egan, "A Temporary Force to Be Reckoned With," *New York Times*, May 20, 1996, pp. D1, 8.

p. 216   Instead, "competencies" and "skill sets": Susan Albert Mohrman and Susan G. Cohen, "When People Get Out of the Box: New Attachments to Co-Workers," CEO publication G 94-19 (262) (Los Angeles: University of Southern California, Center for Effective Organizations), March 1994.

APPENDIX: TOOLS FOR MEASURING AND MANAGING INTELLECTUAL CAPITAL

p. 222   "The more stuff": Interview with Michael Brown, May 16, 1996.

p. 226   Federal Reserve chairman Alan Greenspan: David Hale, "Will Delayed Fed Tightening Set the Stage for an October Stock Market Crash?" Zurich Kemper Investments, June 21, 1996, p. 5.

p. 229   *gross margin* from new products: Robert S. Kaplan, "Devising a Balanced Scorecard Matched to Business Strategy," *Planning Review*, vol. 22, no. 5, September–October 1994, p. 19.

p. 231   Celemi International: The company can be reached at Box 50, S-230 42 Tygelsjö, Sweden, or on the World Wide Web: http://www.celemi.se.

p. 240   "Measurements of this sort": Quoted in Thomas A. Stewart, "After All You've Done for Your Customers, Why Are They Still Unhappy?" *Fortune*, December 11, 1995, p. 178.

p. 240   Measuring alliances: Some of these ideas are adapted from Jordan Lewis, *The Connected Corporation* (New York: Free Press, 1995), esp. pp. 133–41.

p. 241   Reichheld's work: See Frederick R. Reichheld, *The Loyalty Effect: Growth, Profits, and Lasting Value* (Boston: Harvard Business School Press, 1996).

p. 243   Reichheld and his colleagues at Bain: Reichheld, op. cit, exhibit 2-1.